全国高等学校外语教师丛书·理论系列

语料库语言学 群言集

Vander Viana（巴西）
Sonia Zyngier（巴西）　编
Geoff Barnbrook（英）

Perspectives on Corpus Linguistics

外语教学与研究出版社
FOREIGN LANGUAGE TEACHING AND RESEARCH PRESS
北京 BEIJING

京权图字：01-2016-2995

Original edition: "Perspectives on Corpus Linguistics" edited by Vander Viana, Sonia Zyngier and Geoff Barnbrook. ©2011
John Benjamins Publishing Company, Amsterdam/Philadelphia.
Reprinted by permission for distribution in the People's Republic of China only.

图书在版编目（CIP）数据

语料库语言学群言集：英、汉 ／（巴西）范德·维亚纳（Vander Viana），（巴西）索尼娅·金吉尔（Sonia Zyngier），（英）杰夫·巴恩布鲁克（Geoff Barnbrook）编. —— 北京：外语教学与研究出版社，2016.7（2018.4 重印）
（全国高等学校外语教师丛书. 理论指导系列）
ISBN 978-7-5135-7813-4

I. ①语… II. ①范… ②索… ③杰… III. ①语料库－语言学－文集－英、汉 IV. ①H0-53

中国版本图书馆 CIP 数据核字（2016）第 166107 号

出 版 人　蔡剑峰
项目负责　解碧琰
责任编辑　毕　争
责任校对　董一书
封面设计　外研社设计部　彩奇风
出版发行　外语教学与研究出版社
社　　址　北京市西三环北路 19 号（100089）
网　　址　http://www.fltrp.com
印　　刷　北京九州迅驰传媒文化有限公司
开　　本　650×980　1/16
印　　张　20
版　　次　2016 年 8 月第 1 版　2018 年 4 月第 3 次印刷
书　　号　ISBN 978-7-5135-7813-4
定　　价　73.90 元

购书咨询：（010）88819926　电子邮箱：club@fltrp.com
外研书店：https://waiyants.tmall.com
凡印刷、装订质量问题，请联系我社印制部
联系电话：（010）61207896　电子邮箱：zhijian@fltrp.com
凡侵权、盗版书籍线索，请联系我社法律事务部
举报电话：（010）88817519　电子邮箱：banquan@fltrp.com
法律顾问：立方律师事务所　刘旭东律师
　　　　　中咨律师事务所　殷　斌律师
物料号：278130101

To Stig Johansson,
In recognition of his generosity

Contents

总序

  "全国高等学校外语教师丛书"是外语教学与研究出版社高等英语教育出版分社近期精心策划、隆重推出的系列丛书，包含理论指导、科研方法和教学研究三个子系列。本套丛书既包括学界专家精心挑选的国外引进著作，又有特邀国内学者执笔完成的"命题作文"。作为开放的系列丛书，该丛书还将根据外语教学与科研的发展不断增加新的专题，以便教师研修与提高。

  笔者有幸参与了这套系列丛书的策划工作。在策划过程中，我们分析了高校英语教师面临的困难与挑战，考察了一线教师的需求，最终确立这套丛书选题的指导思想为：想外语教师所想，急外语教师所急，顺应广大教师的发展需求；确立这套丛书的写作特色为：突出科学性、可读性和操作性，做到举重若轻，条理清晰，例证丰富，深入浅出。

  第一个子系列是"理论指导"。该系列力图为教师提供某学科或某领域的研究概貌，期盼读者能用较短的时间了解某领域的核心知识点与前沿研究课题。以《二语习得重点问题研究》一书为例。该书不求面面俱到，只求抓住二语习得研究领域中的热点、要点和富有争议的问题，动态展开叙述。每一章的写作以不同意见的争辩为出发点，对取向相左的理论、实证研究结果差异进行分析、梳理和评述，最后介绍或者展望国内外的最新发展趋势。全书阐述清晰，深入浅出，易读易懂。再比如《认知语言学与二语教学》一书，全书分为理论篇、教学篇与研究篇三个部分。理论篇阐述认知语言学视角下的语言观、教学观与学习观，以及与二语教学相关的认知语言学中的主要概念与理论；教学篇选用认知语言学领域比较成熟的理论，探讨应用到中国英语教学实践的可能性；教学研究篇包括国内外将认知语言学理论应用到教学实践中的研究综述、研究方法介绍以及对未来研究的展望。

第二个子系列是"科研方法"。该系列介绍了多种研究方法，通常是一本书介绍一种方法，例如问卷调查、个案研究、行动研究、有声思维、语料库研究、微变化研究和启动研究等。也有的书涉及多种方法，综合描述量化研究或者质化研究，例如：《应用语言学中的质性研究与分析》、《应用语言学中的量化研究与分析》和《第二语言研究中的数据收集方法》等。凡入选本系列丛书的著作人，无论是国外著者还是国内著者，均有高度的读者意识，乐于为一线教师开展教学科研服务，力求做到帮助读者"排忧解难"。例如，澳大利亚安妮·伯恩斯教授撰写的《英语教学中的行动研究方法》一书，从一线教师的视角，讨论行动研究的各个环节，每章均有"反思时刻"、"行动时刻"等新颖形式设计。同时，全书运用了丰富例证来解释理论概念，便于读者理解、思考和消化所读内容。凡是应邀撰写研究方法系列的中国著作人均有博士学位，并对自己阐述的研究方法有着丰富的实践经验。他们有的运用了书中的研究方法完成了硕士、博士论文，有的是采用书中的研究方法从事过重大科研项目。以秦晓晴教授撰写的《外语教学问卷调查法》一书为例，该书著者将系统性与实用性有机结合，根据实施问卷调查法的流程，系统地介绍了问卷调查研究中问题的提出、问卷项目设计、问卷试测、问卷实施、问卷整理及数据准备、问卷评价以及问卷数据汇总及统计分析方法选择等环节。书中各个环节的描述都配有易于理解的研究实例。

第三个子系列是"教学研究"。该系列与前两个系列相比，有两点显著不同：第一，本系列侧重同步培养教师的教学能力与教学研究能力；

第二，本系列所有著作的撰稿人主要为中国学者。有些著者虽然目前在海外工作和生活，但他们出国前曾在国内高校任教，也经常回国参与国内的教学与研究工作。本系列包括《英语听力教学与研究》、《英语写作教学与研究》、《英语阅读教学与研究》、《英语口语教学与研究》、《口译教学与研究》等。以《英语听力教学与研究》一书为例，著者王艳博士拥有十多年的听力教学经验，同时听力教学研究又是她博士论文的选题领域。《英语听力教学与研究》一书，浓缩了她多年来听力教学与听力教学研究的宝贵经验。全书分为两部分：教学篇与研究篇。教学篇中涉及了听力教学的各个重要环节以及学生在听力学习中可能碰到的困难与应对的办法，所选用的案例均来自著者课堂教学的真实活动。研究篇中既有著者的听力教学研究案例，也有著者从国内外文献中筛选出的符合中国国情的听力教学研究案例，综合在一起加以分析阐述。

教育大计，教师为本。"全国高等学校外语教师丛书"内容全面，出版及时，必将成为高校教师提升自我教学能力、研究能力与合作能力的良师益友。笔者相信本套丛书的出版对高校外语教师个人专业能力的提高，对教师队伍整体素质的提高，必将起到积极的推动作用。

文秋芳

北京外国语大学中国外语教育研究中心

2011年7月3日

导读

　　《语料库语言学群言集》一书收录了对 14 位国际知名语料库语言学专家的书面访谈，外加该书第一主编 Vander Viana 的一篇论文作为结尾，全书正文共计 15 章。另有 Ronald Carter 所写的序言及三位编者的前言。

　　该书编者在采访 14 位语料库研究学者时，请每位学者围绕 10 个给定的问题作答，其中七个问题为共答题，另三个问题则因各人专业特色而异。

1. "语料库十问"之共答七问：语料库语言学的本体

　　14 位学者都必须回答的七个问题是：

1) Where do you place the roots of Corpus Linguistics? And to what do you attribute the growth of interest in the area?（您认为语料库语言学的学术源头在哪里？您认为这个领域持续受人青睐的原因是什么？）

2) Is Corpus Linguistics a science or a methodology? Where would you situate Corpus Linguistics in the scientific or methodological panorama?（语料库语言学是一门学科还是一种方法论？在学科和方法论的大背景下，您会将语料库语言学置于怎样的地位？）

3) How representative can a corpus be?（语料库应当具有怎样的代表性？）

4) How far should an analyst rely on intuition?（分析者应在多大程度上倚赖个人直觉？）

5）What kind of questions should an analyst think of?（分析者应关注哪些研究选题？）

6）What are the strengths and weaknesses of corpus analysis?（语料库分析的强项和弱点有哪些？）

7）What is the future of Corpus Linguistics?（语料库语言学的未来将会怎样？）

这些问题涉及语料库语言学的核心学科属性，从学科起源、语料库自身特点和研究者素质谈起，一直延伸至语料库语言学的未来发展方向。

问题 1 和问题 2 探讨的是语料库语言学在语言学史上的位置，包括它自身的学科特性和方法论意义。受访的 14 位学者中，有些认为语料库是计算机时代的产物，语料库语言学的历史可以追溯到 20 世纪 60 年代美国布朗大学的美国书面英语语料库项目。然而，更多的学者倾向于将采集真实语言素材、运用量化统计方法描写和分析语言的历史追溯到 20 世纪上半叶，特别是以 Bloomfield 和 Boas 等为代表的美国结构主义学者所开展的语言描写研究。应当说，就语料库语言学的研究理念而言，语料库语言学并非是在机读语料库出现之后才产生的，但机读语料库和相关语料库分析工具的出现大大促进了语料库语言学的发展。

问题 3 关注的是语料库作为语言资源（resource）的这一属性。语料库的海量规模往往为人津津乐道，然而除去"体量巨大"这一优势，语料取样代表性的价值更为关键。可是"代表性"（representativeness）这一概念着实难以界定。不同学者对取样代表性的认识分歧不小，受访者们对这一问题的回答，很大程度上是各自学术背景的投射。从事语言教学研究、翻译研究和语法研究的学者，对教学型语料、翻译或多语语料以及通用语言事实的需求各不相同，因此对语料库的代表性理解自然不同。可见，语料库取样代表性有其相对性，很大程度上取决于研究目的。

问题 4 和问题 5 涉及的是语料库语言学的研究（research）属性，或者说学科性。其中问题 4 谈到语料库语言学对研究者的要求。面对海量数据以及量化分析结果，研究者是做一个客观描述者，还是结合个人语感以及相关语言学理论对数据加以分析和阐释，这其中隐含了语料库语言学领域内部"基于语料库"（corpus-based）和"语料库驱动"（corpus-driven）两种学术路径的迥异观点（参阅梁茂成、李文中、许家金 2010：第 6 章；梁茂成 2012）。前者不排斥个人知识和语言学理论介入语料分析，后者则主张少用或不用已有的理论。目前多数研究是按基于语料库的思路开展的。然而，若能有更多人坚持按语料库驱动的思路开展研究，则更有可能得到原创性的语言学发现。

问题 5 试图了解的是语料库语言学擅长解决哪些研究问题。这一问题引发了 14 种不同的答案。不同学术背景的学者向读者们展示了语料库语言学应用的广阔前景。

通常一个研究领域优势突出，弱点也会比较明显。问题 6 谈的就是这个问题。语料库语言学的长处似乎尽人皆知，倒是它的局限性更值得一说。有意思的是，不少作者在面对这个题目时，并不承认语料库语言学自身有什么明显的缺点或不足。

比如，Leech[1]（见 179 页）明确指出："I do not see any weaknesses in Corpus Linguistics *per se*.（我不认为语料库语言学本身有什么缺陷。）"Leech 认为很多时候问题出在对语料库语言学的应用上，而语料库作为一种数据源自身并没有什么问题。他反对将语料库作为语言学家的唯一数据和证据来源，他认为，如能结合语感判断、诱导数据（elicited data，包括心理语言学实验数据）等方法，可以更有效地推进这一学科的发展。对于有人认为语料库研究只注重对语言事实进行描述，不注重

---

1 Geoffrey Leech教授于2014年8月19日病逝。此次《群言集》在中国出版之时，为保持本书原版状态，书中涉及Leech教授的内容未作任何改动。

理论建构的言论，Leech 以 *Corpus Linguistics and Linguistic Theory* 这个杂志的创立为例，说明其实已经有越来越多的研究在关注语料库数据与语言学理论的结合。对于 Widdowson 等人对语料库分析脱离语境的批评，Leech 表示这只是因现阶段技术所限，目前很多语料库研究更关注文本内部词汇语法特征的频数分析，事实上语料库语言学从来不排斥包含更完整语境信息的音视频材料。随着语音识别技术的发展，语义和语篇自动分析技术的发展，基于语料库的研究一定会发挥更大的作用。

再如 Gries（见 98 页）在谈及这一问题时指出，如果说语料库语言学有什么缺陷的话，那么问题主要在于研究者们对语料库及语料库方法使用得不够恰当，而不应归咎于语料库语言学本身。比如，Gries 注意到，很多已发表的研究中统计方法运用不尽合理。

在谈及语料库的未来走向（问题 7）时，受访者们都期待有更多、规模更大、语境信息更丰富的语料库以及更先进的语料库工具出现，期待语料库能解决更多的语言学问题。与此同时，学者们似乎越来越倾向于淡化语料库语言学的学科地位。比如 Leech（见 181 页）说道："...Corpus Linguistics, as a separate area of linguistics, will simply melt away, as a sub-branch of linguistics, because using corpora will be the most obvious natural way to do linguistics.（语料库语言学作为语言学的一个独立的分支领域，很自然会消解掉，因为运用语料库从事语言学研究是再显而易见和再自然不过的做法了。）"Sampson（见 226 页）也有类似的观点，他提到："... in a sense I believe that Corpus Linguistics as such has not got a future. ... I would hope that its future is simply to fade away as a concept, because all concerned will take corpora for granted as one important set of tools in any linguist's toolbox.（照此我认为，某种意义上，语料库语言学没有未来。我希望语料库语言学这一概念最终消逝，因为那时所有有关的语言学家，都理所当然地将语料库视为其工具箱中的一套重要工具。）"

然而，Louw（见 204 页）对于上述这种认识表现出深深的担忧，他觉得上述"工具论"或"方法论"是对语料库语言学庸俗不堪的（insultingly mundane）、下里巴人式的（pedestrian）、混淆不清的（hybridising）、言不由衷的（dishonest）认识。Louw 觉得现在对语料库的看法将会摒弃掉 Firth、Malinowski 和 Sinclair 开创的"搭配生义"（meaning by collocation）这样具有远见卓识的观念（参阅李文中 2016）。Louw 慨叹，语料库语言学的巅峰时代在 20 世纪 80 年代，那时伯明翰大学正在开展 COBUILD 语料库项目。他希望学者加强对语义韵和词语搭配的研究和应用。

伯明翰大学的 Teubert 和我国一些受 Sinclair 学术思想影响的学者也持有与 Louw 相近的观点，认 Sinclair 的语料库研究思想为正宗，其余都是误用或是盗用语料库语言学这个概念（参阅 Mukherjee 2010：371）。

在国内外语料库研究学界，受 Sinclair 学术思想影响的语料库学者虽人数不多，但影响不小。从学术发展的大势来看，不同流派或不同学术观点的存在，正是学术繁荣的迹象。这本《群言集》，不只收一家之言，足见其包容性。

我们认为，运用语料库以及语料库方法开展语言学研究，要比 Sinclair 的搭配研究和 COBUILD 相关课题来得更早。1959 年开始的"英语用法调查"（Survey of English Usage）和 1962 年开始的布朗语料库项目早为大家所熟知。从《群言集》的"语料库十问"的第一问中，大家可以读到很多更早的语料库研究课题。即便在我国，相关研究开展也有近一个世纪的历史（参阅 Xu 2015）。

Leech（见 173 页）将语料库语言学概括为 a methodologically-oriented branch of linguistics（具有很强方法论导向的语言学分支）。他不认为语料库语言学是个简单的方法论，他通过哈勃太空望远镜的例子说明，就像天文望远镜可以促成或大大推动天文学或天体物理学这些学科的发展一样，技术的发展跟学科的建立，两者互为表里，不可割裂。

上述七个问题可以说都是根本性话题，因此，该书虽是五年前出版，但丝毫没有过时之虞。虽然每章都是相同的话题，我们却可以读到迥然不同的回答，丝毫不会有重复单调之感。

2. "语料库十问"之个性三问：作者阵容及特色领域

2.1 作者阵容

除了共答题，每位受访者还从各自研究领域出发，就三个个性化题目作了论述。这些个性化论题恰能反映各位受访学者丰富的学科背景，以及该书之兼容并包。

该书作者阵容可谓梦之队。且不以语料库研究成就论，Geoffrey Leech (1936—2014) 一生在英语语法、语义学、语用学、文体学、语料库语言学等诸多方面都作出了杰出贡献。他主要完成或合作完成的代表作有：《英语语法大全》(*A Comprehensive Grammar of the English Language*)、《语义学》(*Semantics*)、《语用学原理》(*Principles of Pragmatics*)、《小说文体论》(*Style in Fiction*) 和"英国国家语料库"(British National Corpus, BNC)。《英语语法大全》，俗称"夸克语法"，长期以来是我国语法教学界的权威基准；《语义学》中列举的七种意义已成为语言学学生的专业常识；《语用学原理》中提出的"礼貌原则"是礼貌研究的重要基石；《小说文体论》是文体学领域当仁不让的第一教材；"英国国家语料库"是近 20 年来语料库领域的业界标杆。Leech 可以称得上是一位世界级语言学家。

Stig Johansson (1939—2010) 是英语语法和对比语言学领域的杰出学者。

Ken Hyland 是学术话语领域最重要的学者之一。

John Swales 是体裁分析的开创者。

若以语料库研究的成就论，受访者中有语料库领域影响最大的分析工具 WordSmith Tools 的作者 Mike Scott，有"网络语料库"（Web as Corpus）时代最具影响的在线语料库平台"杨百翰大学语料库平台"（http://corpus.byu.edu）的创建者 Mark Davis，有基于语料库的认知语言学研究代表人物 Stefan Th. Gries，有将语料库与话语分析和社会语言学相结合的代表性学者之一 Paul Baker，还有语料库翻译学代表学者 Sara Laviosa，等等。

另外，Stefan Th. Gries 和 Bill Louw 还是 2008 年在 Corpora List（语料库邮件列表）讨论组上发起著名的"新兵训练营大论战"（Bootcamp Debate 或 Bootcamp Discourse）的对立双方。他们给《群言集》供稿，使得这本书能更全面地反映学界声音。

上述阵容可谓豪华，称得上全明星团队。若是受访者中还能包括 Sylviane Granger、John Sinclair、Mona Baker、Douglas Biber、Tony McEnery 则几乎可以称为完美。事实上《群言集》缘起于本书第一编者 Vander Viana 对 Sylviane Granger 的题为 "Corpus linguistics, language learning and ELT" 的访谈（Granger & Viana 2007）。读者可从网络上下载阅读。John Sinclair 的思想已部分地通过 Bill Louw 的访谈阐述出来。Mona Baker 的语料库翻译学思想也通过其弟子 Sara Laviosa 的访谈传达出来。Douglas Biber 的基于语料库的语域变异研究也通过其合作者 Susan Conrad 的访谈得以展示。Tony McEnery 的学术观点已有 Geoffrey Leech 和 Paul Baker 两位代言人。

2.2 特色领域

该书编者在前言中通过三张表格，将《群言集》各章涉及的话题、领域作了极好的概括。因此在这里译出，以方便读者了解该书内容，并根据个人兴趣选择阅读。

表 1. 研究所用语料及方法

话题	Topic	受访者
学习者语料库	Learner corpora	Guy Aston
平行和可比语料库	Parallel and comparable corpora	Stig Johansson
适用于译者的语料库	Suitable corpora for translators	Sara Laviosa
通用语料库及工具	Public-domain corpora and tools	Mark Davies
（元信息）标记	Markup	Guy Aston
（语言学）标注	Annotation	Geoffrey Leech
树库	Treebanks	Geoffrey Sampson
语料库对比	Corpus comparison	Stefan Th. Gries
对研究者的技术要求	Technological mastery and requirements	Mark Davies
技术发展速度	Speed of technological development	Mike Scott
编程知识	Programming knowledge	Stefan Th. Gries
统计学知识的掌握	Statistics control	Stefan Th. Gries

表 2. 各章节所涉及的语言学研究领域

话题	Topic	受访者
历史语言学	Historical Linguistics	Mark Davies
语用学	Pragmatics	Geoffrey Leech
句法学	Syntax	Geoffrey Sampson
社会语言学	Sociolinguistics	Paul Baker
话语分析	Discourse Analysis	Mike Scott
批判话语分析	Critical Discourse Analysis	Paul Baker
对比修辞	Contrastive Rhetoric	John Swales
隐喻	Metaphor	Tony Berber Sardinha
体裁	Genres	John Swales
语域	Registers	Susan Conrad

（待续）

（续表）

话题	Topic	受访者
语言复杂度	Language complexity	Geoffrey Sampson
专门用途英语	English for Specific Purposes	Mike Scott
写作中的人际特征	Interpersonal features in writing	Ken Hyland
跨语言研究	Cross-linguistic research	Stig Johansson
翻译研究	Translation studies	Sara Laviosa
语料库语言学视角下的语言变化	Changes in Corpus Linguistics	Stig Johansson
发展中国家的语料库	Corpora in developing countries	Tony Berber Sardinha

表 3. 语料库语言学在相关学科中的应用

话题	Topic	受访者
性别研究	Gender	Paul Baker
文学研究的社会功能	Social functions in literary research	Bill Louw
知识的社会建构	Social construction of knowledge	Ken Hyland
对传统文学概念的挑战	Challenges to traditional literary concepts	Bill Louw
文体研究	Style	Geoffrey Leech
大学中的学术语言素养	Literacy at the university	Ken Hyland
学术语言素养及教学	Academic literacy and pedagogy	John Swales
学生自主性	Student autonomy	Guy Aston
教师教育	Teacher education	Susan Conrad
大学文学课程	University literature curriculum	Bill Louw
英语 / 西班牙语外语教材研究	Teaching materials for English/ Spanish as a foreign language	Tony Berber Sardinha
专业学术能力训练	Professional practice	Susan Conrad
语料库与传统翻译研究资源	Corpora vs. traditional translation resources	Sara Laviosa

从上述三张表格中我们可以看到，我国（包括中国香港特别行政区和中国台湾地区）学者，乃至整个东亚以及东南亚地区语料库学者的研究并没有走向世界的主流舞台。其中原因之一，还是我国及周边地区和国家的学者迄今在国际上用英文发表论著的数量尚不够多。另外，具有自身独特风貌的语料库研究传统并没有形成。巴西学者 Tony Berber Sardinha 似乎并不能代表发展中国家这个广大的群体。长期在中国香港任教的 Ken Hyland 的学术思想和观念还是源自英国。值得欣慰的是，我国学者在国际上发表论著的上升势头十分强劲。不久的将来，语料库语言学会在世界更广大的地区兴盛起来。

3. 对《群言集》的评价与阅读建议

《群言集》一书的编辑体例应当是当今读者所乐见的。每一章各自独立，读者可根据喜好选读，而不必一气读完。《群言集》基本上是同题讨论，各章相同话题的讨论内容可以相互参照。

从一般阅读经验来看，论文集的质量和可读性往往不及自成一体的专著。然而，这本《群言集》却卓然不群，使读者颇有读一书而览众山之感。

除了通读和根据个人研究兴趣选读相关章节外，书中 Geoffrey Leech、Stig Johansson 和 Stefan Th. Gries 这三位学者的访谈尤其值得推荐。前两位是已故的资深语言学家，在语料库语言学中浸淫达半个世纪，对语料库语言学的认识更为全面，观点更为平衡。Stefan Th. Gries 则是近十年左右崭露头角，当前炙手可热的中年语料库学者。他和同行学者一道，不断将语料库相关的统计方法往前推进，更重要的是，他将扎实的认知语言学背景与语料库量化分析手段进行了充分有效的结合。

《群言集》属于命题作文，各人因为时间安排问题、重视程度的差异，所作出的回答质量终究还是有高下。当然，上述对访谈内容的评价很容易失于主观。导读作者只是一家之言，生怕自喻专家而误导读者。聪明的读者定然能自辨内容优劣。

北京外国语大学中国外语教育研究中心在编辑《语料库语言学》期刊时，曾策划"专家视点"和"同题共议"栏目，与本书策划的主题十分相似，着重关注中国语料库学者，也算是中国版的《群言集》，是对《群言集》的本土化补充。其中包括：桂诗春语料库语言学答客问、肖忠华语料库语言学答客问、卫乃兴谈语料库语言学的本体与方法、梁茂成谈语料库语言学与计算机技术、李文中谈基于语料库的文化表述研究等。诸位如果对上述话题感兴趣，也可以从期刊网址（http://ylyy.chinajournal.net.cn）免费下载阅读。

许家金

北京外国语大学中国外语教育研究中心

2016 年 5 月

参考文献

Granger, S. & Viana, V. 2007. Corpus Linguistics, language learning and ELT: An interview with Sylviane Granger. *Mindbite* (1): 11–14.

Mukherjee, J. 2010. Corpus linguistics versus corpus dogmatism – pace Wolfgang Teubert. *International Journal of Corpus Linguistics* 15(3): 370–378.

Xu, Jiajin. 2015. Corpus-Based Chinese studies: A historical review from the 1920s to the present. *Chinese Language and Discourse* 6(2): 218–244.

李文中，2016，"新弗斯语料库语言学"考辩，《外国语》（2）：30–38。

梁茂成，2012，语料库语言学研究的两种范式：渊源、分歧及前景，《外语教学与研究》（3）：323–335。

梁茂成、李文中、许家金，2010，《语料库应用教程》，北京：外语教学与研究出版社。

Foreword

There are many books currently available that are devoted to the theory and practice of Corpus Linguistics. This volume is different, indeed unique, in eliciting responses to key questions about the field from a wide range of distinguished practitioners. It provides a valuable record of reflection on past developments, an index of current thinking and a map for future possibilities and all in relation to a field which is one of the fastest growing areas in the domain of language study. The volume lucidly addresses key questions which are of interest both to those new to the field and to experienced professionals alike.

The sheer diversity of responses provided by contributors to the volume provides a guide to the multiple and varied theories and practices associated with Corpus Linguistics. At the same time, however, reading through the responses in sequence reveals how unified the field is in its recognition of strengths and weaknesses, how much agreement there is about the need for improved methods and practices, and the extent to which contributors converge in their view of future prospects. Given the remarkable growth of the field in the last twenty years, the ever-increasing computational and analytic power currently available and the fact that some advocates are now saying that Corpus Linguistics *is* linguistics or should be linguistics or that linguistics in any of its manifestations cannot be practised without being corpus-informed, the contributors are helpfully measured in their responses and reflections, are not over-zealous in their claims and are constantly alert to the fact that the field requires both consolidation and further extension and expansion. The need for better automated transcription and corpus annotation, the need for more spoken and multimodal corpora, the need for fuller engagement with linguistic theory and the need for corpora to embrace more than English as the main language of description and investigation are just some of the examples on which there is agreement. At the same time several contributors also remind us how new the field is, at least in terms of its computationally-driven manifestations and in terms of user-friendly software interfaces, and that the term 'Corpus Linguistics' was not used much before the 1990s.

As a whole the volume amply illustrates the extent to which Corpus Linguistics challenges many current orthodoxies and paradigms (especially within Chomskyan models for language study), meeting the challenge with a range of examples and further questions relevant to interdisciplinary endeavours in the field of translations and literary studies, English for academic purposes, language teaching and learning, as well as a whole host of domains within communications studies. What is underlined here time and again is that the widest possible range of naturally-occurring utterances are needed in order to begin to answer such challenges and that consideration of other data types, while welcomed, can only be countenanced alongside such real language data. The days of invented or concocted data are well and truly numbered but 'evidence' in the form of multimillion word data sets is rightly treated with a degree of caution by all the contributors to this volume, with some contributors underlining the value of smaller specialised corpora, of learner corpora, of corpora of expert speakers or speakers with English as a lingua franca as opposed to native speaker-based corpora. The advent of web-based corpora further raises issues of representativeness and what is meant by 'facts' about the language as a whole.

Contributors also advance debate about the different value and values attached to corpora. Is Corpus Linguistics an end in itself, advancing our understanding of patterns of language in ways beyond human intuition and observation? Or is Corpus Linguistics a means to an end, informing and advancing our engagement with a wide variety of texts and text types? To what extent can corpus methods be aligned with other quantitative and qualitative research methods and to what extent can corpus data sit comfortably alongside elicited or introspective data? The book bristles with powerful insights, good practical ideas, exciting theory building, and endlessly helpful reflections.

The editors are to be congratulated for the originality of their idea of designing the book around key questions (both common to all and helpfully specific to individuals), for assembling such an interesting cast list of participants and from beginning to end for ensuring the clarity and accessibility of the process.

Prof. Ronald Carter
University of Nottingham

Preface

Humans are naturally curious beings in search of knowledge. We assume that those who have started to read these first pages may wonder about how this book came together. Its original concept goes back to an interview carried out by one of the editors with Sylviane Granger for a newsletter aimed at teachers of English as a foreign language (see Granger & Viana 2007). By the time this interview was published, it became clear that there was a growing need to compare and contrast the opinion of various scholars on different aspects of the area, which had been taken for granted or assumed to be part of commonsense knowledge. In doing that, we assumed that we would arrive at an overall appreciation of how Corpus Linguistics has impacted language research as well as of the interrelations and interconnections it allows.

Before the book arrived at its printed form, we contacted several renowned professionals whose corpus research has been influential in our field, and asked them whether they were willing to participate in this project. We would like to take the opportunity here to thank wholeheartedly the scholars who opened a slot in their agendas to undertake this writing commitment and who helped us shape this volume. We are also grateful to Elena Tognini-Bonelli, our series editor, and Kees Vaes, John Benjamins representative, for their unrestricted support to this project, and to Ronald Carter for writing the foreword.

This collection is posthumously dedicated to Stig Johansson, who, despite health problems, was among the first to accept our invitation with enthusiasm. In April 2010, when this book was still in progress, news arrived of his passing away. His contributions to the field of Corpus Linguistics and his professional generosity will never be forgotten.

In terms of its format, the present volume brings together fourteen interviews with well-known linguists. As editors, we had the feeling of holding a round table. Perhaps the main difference between this final written version and the spoken mode of a round table is that there is no direct discussion between the guests. Instead, this task is left to the reader, who will be able to arrive at an overall understanding of the topics discussed by piecing together the various approaches and perspectives.

We would like to make clear that a volume such as this one requires a special approach from the editors. Some degree of editing was needed in the replies so that the contributions became a kind of hybrid between interviews and essays. In several cases, after reading the first draft of the text, additional questions were posed to the guests in order to make their positions on a number of issues more explicit. Hopefully, this strategy has resulted in a better understanding of the points raised in the following pages. However, as no restriction has been imposed in terms of the content itself, the opinions expressed in the interviews are exclusively those of the interviewees. Because of the different nature of this collection, we were careful not to exercise any constraint on our guests' statements, even when they ran counter to our own positions as corpus researchers.

As this volume is aimed both at experts and novices in Corpus Linguistics, we paid special attention to clarity of expression. To this end, we asked the contributors to explain (sometimes in footnotes) the meaning of concepts which might be taken for granted by those already working in the field. Ample exemplification was also requested to help readers see the theoretical points raised. As in a normal essay, the interviewees were also asked to refer to published sources where readers could examine in more detail the issues covered. When our guests felt these additions were unnecessary, we respected their position and did not alter their original contributions.

Perspectives on Corpus Linguistics is of worldwide interest and application: it brings together researchers with different backgrounds and experiences, as their brief biographies at the end of the volume indicate. The foreword situates Corpus Linguistics and provides a framework for the entire volume. Each chapter is preceded by a title and a brief introduction written by the editors. The title signals the particularities of each interview while the introduction summarises the main points. They are intentionally concise so as to avoid preempting the ideas to be presented while arousing the readers' curiosity. The interviews which follow this preface have been ordered alphabetically by contributors' surnames.

Each interview consists of a set of ten questions, seven of which are common to all guests. These general themes can be grouped into four main clusters. We begin by enquiring about the area of Corpus Linguistics in a broader sense. Our interviewees detail their historical understanding of its development by pointing out where they place its roots and which factors they see as most relevant to its current popularity. We then address a recurrent theme in Corpus Linguistics: its status. This relates to the crucial issue of whether it constitutes a branch of Linguistics, a method, a methodology, a discipline, an approach, or something else.

The second area covered by the general questions refers to the method employed in carrying out corpus research and addresses two major issues in the field. We ask our guests how they understand corpora to be representative of a language (or a specific part of it) and, most importantly, how this goal may be achieved (if it is at all possible). The interviewees also consider the role intuition plays in corpus analysis as it has always been a slippery and complex topic.

We then move to two general issues relating to the actual performance of corpus research. First, the guests identify the research questions one should consider when carrying out corpus work. Next, they reflect on what is gained and lost in undertaking such work. The goal is to allow them to highlight what they think can be achieved by the use of corpora and what is still left out.

Directly related to the previous question, the last one in this general set looks forward to the future of Corpus Linguistics. In this part, the guests comment on the directions they believe we should be taking in the future. Some descriptions might seem hard to visualise as we do not know how current technology may change and enable us to achieve the goals which some interviewees project. However, what could be seen as science fiction now may not be so. Had we presented most current corpus approaches in a book some fifty years ago, perhaps our readers would not have believed them possible then.

As far as the three specific questions are concerned, a variety of topics are presented, which we group below into three categories. The first deals with materials and methods which are currently used in Corpus Linguistics. Table 1 presents a summary of the topics in this category.

Table 1. Materials and methods in Corpus Linguistics

Topic	Interviewee
Learner corpora	Guy Aston
Parallel and comparable corpora	Stig Johansson
Suitable corpora for translators	Sara Laviosa
Public-domain corpora and tools	Mark Davies

(continued)

(continued)

Topic	Interviewee
Markup	Guy Aston
Annotation	Geoffrey Leech
Treebanks	Geoffrey Sampson
Corpus comparison	Stefan Th. Gries
Technological mastery and requirements	Mark Davies
Speed of technological development	Mike Scott
Programming knowledge	Stefan Th. Gries
Statistics control	Stefan Th. Gries

As can be inferred from Table 1, a few questions deal with different types of corpora and to what extent they should be made available to the wider community of linguists. Some consideration is also given to the extra information that can be added to corpora when they are compiled.

The second group deals with specific aspects of research in Linguistics. Here, the interviewees comment on the advantages and disadvantages of using corpora to approach diverse features and levels of languages, as summarised in Table 2 below.

Table 2. Specific aspects in Linguistics

Topic	Interviewee
Historical Linguistics	Mark Davies
Pragmatics	Geoffrey Leech
Syntax	Geoffrey Sampson
Sociolinguistics	Paul Baker
Discourse Analysis	Mike Scott
Critical Discourse Analysis	Paul Baker
Contrastive Rhetoric	John Swales
Metaphor	Tony Berber Sardinha
Genres	John Swales
Registers	Susan Conrad

(continued)

(continued)

Topic	Interviewee
Language complexity	Geoffrey Sampson
English for Specific Purposes	Mike Scott
Interpersonal features in writing	Ken Hyland
Cross-linguistic research	Stig Johansson
Translation studies	Sara Laviosa
Changes in Corpus Linguistics	Stig Johansson
Corpora in developing countries	Tony Berber Sardinha

The questions in this second group include well-known branches of Linguistics (such as Pragmatics and Syntax) and other already familiar concepts (for instance, genre and register). Similar to the first group, the questions here also address languages other than English as, for instance, in the discussion of cross-linguistic investigations and of the use of corpora in translation studies.

In the third category, the specific questions point out to broader issues in order to show how corpora may be used in other areas of investigation, as briefly indicated in Table 3.

Table 3. Applied uses of corpora

Topic	Interviewee
Gender	Paul Baker
Social functions in literary research	Bill Louw
Social construction of knowledge	Ken Hyland
Challenges to traditional literary concepts	Bill Louw
Style	Geoffrey Leech
Literacy at the university	Ken Hyland
Academic literacy and pedagogy	John Swales
Student autonomy	Guy Aston
Teacher education	Susan Conrad
University literature curriculum	Bill Louw
Teaching materials for English/Spanish as a foreign language	Tony Berber Sardinha

(continued)

(continued)

Topic	Interviewee
Professional practice	Susan Conrad
Corpora vs. traditional translation resources	Sara Laviosa

From a general perspective, the questions in this third category point to interdisciplinary uses of Corpus Linguistics, indicating how it may be applied, for instance, in the study of literature and social aspects. Another major concern here is with pedagogical matters, when the interviewees discuss the usefulness of the corpus approach to learners of language, literature, and other professional areas.

In order that readers have a deeper look into what all the interviews may be suggesting, the final chapter presents the underpinnings which surge after reading the fourteen contributions. To this end, five strands that tie them together are described as the politics of Corpus Linguistics, and the author reflects on the implications of this political agenda.

At this stage, we hope readers will agree with our initial statement that there was much ground to be covered. As corpus-based investigations have become worldwide and as researchers continuously resort to them to suit a wide range of needs, we expect this publication will provide a more complete picture of where we stand 20 years after the publication of Sinclair's (1991) seminal *Corpus, Concordance, Collocation*.

This volume has been a truly collaborative enterprise and there is perhaps nothing better than a painting to illustrate the rationale behind it. The reader will probably be familiar with Seurat's *A Sunday Afternoon on the Island of La Grande Jatte*, a fine example of the art of Pointillism. On a huge canvas, Seurat shows a wide range of middle class people at a park on an island in the Seine, on which art historian Meyer Schapiro (1978: 103) comments:

> One can enjoy in the *Grande Jatte* many pictures each of which is a world in itself; every segment contains surprising inventions in the large shapes and the small, in the grouping and linking of parts, down to the patterning of the dots. The richness of Seurat lies not only in the variety of forms, but in the unexpected range of qualities and content within the same work: from the articulated and formed to its ground in the relatively homogeneous dots; an austere construction, yet so much of nature and human life; [...]

Like the dots in Seurat's painting, each of the interviews in this book is a world of its own. Although a similar set of questions is answered by fourteen eminent linguists, each one provides a different point of entry, a diverse view, or a unique perspective. If we are ever to arrive at a complete picture of what the area of Corpus Linguistics is like in the first decade of the 21st century, we can only arrive at it – as with Seurat's painting – by placing each fine and precise statement on a larger 'canvas' so that readers may construct a composite image.

In a different way from the painting, however, readers will notice that some areas are more easily identifiable while others are not so clearly defined. These are some of the connections and controversies that may be found in the area. The former helps us identify the directions the community of corpus researchers is taking. The latter indicates which areas still need our attention. It is only by bringing both aspects to the fore that we will be able to see, with the perspective of distance, the larger scenario of Corpus Linguistics at its current stage.

Vander Viana
Sonia Zyngier
Geoff Barnbrook

References

Granger, S. & Viana, V. 2007. Corpus Linguistics, language learning and ELT: An interview with Sylviane Granger. *Mindbite* (1): 11–14. <http://sites-test.uclouvain.be/cecl/archives/Interview_for_Mindbite.pdf>

Schapiro, M. 1978. *Modern Art: 19th & 20th Centuries*. London: Chatto & Windus.

Sinclair, J. 1991. *Corpus, Concordance, Collocation*. Oxford: OUP.

Applied Corpus Linguistics and the learning experience

The interview with Guy Aston, Professor of English Language and Translation at the University of Bologna (Italy), which opens the present volume, introduces us to an applied perspective of Corpus Linguistics. Differently from the other contributors, he emphasises the role of teaching and learning as an integral part in doing corpus studies. One might consider this to be commonsensical given that two of his specific questions deal with such topics (namely, learner corpora and student autonomy). Aston's concern for learners, however, pervades his interview, as, for instance, when he highlights the role of the language classroom in the development of Corpus Linguistics, in the concept of representativeness, in the advantages and disadvantages of the corpus approach, and in encoding corpora with extra information. All in all, Aston's statements encourage us to consider the impact of Corpus Linguistics beyond the research paradigm. His interview leads us to reflect on the potentials of corpora to our (language) classrooms and how our research may inform our own teaching practice.

1. Where do you place the roots of Corpus Linguistics? And to what do you attribute the growth of interest in the area?

The first concordance was probably that compiled for the Vulgate Bible in the 13th century by Hugh of St. Cher, who employed 500 monks to list almost every word in the Bible with the points where it was used. It thus seems right to see him as the first corpus linguist. The scale of his crowd-sourcing method explains why Corpus Linguistics has only become widespread since the arrival of computers and electronic texts. Today, Hugh could do the same job on his own with an everyday PC in a matter of minutes, using freely available electronic text and concordancing software (though printing out the results might take rather longer).

Like Hugh, whose interest was biblical exegesis, most corpus linguists are interested in applications of corpora rather than in corpora *per se*. This was obviously the case at the end of the last century, where what became the two main 'reference corpora' for English, the Bank of English and the British National Corpus, were both set up in collaboration with commercial publishers, who saw them as the basis for a new generation of dictionaries. The main provider of corpora in America, the Linguistic Data Consortium, was (and is) instead oriented towards the production of corpus resources for natural language processing applications, such as automatic speech recognition, text summarisation, and machine translation.

At the same time, there was a growing interest in corpora as a tool in the language learning classroom, particularly due to the work of Tim Johns, whose 'data-driven learning' approach exploited relatively small corpora to generate concordances from which learners could work out linguistic regularities for themselves. Johns' (1991) view of 'the learner as researcher' was complemented by a tendency for teaching materials to adopt syllabuses exploiting corpus-based research, privileging those features which appeared most frequently in native speaker corpora, or most problematic in corpora of learner data. The size of the ELT market has made it one of the major corpus users today, and has led to a growing popularisation of the corpus concept: the *100-go* English conversation programme on Japanese television, starring a 'Mr Corpus' puppet who provided frequency information and concordance examples, had an audience of over a million viewers (Tono 2011).

This focus on application is not to downgrade corpus-based work in theoretical and descriptive linguistics, which has also had notable impact on the application areas mentioned. Few books on Corpus Linguistics fail to pay homage to the work of John Sinclair, whose development of Firth's (1957) notions of collocation and colligation in the 'idiom principle' (Sinclair 1991) has widely influenced work in applied as well as descriptive linguistics, leading to a view of lexis and grammar as a continuum rather than an opposition. Corpus analysis has provided an empirical basis for much contemporary research on language, employing data-based methods which emphasise statistical regularities rather than combinatory rules.

2. Is Corpus Linguistics a science or a methodology? Where would you situate Corpus Linguistics in the scientific or methodological panorama?

The answer to this question can only be: both. Given its predominant concern with applications, Corpus Linguistics must be viewed as a methodology, whether employed to provide data for dictionaries and grammars, to produce language teaching syllabuses and materials, or for natural language processing procedures of speech recognition, automatic text categorisation/summarisation, machine translation, or authorship attribution. On the other hand, Corpus Linguistics is a science inasmuch as it has a particular object of study, namely language as it is actually used in naturally-occurring speech and writing: its focus on actual texts as its primary data (Sinclair 2004) distinguishes it from many other traditions in linguistics, notably from the Chomskyan focus on knowledge of language. For Corpus Linguistics, language is in the first place something which is used rather than known, and the primary concern is to identify patterns of use in selected bodies of text from some population of language use, and the principles by which those patterns are constructed. As such, it is a science, while in its various applications – in natural language processing, language pedagogy, forensic linguistics, etc. – I see it as a methodology, where its use is guided primarily by concerns of practical effectiveness and theories from other fields. One of the interesting things about the wide range of areas in which corpus linguistic methods are employed is that if you are interested in one application area, you can often learn things from other areas: there is a lot of scope for interdisciplinarity in applied Corpus Linguistics.

3. How representative can a corpus be?

A corpus which includes all the members of a textual population is fully representative. This is true of cases like the Bible, extant Old English poetry, and perhaps the works of Shakespeare (though in this case we must first agree what the textual population consists of). There are other fairly clear instances, such as a corpus of all the materials used – or produced in class – by a particular group of students, or of all the speeches delivered in the European Parliament in the last 14 years and their official translations (Koehn 2005). But in most cases, a corpus includes only a sample from the target population, which it may represent with varying degrees of adequacy. By definition, any corpus is only perfectly representative of itself.

Deciding whether a corpus which does not include the entire textual population we are concerned with can be said to represent it adequately is not just a matter of evaluating the sampling policy, but also of defining the population. With any sample corpus, it is easy to find text types which seem under- or over-represented: of the two main corpora designed to represent contemporary British English in the 1990s, the Bank of English was widely criticised as containing an excessive amount of journalism, and both it and the BNC as having too little speech. In both cases, the reasons were primarily economic ones: constructing corpora is an expensive business. Populations change over time: the BNC has been criticised as past its sell-by date since it does not include new text types like blogs and text messages, or recent neologisms (uses of 'web' in the BNC refer to spiders rather than the Internet) – and obviously its sample of teenager speech, collected around 1990, tells us little about the speech of teenagers today.

One way to improve representativeness may be to increase corpus size. A larger sample is more likely to capture more of the characteristics of a population, and some web-derived corpora now run to billions of words. But a sampling strategy which under- or over-represents certain areas of the population we are interested in will still be inadequate by definition, regardless of size. Corpus linguists are fond of saying that there is no data like more data – but it clearly needs to be the right data. Thus, while Web-as-Corpus initiatives have enabled cheap automatic construction of far larger corpora than those of the1990s, it is doubtful that they satisfactorily represent contemporary English as a whole – merely the English of the web, where there are not many transcripts of casual conversation, and the most common use of the word 'home' is likely to refer to home pages.

We can only really talk about representativeness if we have an adequate description of the population we are trying to represent. We do not have such a description for the works of Shakespeare, let alone contemporary language use, and the word 'representative' is much less used by corpus linguists now than it was twenty years ago. Corpora are what they are: they represent themselves, and different corpora will give different results. From this point of view, it is striking how few analyses use multiple corpora which purport to derive from the same population and compare the results, or consider the extent to which we should expect results from such comparisons to coincide. The important thing for users is to be aware of what the corpora they are using contain, and of how/why they have been designed and constructed, and to be consequently cautious in making generalisations about the population as a whole. If something happens a lot in a large corpus, it probably happens quite a lot in the population from which that corpus is drawn. If it does not happen in the corpus, that does not mean that it never happens in the population (though it probably does not happen as often as things that happen a lot in the corpus).

Assessing the reliability of corpus data ultimately often remains a matter of intuition – whether the results seem compatible with the analyst's experience of the textual population involved.

From the point of view of the applied corpus linguist, the real questions may in any case be less straightforward. In language teaching and learning, for instance, we would arguably like corpora to be representative of the textual population which language learners need to deal with, but at the same time to be ones whose use will help promote learning. These objectives may not be fully compatible: it may be more important that the texts included are relatively easy to understand and relate to, rather than that they constitute a representative sample of the target language. Anyone who has worked with corpora of casual conversation knows that even a native speaker often has no idea what is going on from a transcript. Appropriacy for purpose may be more important than representativeness *in se*.

4. How far should an analyst rely on intuition?

While necessary, intuition is proverbially inaccurate. We look things up in corpora and fail to find what we were expecting, and find things which we were not expecting. Intuition seems particularly unreliable for speech, where what we imagine people say is often the idealised speech of written journalism and fiction, which often differs substantially from the real thing, with its filled and unfilled pauses, false starts and repetitions. Our intuition also tends to privilege literal over metaphorical meanings, and the prototypical uses listed in prescriptive grammars and textbooks. Our intuition tends to focus on one use at a time, forgetting others than the one we first thought of – particularly uses in other text types and context types. Intuition is also notoriously unreliable as to the relative frequency of different features, and obviously, is hopeless with regard to text and context types with which we are not familiar. On the other hand, however, when we look at corpus findings we do often find that they match our intuitions retrospectively, as we recognise familiar patterns and mutter 'of course, why didn't I think of that?'.

For this last reason, one of the roles of intuition in corpus analysis is to test corpus findings. If we find that a particular use is more (or less) frequent in a corpus than we would have expected, it may be appropriate to examine its distribution across texts and across text types, and to see if the results are biased by the composition of the corpus, due to the presence/absence of a particular text or text type. Our results may also be distorted by the way we have formulated our queries, which have effectively excluded cases we are interested in or included ones which are irrelevant to our purposes.

Intuition is also important in formulating queries. Familiarity with the language and text type concerned, as well as with the corpora and query software, may help us strike a balance between recall (finding all the cases we are interested in) and precision (finding only cases we are interested in). Take 'strike a balance between'. If we want to investigate the use of this expression in a corpus, we need to consider a range of possible variants in order to maximise recall – different forms of the verb 'strike', possible modifications of 'balance' (might it also occur with adjectives, with the definite article, or in the plural?), omission of 'between', passivisation, insertion of adverbial elements, etc. These are all decisions which are aided by experience and intuition, and will determine whether we find such BNC instances as:

> *She described the Maastricht Treaty as striking the 'necessary balance' between the conflicting interests of the 12 EC members.*   (HLK: 2233)

> *In dealings with other people a balance needs to be struck, therefore, between standing up for your own rights whilst respecting other people's.*   (B2F: 1547)

Intuition can similarly help us decide how far we should restrict a query in order to reduce recall and improve precision. It is often necessary to find ways of eliminating trees to find the wood. A search for co-occurrences of 'wood' and 'trees' in a span of five words in the BNC finds as many literal as metaphorical uses: it is only when we add the lemma 'see' to the query that it becomes a reasonably precise means of investigating the metaphor. But then, as you may notice from the sentence you are currently reading, we also lose sight of trees in other bits of the same wood.

5. What kind of questions should an analyst think of?

The immediate answer is: questions which are appropriate to the analyst's purposes, whatever these may be. Because intuition is unreliable, it is a good idea also to pose questions to which you think you already know the answers. Deciding what you want to find out is the first problem. The second is selecting a suitable corpus or corpora for the job. The third is deciding how that problem can be formulated as a query or set of queries, and eventually refined as necessary (there are of course further problems about how best to do this). And then there all the questions are involved in interpreting the results.

There are also questions which do not derive from a prior purpose, but may accidentally arise *en route*, motivated by pure curiosity. Both the typical outputs provided by corpus software, namely concordances and counts of various kinds, will offer all sorts of information as well as – or instead of – that which was initially sought for, and it is rare not to encounter things among them which are unexpected, but nonetheless potentially relevant to the analyst in some wider context. One example is in translation. When using a corpus to test a particular translation hypothesis, particularly where that corpus contains texts similar to the one being translated, the user may well discover that the context of an instance in the corpus provides a solution to another problem in that (or in a similar) translation. We can learn other things from corpora than those we were looking for. In the final example in the previous answer, I was struck by the use of 'whilst' +V-ing to link the two alternatives between which a balance needs to be struck. In the BNC, I found that 'whilst' is 10 times less frequent than 'while', and that it is particularly rare in spoken conversation, newspapers and fiction. While the most frequent verb lemmas following 'while' are 'wait', 'go', 'make', 'work', 'remain', 'take' and 'try', those most frequently following 'whilst' are 'work', 'maintain', 'retain', 'remain', 'make', 'try' and 'recognise'. The differences between these lists highlight the use of 'whilst' in contrasts, such as

The Grand offers many modern facilities whilst retaining its Victorian grandeur.

(EFE: 30)

And this concordance line could easily lead to further questions: does 'grandeur' always have such positive associations? (Its most significant collocate in the BNC is 'delusions'.) What are the most significant collocates of 'Victorian' as a premodifier? ('era'/'terraced house(s)'/'gothic'/'mansion'/ 'prudery'). Arguably, this list tells us something about the stereotype of Victorian Britain, providing cultural as well as purely linguistic information which might be of use to the language teacher or learner, as well as the amateur anthropologist.

Corpus use is essentially an open-ended process. In the area in which I use corpora, that of language and translation teaching and learning, one of the questions the corpus user has to ask is thus whether something is worth learning. Is this phenomenon sufficiently frequent to make it worth investigating? Is it relevant in the text types I am trying to master? In other words, is it all worth the effort? The enormous range of things that might be explored has to be narrowed down by considerations which are external to Corpus Linguistics itself, but depend on the analyst's purposes.

6. What are the strengths and weaknesses of corpus analysis?

Given the growing size of corpora, corpus analysis is increasingly quantitative, tending to focus on those features which are readily identifiable and countable for a computer. This generally means word forms (readily identified by the relatively unambiguous feature of spacing), and their co-occurrences with other word forms as collocations, n-grams, etc. These frequency counts can then be compared with those obtained for other words and co-occurrences, or with those for different corpora or sub-corpora, in order to identify statistically significant differences. This approach has provided many insights into collocational and colligational patterns (witness the emphasis on collocations and colligations in corpus-based dictionaries and grammars), and into the distribution of linguistic features across different text types, different language users, and different language varieties (Biber et al. 1999).

A major strength of corpus analysis is that such counts can highlight patterns which may have eluded intuition. Thus it is doubtful whether the frequent use of the verb 'tend' in conversation would have been noted (and empirically demonstrated) without quantitative analysis of corpus data (McCarthy & Carter 1995). I shall not go into the question here of the relative appropriacy of the various statistical tests used in evaluating counts, other than to note that such tests tend to assess frequencies for significance by reference to a null hypothesis of random occurrence – even though random occurrence is near-impossible in language use (Kilgariff 2005). In consequence, it seems implicitly agreed that only those differences which are highly significant statistically should be taken seriously.

It must also be borne in mind that quantitative analyses tend to be based on counts of forms without distinguishing meanings. They simply count what can easily be counted. Thus studies of the distribution of first person pronouns in different text types rarely distinguish between inclusive/exclusive 'we' ('we all have to die sooner or later' vs. 'we all miss you').

One recurrent focus of recent quantitative analyses has been n-grams, i.e. recurrent multi-word sequences. This has led to the production of lists of 'multi-word units' or 'formulae' associated with particular text types, with proposals [following Sinclair's (1991) notion of the 'idiom principle'] that they be treated as part of the lexicon in natural language processing, and taught as such to language learners. Leaving aside the question of the level of recurrence required for a sequence to constitute a multi-word unit rather than an *ad hoc* composite, such a simple counting approach overlooks the possibility of variation within these units (in strident contrast, for example, with the tendency to conflate different forms of the same lemma in single-word lexical analysis). Thus, while 'have a nice day' is undoubtedly a frequent formula, in the BNC we also find fair numbers of the variants 'have a good/lovely/ wonderful day', not to mention 'have a snazzy day'. The variation here does not seem totally free: the range of words that replace 'nice' appears limited to more or less synonymous adjectives, all without pre-modification: there are no cases of 'have a very nice (or 'very good/lovely/wonderful/snazzy') day' in the BNC. A more complicated example is that of proverbs, which are regularly varied and abbreviated to match the particular context, and rarely occur in their prototypical form, which the addressee is assumed to be able to retrieve from a partial citation. But because automatic counting procedures are comparatively primitive, regularities of these kinds tend to be overlooked by n-gram analysts – unless they design their queries to take account of possible variations, which implies manually inspecting the results.

The essential limit of quantitative analyses is that they present the user with numbers rather than instances of use. It is only by inspecting occurrences that the user can decide whether the right things are being counted, and relate forms to meanings. Otherwise, purely quantitative results risk total decontextualisation, and hence defy validation through intuition and experience.

7. What is the future of Corpus Linguistics?

The future of Corpus Linguistics will largely be determined by its practical applications. Developments of the semantic web, using meaning- rather than form-based search criteria, seem likely to use corpus-based methods to classify texts, along the lines of those developed by Biber et al. (1998) to distinguish registers, or by Baroni & Bernardini (2006) to distinguish original texts from translations. The recently increased effectiveness of machine translation systems (notably Google's) derives from analyses of massive automatically-compiled parallel corpora, which are continually augmented on the basis of user feedback, and similar crowd-sourcing methods are likely to be employed in the construction of ontologies for the semantic web. The development of speech recognition and classification systems seems set to require mammoth multimedia corpora, and may eventually also lead to effective speech-to-speech translation. Corpus Linguistics will be called on to assist in the process of elaborating appropriate algorithms, and there will be indirect feedback into research on text and speech comprehension and production. There also seems little doubt that in future, most corpora will be compiled from texts available on the Internet, largely using automatic procedures. Consequently, corpus construction will depend to a large extent on the search algorithms of Google, Bing and Yahoo, and the extent to which commercial interests limit the nature of the texts – and hence the corpora – which can be made available.

From the perspective of language teaching and learning, one direction which seems important is that of multimedia corpora of speech, where audio (and even video) are aligned with their transcriptions, so that as well as reading a concordance line, the user can immediately hear the corresponding audio segment. A project is currently underway to achieve this for the BNC spoken data (Coleman 2010). Corpora consisting solely of transcripts are a very limited resource for learners seeking to develop active and passive oral proficiency, since they provide little or no information as to pronunciation features (including stress and intonation), and are decontextualised with respect to the actual processes of speaking and listening. Recent work in phraseology has highlighted ways in which fluency in speaking and listening seems largely based on a use of multi-word sequences which are produced and interpreted as single units, with their own distinctive patterns of pronunciation and variation (Lin & Adolphs 2009). These range from functional units such as 'as far as I know' and 'one of the things that' to referential ones such as 'global warming' and 'coal-fired power stations'. Dictionaries and textbooks rarely provide information as to the pronunciation of units like these (e.g. which syllable bears the primary stress), but aligned speech corpora will enable learners to access multiple instances and hear them in context, just as they will enable corpus analysts to identify these units and their behaviours more effectively.

The availability of automatic corpus construction tools (Baroni & Bernardini 2004) will also increasingly place teachers and learners in a position to construct their own specialised corpora in order to assist them in projects dealing with a particular topic and/or text type, be it in order to extract terminology and identify recurrent formulae, or to check the appropriacy of their own textual productions. But in order to maximise the value of such corpora, it is essential for ways to be found of solving a problem raised nearly twenty years ago by Leech (1997), namely that of ranking corpus data by its simplicity/difficulty, either through markup or through on-the-fly filtering, so that learners can be presented with instances which are appropriate to their level of proficiency. There are few things more demotivating for the average learner than to be faced with screenfuls of incomprehensible concordance lines. To help establish such difficulty levels, an important role may be played by learner corpora, as a source of information as to what can be assumed to be relatively unproblematic for learners at a particular level.

8. What are the advantages and the challenges of setting up learner corpora? And how have they impacted research in Applied Linguistics?

Learner corpora can reveal much about learner language, showing recurrent patterns of various kinds which are potentially fascinating for those interested in cross-language interference, in interlanguage, and in second language acquisition in general. However, the methods used to compile such corpora, and the interpretations of data derived from them in applied linguistic research, merit reflection. First, most learner corpora consist of essays written by learners, or of transcripts of interviews with learners (following the ICLE model: Granger 1998). While the homogeneity of these text types clearly facilitates comparison of different learner groups, it seems legitimate to question whether they provide adequate evidence of learners' real-life communicative abilities. Most written learner corpora consist of data gathered in pseudo-examination contexts, in which learners may understandably opt to 'play safe', avoiding risks and relying on behaviour in which they feel most confident and most likely to make a good impression. The same is true of spoken interviews, where the behaviour of the interviewer is not generally taken into consideration as a variable affecting the learner's production. While such corpora are relatively easy to compile, are they really the kinds we need?

The choice of construction criteria for learner corpora depends on their intended use. A striking tendency of the literature based on such corpora is its focus on negative features – perceived inadequacies in learner behaviour. Studies have focused on what learners get wrong, drawing conclusions about what they need to be better taught. One approach has coded and counted perceived learner errors – from misspellings to incorrect collocations and rhetorical inappropriacies. Such codings are far from straightforward, since they first involve hypothesising what the learner should have written or said (and hence what they wanted to say, which may be far from obvious), and then categorising and counting the errors of different types. This is far from simple, since more than one error may underlie a particular 'faulty' portion of text. Any teacher who has compared his/her own correction of a piece of learner writing with that of a colleague will recognise the subjectivity of error correction, and, hence, the difficulty of achieving replicability.

A more reliable approach, which avoids this interpretative trap, has focused on the frequencies of particular features, comparing these frequencies with those found in data produced by more proficient learners, learners of different backgrounds, or by native speakers. This approach has led to the employment of the damning terms 'overuse' and 'underuse' of particular features by learners in comparison with some reference group. But it remains to be shown that learners should be judged on the basis of their conformity to the behaviour of a particular reference group, or indeed to a statistical norm: even learners have a right to a personal identity, and to use language creatively to assert it. In any case, the things that particular learners (or learner groups) are accused of underusing or overusing are once more the things which are easy for corpus analysts to count: particular lexical items, collocations and grammatical structures. There has been little attempt to describe under/overuse in pragmatic terms. Do learners try to explain what they mean more often? Do they clarify reference more often? Do they reformulate more often? Do they apologise more often for their linguistic shortcomings? If they do these things, they are arguably adopting sensible strategies of communication given their limited linguistic skills. However, many analyses of learner corpora have treated all quantitative differences from reference group behaviour as undesirable – as things that learners should learn not to do, rather than as things that may help them communicate and learn more effectively.

Analyses in terms of errors or of underuse/overuse of specific features both take a negative view of learner behaviour. For those who remember the course of applied linguistics in the last century, this view looks suspiciously familiar. Some thirty years ago, the birth of interlanguage studies put a (temporary) end to traditional error analysis as a research approach (Corder 1981). Rather than trying to describe and correct what learners did wrong, applied linguists became interested in what they did right from a communication and learning perspective, and how, as a result, they managed to improve. But such interest has been missing from much work on learner corpora. Those focusing on error have paid too little attention to success – what are the things that learners get right, or that allow them to solve their communication problems even while making mistakes? Those who turn their attention to frequency of use have rarely asked *why* learners underuse/overuse particular features, and whether these tendencies may not result from the particular contexts in which they find themselves as learners. Rather than comparing their performances with those of native speakers, it might well be more appropriate to compare them with performances by successful users of English as a Lingua Franca, and in real-life situations rather than in artificial classroom tasks.

This is not to deny the positive impact on applied linguistics of much work based on learner corpora. Quantitative accounts of learner language provide important material for reflection by teachers, materials writers – and indeed learners themselves, who are often highly motivated to avoid errors and the overuse of particular features, particularly in their productions in educational contexts. But learner corpora also need to be designed, analysed and interpreted in the light of current theories of language learning.

9. In what way(s) can corpus work help student autonomy?

It was Tim Johns (1991) who first proposed a view of the learner as researcher, in a process of 'data-driven learning'. The possibility for learners to perform their own analyses and reach their own conclusions can be highly motivating for the sense of empowerment it provides, since it puts the learner in a position to contradict their teachers and textbooks. The teacher's role can largely cease to be that of an authority about the language, becoming primarily that of an authority on learning methods – an aide to students in their autonomous learning process. Students often have better computer skills than their teachers, and many students may derive more from first-hand corpus work than their teachers may expect. What they have to learn is to pose relevant questions, to translate these questions into appropriate corpus queries, and to analyse and interpret the results of these queries in order to draw conclusions which are useful for their learning purposes.

In the first place, students need to understand what kinds of information corpora can provide, and how this compares with that available from other tools, such as dictionaries or Google searches. Research in Corpus Linguistics has provided many useful indications, particularly at the lexical level, where the notions of the 'phraseological item' (Sinclair 2008) and 'lexical priming' (Hoey 2005) point to a focus on collocation, colligation, semantic preference and semantic prosody, as well as on associations with particular text types and textual positions. These are all features which the learner can be taught to look for in selecting appropriate corpora or subcorpora, formulating appropriate queries to balance recall and precision, and exploiting sorting and listing techniques to identify recurrent patterns in concordances. Does this mean that the learner should be trained as a corpus linguist? In part, yes; but in part, no. Unlike the lexicographer, the learner's objective is not necessarily one of accounting for all the data, merely to identify some of the patterns which recur in it, patterns of which they can recognise a utility for their own purposes. The learner needs to view corpus data by asking 'What can I take away from all of this which would be useful to me?' – a frequent collocation, a frequent textual position, or a strange exception.

The key questions are nearly always functional ones. What items can perform this function? What can this item be used to do? And the answers to these two questions can only be found by examining an item's contexts of use. With respect to the first of these questions, students need to learn to exploit collocates. Where they do not know exactly what item they are looking for, they should try looking for other items which are likely to co-occur with the unknown one. If you do not know what word to use to denote the piece of glass in a window, listing the noun collocates of 'window' can provide clues: in the BNC the most significant collocates of 'window' are 'sill' and 'pane'. With respect to the second question, students need practice in designing queries with adequate recall, considering possible variants and ambiguities, and exploiting any available markup. Some of the first things I teach students learning to use corpora are to list the possible parts of speech for a particular word form, to list the possible forms of a lemma, and to list the possible positions of an adjective. In interpreting results, understanding the function of an item will often involve inspecting a larger context than that provided by an online KWIC concordance. This implies limiting the number of instances which have to be examined, and encouraging students to work with random sets. Such qualitative study can then be followed up with quantitative analysis to confirm or disconfirm findings based on a limited number of instances, if necessary refining queries to focus on particular patterns.

The need to examine and read relevant instances in an adequate context poses a number of problems in proposing corpora for learner use. For instance, it may help if the learner limits queries to a particular text type which is familiar to them, or indeed constructs a corpus for themselves containing only texts of a particular type or from a particular domain (Baroni & Bernardini 2004) – from many points of view, small and specialised is beautiful where corpora for learners are concerned (Aston 1997). It may also help if they first eliminate instances involving other uses of the search expression – for instance by restricting their query to a particular part of speech, or by manually eliminating other senses. Take the word 'atmosphere'. This is used in both a literal and a metaphorical sense, but in a large mixed corpus such as the BNC the latter is much more frequent. Once we eliminate the literal uses from a random set, it becomes apparent that in its metaphorical use, 'atmosphere' is not a neutral term. It generally has a clear semantic prosody – either a 'relaxed/ friendly/family/good/informal/welcoming/special atmosphere', or a 'charged/ tense/strained/hostile' one.

Looking at particular instances in context may arouse the learner's curiosity – what is this text and what is it about? Why is this particular instance seemingly different from the general pattern? In other words, it may encourage serendipitous exploration. We should never forget that a corpus is a resource from which learners may learn many other things than those they were originally looking for. Since corpora provide samples of language to be examined, not examples of particular features – as found in grammars and textbooks (or hopefully in dictionaries) (Gavioli 2005), they take longer to use, but can be far more rewarding.

10. What are the challenges and potentials of encoding corpora?

Markup adds information to corpus texts, usually of a lexicogrammatical, text-structural, or contextual nature. Lexicogrammatical markup may involve adding information for (a) each word form as to part of speech, lemma (the headword from which each word form derives), word sense and semantic class; and (b) syntactic segmentation (into clause and phrase units, often continuing down to the word or morpheme level), with categorisation of their syntactic roles. Text-structural markup typically indicates sentence boundaries, paragraphs, sections, headings/captions/notes/quotations, etc., and for spoken transcripts utterance-breaks (and their speakers), along with non-verbal and paralinguistic features such as pauses and hesitations, laughter, coughs, background noises, emphasis, accent and the like. Contextual markup provides text categorisations, bibliographic information, details concerning the setting and the participants, as well as information concerning the markup procedures employed. While methods used to indicate markup vary considerably, the TEI guidelines offer a widely-accepted set of norms.

Corpora designed or adapted for particular uses may also include markup specifically designed for those uses. One case is the markup of errors in learner corpora. Parallel corpora typically include alignment markup, indicating correspondences between text-segments in one language and text-segments in another language. In speech corpora, markup may similarly indicate correspondences between transcript segments and segments of the original audio, as well as temporal relationships between different parts of the transcript (e.g. overlapping and latched turns).

Where carried out manually, markup is a tedious and expensive business, so researchers tend only to mark up those things they are interested in, or for which reasonably reliable automatic procedures are available. Seen from a language teaching and learning perspective, what features would one like to be marked up in corpora? Within a communicative approach, the obvious desirable is pragmatic or discourse function. For instance, it would be useful to retrieve all the occurrences of a particular speech-act type (a segment of the ICE spoken corpus of Irish English has been manually marked up in this way – see the forthcoming reference to SPICE-Ireland in Kallen & Kirk 2008), rather than simply relying on presumed form-function correspondences. The latter rarely have effective recall: if we search for instances of 'advice-giving' by looking for a list of forms ('I advise', 'if I were you', 'you should/ought to', etc.), not only will we miss instances where advice is given in other ways, but precision may also be low, given the number of potential functions of an expression like 'you should'. Or again, in learner corpora it would be nice to have markup of conversational repair sequences, in which mistakes and misunderstandings are resolved: do learners use the same strategies to deal with these problems as native or successful ELF speakers?

Markup at the lexicogrammatical level can improve the recall and precision of many queries. For learners, it is useful to be able to search for any form of a particular lemma, or a particular sense of a word – how else can one retrieve occurrences of the noun 'will' (in the sense of 'desire'/'wish'), while excluding the modal verb, the main verb, the proper noun, and the 'testament' noun sense? At the same time, the learner needs to be made aware of all these other possibilities and their relative probabilities, and exercises in classifying concordance lines by word-sense while ignoring markup are arguably an important part of learner training. Similarly, syntactic markup can facilitate the retrieval of particular syntactic constructions. And markup of text structure and context can facilitate queries concerning, for example, the syntax of newspaper headlines or the organisation of research article abstracts. So markup seems a good thing, provided that it is reasonably reliable and that it can when so wished be ignored, so as to place the learner in the position of the reader of the text.

One striking fact about the current corpus landscape is the lack of aligned speech corpora. Most language learners want to speak and understand speech, and access to audio parallel to transcripts would make corpus use a much more effective learning aid. Another area where little is available is that of parallel translation corpora, where again there are no widespread simple query tools. Such corpora can play an important role not only in translator training but also in language learning, by highlighting cross-language contrasts and by making foreign language data more readily comprehensible (Frankenberg-Garcia 2005).

Many of these problems are objects of research in natural language processing, where procedures for audio and translation alignment, the recognition of text and lexicogrammatical structure, and identification of discourse function are slowly being developed and improved. Hopefully, they will become sufficiently reliable to allow corpora to be automatically marked up in a greater variety of ways, according to the purposes of the user.

References

Aston, G. 1997. Small and large corpora in language learning. In *PALC '97: Practical Applications in Language Corpora*, B. Lewandowska-Tomasczczyk & P. J. Melia (eds), 51–62. Lódź: Lódź University Press.

Baroni, M. & Bernardini, S. 2004. BootCaT: Bootstrapping corpora and terms from the web. *Proceedings of LREC 2004.* <http://sslmit.unibo.it/~baroni/publications/lrec2004/bootcat_lrec_2004.pdf>

Baroni, M. & Bernardini, S. 2006. A new approach to the study of translationese: Machine-Learning the difference between original and translated text. *Literary and Linguistic Computing* 21(3): 259–274.

Biber, D., Conrad, S. & Reppen, R. 1998. *Corpus Linguistics: Investigating Language Structure and Use.* Cambridge: CUP.

Biber, D., Johansson, S., Leech, G., Conrad, S. & Finegan, E. 1999. *Longman Grammar of Spoken and Written English.* London: Longman.

Coleman, J. 2010. Plans for an audio search engine. *Digital Planet,* 5 January

2010. <www.bbc.co.uk/iplayer/console/p005m6zn>

Corder, S. P. 1981. *Error Analysis and Interlanguage.* Oxford: OUP.

Firth, J. R. 1957. *Papers in Linguistics 1934–1951.* London: OUP.

Frankenberg-Garcia, A. 2005. Pedagogical uses of monolingual and parallel concordances. *ELT Journal* 59(3): 189–198.

Gavioli, L. 2005. *Exploiting Corpora for ESP Learning* [Studies in Corpus Linguistics 21]. Amsterdam: John Benjamins.

Granger, S. 1998. *Learner English on Computer.* London: Longman.

Hoey, M. 2005. *Lexical Priming.* London: Routledge.

Johns, T. 1991. Should you be persuaded: Two examples of data-driven learning. In *Classroom Concordancing*, T. Johns & P. King (eds). *ELR Journal* 4: 1–16.

Kallen, J. L. & Kirk, J. M. 2008. *ICE-Ireland: A User's Guide.* Belfast: Queen's University.

Kilgariff, A. 2005. Language is never, ever, ever, random. *Corpus Linguistics and Linguistic Theory* 1–2: 263–276.

Koehn, P. 2005. Europarl: A parallel corpus for statistical machine translation. MT Summit 2005. <http://www.statmt.org/europarl/>

Leech, G. N. 1997. Teaching and language corpora: A convergence. In *Teaching and Language Corpora*, A. Wichmann, S. Fligelstone, T. McEnery & G. Knowles (eds), 1–23. London: Longman.

Lin, P. & Adolphs, S. 2009. Sound evidence: Phraseological units in spoken corpora. In *Collocating in Another Language: Multiple Interpretations*, A. Barfield & H. Gyllstad (eds), 34–48. Basingstoke: Palgrave Macmillan.

McCarthy, M. & Carter, R. 1995. Spoken grammar: What is it and how do we teach it? *ELT Journal* 49(3): 207–218.

Sinclair, J. McH. 1991. *Corpus, Concordance, Collocation.* Oxford: OUP.

Sinclair, J. McH. 2004. *Trust the Text.* London: Routledge.

Sinclair, J. McH. 2008. Envoi: The phrase, the whole phrase, and nothing but the phrase. In *Phraseology: An Interdisciplinary Perspective*, S. Granger & F. Meunier (eds), 407–410. Amsterdam: John Benjamins.

Tono, Y. 2011. TALC in action: Recent innovations in corpus-based English language teaching in Japan. In *New Trends in Corpora and Language Learning*, A. Frankenberg-Garcia, L. Flowerdew & G. Aston (eds), 3–25. London: Continuum.

Social involvement in corpus studies

Reader at Lancaster University (United Kingdom), Paul Baker stresses the role corpus research plays in bringing to light social concepts which may underpin texts. The three specific questions he addresses reflect this concern and go hand in hand with his research interests: critical discourse analysis, gender issues and sociolinguistics. He reports on the potential of using corpora to carry out research in areas which have been traditionally viewed as mostly qualitative, favouring the investigation of small samples of language. In line with a social perspective, Baker prefers not to place Corpus Linguistics under a single label (be that 'science', 'methodology' or any other), assuming that it can have a different nature depending on its role in any given project. As a matter of fact, he argues in favour of a less rigid way of conceiving fields of study so that their boundaries become more fluid. Baker believes this perspective will lead the path of future corpus users.

1. Where do you place the roots of Corpus Linguistics? And to what do you attribute the growth of interest in the area?

There were people using methods and ideas that we would view as being similar to Corpus Linguistics as early as a century ago – in the 19th and early 20th centuries early linguists engaged in 'diary studies' where they kept diaries of the developing language of infants, writing down everything that the children said. There is also research referred to in McEnery and Wilson (2001: 3) by Käding published in 1897, which looked at distribution of letters and sequences of letters in an 11-million-word corpus of German (all done without computers!). However, it was not until the emergence of computers (at first slow and primitive ones that were only accessible by elite scientists) that allowed the field to slowly emerge from the 1960s onwards. It is possibly the publication, in 1964, of the Brown University Standard Corpus of Present-Day English (or the Brown Corpus) which contained a million words of written American English in 15 genres from texts published in 1961 that could be said to signify the start of Corpus Linguistics.

I would attribute the growth in interest to the fact that computers have increasingly played such a prominent role in people's lives, particularly since the 1990s. Computers have transformed many academic practices – students now routinely use email to contact lecturers, teaching materials are uploaded onto institutional bulletin boards which also enable 'seminar-like' discussion. Coursework and feedback is submitted electronically. Everyone in academia is now much more familiar with computers, and rather than people feeling that Corpus Linguistics is the preserve of people with a degree in computing or statistics, it is something that almost anyone can try. People are now confident in the analytical techniques that computers can offer, and they are confident in using them. The Internet itself has helped to inform growing numbers of people around the globe about Corpus Linguistics (the journal I edit, *Corpora*, is particularly popular in East Asia), and the emergence of encoding standards like Unicode, as well as software that can work with writing systems like Arabic, Chinese, Bengali etc. have also helped immensely. Additionally, the fact that Corpus Linguistics encompasses a collection of methods that can be applied to many different fields has allowed it to cross over into new areas.

2. Is Corpus Linguistics a science or a methodology? Where would you situate Corpus Linguistics in the scientific or methodological panorama?

I think a case could be made for arguing both. A science is an enterprise for gathering knowledge and organising it into testable laws and theories. It includes observation, experimentation and measurement. It needs to be based on observable phenomena and be capable of being tested under the same conditions by other researchers (replicability). I think Corpus Linguistics embodies these aspects, using naturally occurring data and methods of measurement which are grounded in statistics. The fact that many reference corpora are widely available means that other people can attempt to replicate existing studies.

A methodology refers more to the set of procedures that are associated with a particular approach (although some people view a methodology as also including a set of theories or concepts which relate to a discipline). Again, Corpus Linguistics could be viewed as a methodology – there are various criteria or principles in terms of data collection (balance, representativeness, sampling), as well as techniques such as annotation and analytical routines (collocations, sorting concordances, dispersion). Corpus Linguistics does not have a method that is 'set in stone', however. There is no one step-by-step way that we can carry out the collection and analysis of a corpus. Instead, we can choose from a collection of methods and principles. And in particular, the analytical procedures could be carried out in different orders, or some may not be used at all. Additionally, different cut-off points of significance may be used in our analysis (we may only consider, say, collocates that have an MI score of 3, or we may set our collocational range at four words either side of a search term) and this will obviously impact on the outcomes of our analysis. While this may result in our analysis appearing somewhat unscientific and *ad hoc*, at least we can describe what we did in detail, allowing others to replicate the way we carried out our analysis – or do something differently and then challenge the way we did it.

3. How representative can a corpus be?

It depends on the variety of language that the analyst wants to collect – the more wide ranging the variety, the more difficult it becomes to achieve full representativeness. For projects that have restrictions on time period, author and genre, it becomes easier. To give an example, I have recently collected a corpus of news texts which discuss the topic of Islam. Due to the existence of online archives of news articles, it is possible to enter a search term and specify which newspapers you want to look in and also specify a set of dates. We can then be reasonably confident that the corpus is extremely (if not totally) representative of this genre on that subject from that set of newspapers in the specified time period. Some articles may be missed though – I later spotted an article in the *Guardian* which claimed that young Tory politicians were being trained at a 'Tory madrasa', and because I did not have 'madrasa' in my search term, this text was missed. Additionally an article may potentially only mention Muslims in a very oblique way such as 'those people who cover their faces'. With that said, if you limit claims about representativeness to 'articles which contain the following search terms … ' then at least you are not misleading anybody.

On the other hand, when I built the BE06 corpus, which was designed to be a corpus of written published British English from circa 2006, I followed the model of corpus design that was first used with the Brown Corpus (1 million words of 15 genres of writing, containing 2,000-word samples). It is difficult to claim that this corpus is fully representative of language use – many words in English do not even appear in it, and even the 15 genres do not represent all written published English. With a small corpus like this, I would feel more confident when examining aspects of language which occur frequently. So I was able to compare the BE06 to early corpora like FLOB (from 1991) and LOB (1961) to see whether certain pronouns like *he* and *his* had increased or decreased over time. Because pronouns occur in many texts and are reasonably frequent, it is easier to be confident that any patterns of change you see are representative, rather than being due to idiosyncratic texts being included.

4. How far should an analyst rely on intuition?

A positive feature of Corpus Linguistics research is that you can carry out a piece of analysis on a text or set of texts from a relatively 'naïve' position. Techniques like the elicitation of keywords allow a corpus-driven form of analysis to be carried out, whereby the researcher then has to account for whatever is salient in the data under analysis.

On the other hand, I doubt that much research is ever approached from a completely naïve perspective. Most of us usually have reasons for choosing to look at a particular text or set of texts, and, as language users ourselves, we may already have intuitions (even if they are not always consciously acknowledged). It can be quite tempting at times to try to focus on aspects of a text which fit our preconceptions, and while corpus analysis is better than some forms of analysis at reining in this tendency, it is not perfect. Even if we choose corpus-driven analysis like keywords, we often still will have too many keywords to follow-up, so there needs to be a further selection process.

Intuition in itself can only take us so far. If we have a 'hunch' about something in a corpus, and follow it up, we may find evidence to support our hunch ... or not. If all we want to do is test a hypothesis that we hold, then that is fine. However, there may be other aspects of language in the corpus which are more frequent or salient, and our hunch may not actually be the most interesting feature to have been examined. This is where combining an intuitive approach with a 'naïve' approach, allowing them to inform each other, can be more helpful.

5. What kind of questions should an analyst think of?

A couple of general points first: I often tell my students that when they set themselves a research question, it should be at least answerable. It is quite common to see Corpus Linguistics PhD students in their first year setting themselves questions which their corpus research will simply not be able to answer, because they are too general, vague or ambitious.

With that said, while some analysts begin corpus research with a very specific set of questions, others may approach the data with only a vague idea of what they are interested in, and as a result of their explorations, the questions may emerge or become firmer at a much later stage of the analysis. So, I do not think it is absolutely necessary to begin a research project with very precise questions – and often the answer to a question will result in more questions.

Corpus Linguistics is good at answering questions to do with variation (e.g. how does *x* compare with *y*?, has *x* changed over time?), and particularly questions which relate to amounts (e.g. by how much?, is the difference statistically significant?). I get the impression that Corpus Linguistics, like many other research methods, gets us to view difference as more exciting or important than similarity. So if feature *x* has changed over time or occurs differently in corpus *y* compared to corpus *z*, then that is often seen as a more interesting finding than if there are no differences. When we look at what the corpus software lets us do – we see that we can find things like keywords which point out which words are statistically more frequent in one corpus when compared against another. But it is not so easy to automatically get lists of words where the frequencies are very similar. So, at the moment, when we ask questions, it is sensible to take into account what the software is capable of – but at the same time, we should also think about questions that the software cannot currently tell us, and push for further development of tools.

Finally, a typical corpus analysis which only stays within the corpus is not so good at answering questions which require explanations. So, if I find out that feature *x* has increased over time, the corpus is unlikely to be able to fully explain why this has happened, although looking at examples in the data may offer clues. Instead, the 'why' questions may require us to look elsewhere – at political, social or historical context for example.

6. What are the strengths and weaknesses of corpus analysis?

One of the strengths is that it allows the cognitive and social biases of the researcher to be reduced (although not removed). As researchers, none of us can claim to be completely objective about a piece of research (even the desire to be objective is a 'stance' in itself). However, computers do not have human biases. They can quickly and accurately identify the frequent, salient or widely dispersed items in a corpus and present them to us so we have to account for them. Of course, the human researcher may choose not to examine certain features that the corpus software has brought up, so there still could be subjective selectivity at work. Another strength is in allowing hypotheses to be tested on large amounts of data, which gives researchers much more confidence in making claims.

One weakness is that data collection can be more time-consuming and requires more planning than some other kinds of research. Spoken data is especially difficult to collect and transcribe, and I have seen more corpus linguists making use of Internet data (or online archives) as a result.

Another weakness is that users need to be reasonably familiar with aspects of statistics, text encoding and computer applications, which can put some people off initially. Also, users are dependent on the 'affordances' of the software that they draw on. If their software package is not able to compare frequencies of four corpora together, then this makes it difficult for the average user to do this. Instead, we tend to base our analyses upon what we know the software *can* do, which may drive us to do certain types of analysis like keywords.

Corpora also tend to deliver decontextualised data, so while we see one version of 'the big picture' – lots of concordance lines of the same word, we miss out on how an individual use of a word occurs within its larger context – whether a particular concordance line had a picture on the page it came from, whether that text was later widely referred to or even banned. Of course it is possible to encode this information in the meta-data of each text sample, or to even look for it yourself, but most corpus linguists do not engage with the data in this way. And to be fair, it would be very difficult to do that for every concordance line, especially if our corpus contains lots of texts from many different sources.

Additionally, corpus analysis offers a range of different procedures and cut-off points which can sometimes be overwhelming to users. My own students frequently worry about things like collocational span; or whether they should use mutual information, T-score, both or something else, and then what cut-off points of statistical significance to apply. There is no 'one-model-fits-all' procedure for a corpus analysis, and instead a lot of it can involve feeling your way, trying out different procedures or adjusting parameters to take into account more practical aspects such as time or word-limit restrictions. This could also be viewed as a strength, however, in that users are allowed considerable freedom and creativity.

7. What is the future of Corpus Linguistics?

I can see Corpus Linguistics being more fully integrated into many other fields of Linguistics (such as Feminist Linguistics), as well as being used in other social sciences or Humanities subjects like History, Sociology, Religious Studies or Politics. I think the boundaries between researchers who call themselves corpus linguists and those who are non-corpus linguists will blur somewhat, with many more people viewing themselves as corpus users.

Modern reference corpora are likely to get even larger as more text is routinely formatted for the Internet. Additionally, there will also be much more work carried out on non-English languages, particularly Chinese, Russian, Arabic, Hindi and Bengali.

I can see more interest in diachronic corpus analysis in the future, as more and more reference corpora are collected, with the older ones becoming 'historical', and allowing for comparison with older data sets. We have some very good historical corpus research going on at the moment, but it is difficult to collect large amounts of representative language use from many genres before the 20th century. With spoken data, we have to rely on court transcripts and plays. It will be quite exciting to compare the spoken BNC (10 million words of early 1990s speech) with similar versions collected in the future.

I would hope to see further development of software, particularly integrated tools which allow users to find data from online sources, clean it up, assign meta-linguistic information such as grammatical tags and then enable a wide range of analyses, particularly comparing many corpora together. I would also like to see that tools are developed so that they can easily record and transcribe spoken data – which will lead to an explosion of interest in spoken Corpus Linguistics. Additionally, the development of high definition video recording or 3D recording will enable corpus analysis to be fully multimodal – allowing large scale analyses of gesture, posture and facial expression to be taken into account.

However, it may become harder to collect corpus data, due to text holders becoming concerned about copyright, or realising that there may be money to be made from their texts. Additionally, increasing concerns about ethics make it harder to collect spoken data than it used to be. A project like the spoken section of the BNC, for example, did not require everyone who spoke into the tape recorder to sign ethics forms – only those who were carrying the forms needed to sign them. Today, the ethical procedures would be more stringent, making something like the spoken BNC harder to replicate.

8. How may Corpus Linguistics be combined with critical discourse analysis?

Critical discourse analysis involves studying language as a social practice, and particularly looks at the ways that power and inequalities are maintained or challenged in texts. This can involve examining ways that language is used to persuade people or to set up particular world-views or ideologies as being 'normal' or to represent social actors in certain ways (negatively or positively). A corpus analysis allows us to take a systematic and large-scale approach to critical discourse analysis, by enabling us to consider many more texts than would normally be possible via qualitative research. This can allow us to identify patterns, saliency or frequency in a text which may not be easy to spot via the human eye. For example, if we were interested in the representation of a certain social group in say, the literature of a particular political party, we could gather a corpus of those leaflets and search on terms that reference the social group. We could then use concordances to examine every reference that is made to that group in order to determine whether there were particular repetitive patterns of association that were being made. Additionally, a collocational analysis will tell us about especially recurrent or prominent associations. It might be that the group overwhelmingly collocates with certain negative adjectives, or is represented as being the object of a particular set of verbs. Some scholars (e.g. Stubbs 2001; Hoey 2005) have argued that we come to make sense of the world through exposure to repeated patterns of language. So, a single pairing of two words together may not mean much, but if those pairings occur often enough, gradually members of society start to form associations, which can be quite difficult to deconstruct. The naturalisation of discourse is therefore the result of a 'drip, drip, drip' effect, and Corpus Linguistics is well-placed to expose this effect to us.

Corpus Linguistics, with its reliance on large numbers of texts, can also help us to identify cases of minority positions. These may only occur rarely in a society (or a set of representative texts from a society) and so could be overlooked if we only looked at a few texts. Worse still, there is a small chance that such minority positions could be over-represented if we only considered a few texts. A corpus approach can also help to reduce certain cognitive (and possibly ideological) biases that individual researchers may hold. Research has shown that we tend to notice/remember items that we have first encountered, or elements that are easy to spot, and that we tend to assign more weight to arguments which confirm our own beliefs. We also view media coverage as being biased against issues that we feel strongly about. I do not think it is possible for the corpus approach to completely remove our biases – but at least it forces us to account for any larger-scale or salient patterns that we may not have originally considered.

At the moment, the use of Corpus Linguistics in critical discourse analysis is not standard practice although it is becoming more popular.[1] My own research has combined these fields to examine a number of different areas. For example, I wanted to compare argumentation strategies that were used in UK government debates on banning fox-hunting (see Baker 2006). To do this, I collected a large amount of speech from members of parliament who wanted to keep or ban hunting. I then compared these two sets of speech together in order to obtain lists of keywords – words which were statistically significantly more frequent in one set of data when compared to the other. I found that, surprisingly, many keywords used by those who wanted to keep fox hunting referenced concepts to do with ethics and morality. An investigation of those keywords via more detailed concordance analyses found that they were used to argue that fox hunting was no more or less ethical than many practices that farmers engaged in – a kind of moral relativism strategy. Another piece of research I was involved in was to do with the representation of refugees and asylum seekers in the British press (Gabrielatos & Baker 2008). We found that words like refugees collocated with a number of sets of words which tended to position refugees as problematic in various ways, e.g. as economic burdens (*benefits, claiming, receive*), as illegal (*bogus, illegal, smuggled, detained*), as occurring in very large numbers incorporating water metaphors (*flooding, pouring, streaming*).

9. In what ways have corpus analyses increased the under-standing of gender issues?

At a recent workshop that I organised on corpora and gender for the British Association for Applied Linguistics (BAAL), we discussed how Corpus Linguistics was able to contribute to three aspects of gender research. First, it could tell us something about gendered *usage*, allowing us to answer questions about differences or similarities between male and female language use. Some of this research in the past has relied on small-scale studies or

---

1 See Baker (2006) and Mautner (2009), who give detailed overviews of the potential of the combination of the two fields.

even hypotheses, which have tended to result in generalisations. An analysis of a large spoken corpus which has been speaker-tagged for gender will be able to tell us exactly which words are significantly more frequent in one sex when compared to another, as well as giving more detailed information about distribution (e.g. whether the differences are due to a small number of atypical speakers) and allowing us to cross-reference the information to other identity features as age or social class (if this information is also encoded in the data). This allows us to obtain a much more nuanced view of sex differences and language use, and what such studies have tended to show is that differences tend to be based on gradients rather than absolutes and often connected to people's social roles (e.g. as whether they mainly look after children). Such research can also tell us about similarities rather than differences between the sexes. See, for example, Rayson, Leech and Hodges (1997) and Schmid and Fauth (2003), who both compared male and female differences in lexical usage in the British National Corpus. Additionally, see Harrington (2008), who compared the amount of reported speech that males and females engaged in. While she found that on average females reported the speech of others more, this was due to a small number of atypical females. In fact, for most speakers there was little difference.

Second, Corpus Linguistics approaches can help to tell us about gender *representations* in society – e.g. how are men and women talked or written about, and how these representations change over time. Such research can tell us, for instance, that men tend to be represented in more contexts to do with being powerful or physically active, whereas women tend to be described more in terms of their physical attractiveness (Baker 2010). This type of research can tell us about how notions of 'gender difference' therefore become naturalised in society.

Finally, we could also look at aspects of language use like male bias – to what extent are men and women represented as equal in terms of frequency or opportunity in language. For example, are male pronouns generally more frequent than female pronouns, and what proportion of gendered pronouns are 'generic', standing in for any person? Also, what roles or jobs are labelled as generically male or female (*coalman* vs. *charlady*) for example, and how frequent are such roles referred to in reference corpora? Finally, we could also examine diachronic corpora to obtain an idea of whether various strategies to reduce sexism have been successful. In this sense, have terms like *spokesperson* or *Ms* being widely taken up over time? Closer examination of corpora could reveal the contexts in which such terms are being used and whether they are viewed as problematic. This may give feminist researchers clues regarding the extent to which future strategies will be successful or not (Baker 2010).

10. In which circumstances does Corpus Linguistics enhance the outcome of sociolinguistic studies?

The use of large spoken corpora can be helpful in identifying language patterns associated with particular social groups, providing claims about such groups to be made with more confidence than if smaller numbers of people were examined. Analyses can also allow numerous identity factors to be taken into account at the same time, entitling us to go beyond comparisons of just, say male/female. Corpus-driven studies can help to reveal features of particular groups that may not have been hypothesised.

Additionally, we can study corpora of interactions in order to uncover information that may be beneficial to interactional linguists or people engaging in conversation analysis. For example, we could consult corpora to find out typical contexts that certain discourse markers such as *like* or *well* appear in and how others orient to them. A corpus that has been prosodically annotated could allow us to examine how features such as pitch or volume contribute to the organisation of talk – for example, by allowing us to correlate changes in pitch to say, the introduction of a new topic (Mindt 2000).

We could also use multiple corpora to compare different cultures; for example, how British English differs from American English – see Hofland and Johansson (1982), Leech and Fallon (1992), Nakamura (1993) and Oakes (2003), or changes in the language of a culture over time – see Rey (2001), Leech (2002) and de Haan (2002).

References

Baker, P. 2006. *Using Corpora in Discourse Analysis*. London: Continuum.

Baker, P. 2010. Will *Ms* ever be as frequent as *Mr*? A corpus-based comparison of gendered terms across four diachronic corpora of British English. *Gender and Language* 4(1): 125–149.

de Haan, P. 2002. Whom is not dead? In *New Frontiers of Corpus Research*, P. Peters, P. Collins & A. Smith (eds), 215–228. Amsterdam: Rodopi.

Gabrielatos, C. & Baker, P. 2008. Fleeing, sneaking, flooding: A corpus analysis of discursive constructions of refugees and asylum seekers in the UK Press (1996–2005). *Journal of English Linguistics* 36(1): 5–38.

Harrington, K. 2008. Perpetuating difference? Corpus Linguistics and the gendering of reported dialogue. In *Gender and Language Research Methodologies*, K. Harrington, L. Litosseliti, H. Sauntson & J. Sunderland (eds), 85–102. Basingstoke: Palgrave MacMillan.

Hoey, M. 2005. *Lexical Priming*. London: Routledge.

Hofland, K. & Johansson, K. 1982. *Word Frequencies in British and American English*. Bergen & London: Norwegian Computing Centre for the Humanities & Longman.

Käding J. 1897. *Häufigkeitswörterbuch der deutschen Sprache*. Steglitz: privately published.

Leech, G. 2002. Recent grammatical change in English: Data, description, theory. In *Proceedings of the 2002 ICAME Conference*, K. Aijmer & B. Altenberg (eds), 61–81, Gothenburg.

Leech, G. & Fallon, R. 1992. Computer corpora – what do they tell us about culture? *ICAME Journal* 16: 29–50.

Mautner, G. 2009. Corpora and critical discourse analysis. In *Contemporary Corpus Linguistics*, P. Baker (ed.), 32–46. London: Continuum.

McEnery, T. & Wilson, A. 2001. *Corpus Linguistics*. Edinburgh: Edinburgh University Press.

Mindt, I. 2000. Prosodic cues at speaker turns. In *Corpus Linguistics and Linguistic Theory*, C. Mair & M. Hundt (eds), 255–265. Amsterdam: Rodopi.

Nakamura, J. 1993. Quantitative comparison of modals in the Brown and the LOB corpora. *ICAME Journal* 17: 29–48.

Oakes, M. 2003. Contrasts between US and British English in the 1990s. In *Research and Scholarship in Integration Processes*, E. H. Oleksy & B. Lewandowska-Tomaszczyk (eds), 213–222. Lódź: Lódź University Press.

Rayson, P., Leech, G. & Hodges, M. 1997. Social differentiation in the use of English vocabulary: Some analyses of the conversational component of the British National Corpus. *International Journal of Corpus Linguistics* 2: 133–150.

Rey, J. M. 2001. Changing gender roles in popular culture: Dialogue in *Star Trek* episodes from 1966 to 1993. In *Variation in English: Multi-Dimensional Studies*, D. Biber & S. Conrad (eds), 138–156. London: Longman.

Schmid, H.-J. & Fauth, J. 2003. Women's and men's style: Fact or fiction? New grammatical evidence. Paper presented at the Corpus Linguistics Conference, Lancaster, March 2003.

Stubbs, M. 2001. *Words and Phrases: Corpus Studies of Lexical Semantics*. London: Blackwell.

Corpus Linguistics in South America

Based at the Linguistics Department and at the Applied Linguistics Graduate Programme (both at the Catholic University of São Paulo, Brazil), Tony Berber Sardinha contributes with a South American perspective to the present volume. More specifically, he draws on his teaching/research experience in Brazil to comment on the constraints corpus linguists might experience when working in such an environment as well as on the opportunities they are offered. His interview brings to the fore corpus studies carried out in languages other than English (namely, Portuguese and Spanish) in a variety of answers, ranging from his historical overview of Corpus Linguistics to the way he conceives the future of this field. Based on his programming skills, Berber Sardinha comments on the development of recent software aimed at teaching foreign languages and at identifying metaphors.

1. Where do you place the roots of Corpus Linguistics? And to what do you attribute the growth of interest in the area?

To me, the historic roots of modern Corpus Linguistics go back to the pioneering work of scholars such as John Sinclair, Geoffrey Leech, Jan Svartvik, Charles Fries, and many others. They broke new ground by collecting corpora, developing methods and analysing data during times when the technology was not easily available and the academic environment did not encourage such pursuits. This has been discussed in several papers and books, including McEnery and Wilson (1996), Kennedy (1998), Sampson (2001), Sampson and McCarthy (2004), Stubbs (2009), and my own overview of Corpus Linguistics in Portuguese (Berber Sardinha 2004).

One of the reasons why Corpus Linguistics has grown recently is because of the greater availability of resources. More texts have become available online and this has made it much easier for people to build and explore their own corpora. More corpora have also gone online, for several languages, such as the BNC and COCA for English, CREA for Spanish, and *Corpus*

Brasileiro, Lacio-Web and the Linguateca AC/DC collection for Portuguese, among others. Software for corpus exploration has also become more widely available. As far as desktop applications are considered, WordSmith Tools (Scott 1997) has played an important role in disseminating Corpus Linguistics among researchers but just as importantly among students. In terms of online applications, there is a large array of tools, most for free, which can be accessed on the web, to do basic tasks such as concordancing, word frequency listing and part of speech tagging (the CEPRIL [Centre for Research, Information and Resources in Language] toolkit, for example, offers these), but also more 'advanced' kinds of processing, such as term extraction (implemented in Corpógrafo, zExtractor and eTermos), metaphor retrieval (Metaphor Candidate Identifier) and error detection in learner corpora (Learner Misuse Identifier, these last two available at CEPRIL's website).

The potential for growth does not depend on internal forces only, that is, on theories, methods and resources developed by practitioners, but also on external factors, such as computer science and the whole computer industry, including software, hardware and the web. This means that the field will probably be constantly in motion, being driven by new technologies, which is both challenging and reinvigorating.

2. Is Corpus Linguistics a science or a methodology? Where would you situate Corpus Linguistics in the scientific or methodological panorama?

As far as the first question goes, there is an ongoing debate in the field about whether Corpus Linguistics is a methodology or whether it is more than a set of methods for handling textual corpora. Leech (1992: 105), McEnery and Wilson (1996: 1), and McEnery, Xiao and Tono (2006: 7) refer to it as a methodology; Hoey (1997, cited in Sampson 2001: 6) sees it as 'the route into linguistics'; Biber, Conrad and Reppen (1998) call it an approach; Scott and Thompson (2000: 36) describe it as a means 'for accessing resources'.

My view is that it depends on who uses it and for what purpose. It can be just a method, that is, a set of procedures for collecting and analysing data, in which case it may be used in conjunction with a range of different theories. At the same time, it can make theoretical statements as well, thus going beyond simply being a method: collocation, semantic preference, semantic prosody, dimensions of register variation among others are all theoretical concepts that were either 'discovered' or made evident by means of electronic corpus analysis. These are, in my opinion, theoretical categories in the sense that Halliday (1992/2001) proposes the term, because they seem to be 'general to all languages'. If one adopts these concepts, then he/she is embracing the view that Corpus Linguistics has theoretical status.

I would not go so far as to call Corpus Linguistics a science, because a science is a major field of enquiry, such as anthropology, economics, astronomy, physics, and so on. Corpus Linguistics is a 'domain' of linguistics, which is a science. Readers are referred to Halliday (1992/2001) for an interesting discussion on the status of linguistics as a science, and Bronckart (2008) for what he calls language or text science.

As far as the scientific or methodological panorama is concerned, I would situate it at the crossroads between human and exact sciences, because it is concerned with both the observation of social life via collections of language output and the development of computational means for making sense of such observation. I think there is misunderstanding among some people outside the field, who believe Corpus Linguistics is in the quantitative research paradigm. Some may think that because of the figures and statistics that are usually found in our publications, but CL lies in between the two extremes (quantitative and qualitative). It is quantitative in the sense that it does rely on mathematics for counting and statistics, but it is also qualitative, since a great deal of what corpus linguists do depends on interpreting language data collected in its natural environment, which are characteristics associated with the qualitative paradigm (see Brown 2004 for a discussion on the qualitative/quantitative dimension in Applied Linguistics research).

3. How representative can a corpus be?

Corpora are samples of texts taken from certain linguistic populations. Representativeness is then the degree to which a corpus stands for the population from which it was drawn, which can be conceived of as the totality of language items we want to sample for a particular corpus. These could be tokens, types, texts, genres, etc. It is not to be confused with the speakers of a particular tongue or variety. It is impossible to determine how many words, registers, genres or texts a language comprises. It is very hard to imagine how we could take a census of English or Portuguese, and precisely determine its dimension or contents. How many words are being spoken or written at this very moment, in which genres and registers? How many more have been spoken or written in the past? What varieties have gone out of existence or morphed into other ones? And if we take reception into consideration, how many words have been read or listened to? Hence, for all practical purposes, we have to assume that the exact size and distribution of linguistic features are unknown. We have been aware of these issues for a long time, and the workaround has been to gather increasingly large corpora, because the larger and the more diversified the sample, the closer it will get to the size and diversity of the whole population, thus increasing its representativeness. If we take a whole population as our sample, then it will be 100% representative. For instance, taking the case of essays written by students in a particular school in a given year, if we manage to collect all of these essays, then our corpus will be fully representative such texts for that year in that particular school. Nevertheless, we often do not know the size of the population we are dealing with, and some amount of error is bound to be present. Even very large corpora will have some degree of sampling error, which must be born in mind when interpreting data and making generalisations, because it ultimately means research findings might change if a slightly different text collection was investigated. Apart from these statistical issues, we must bear in mind social factors as well, and always ask ourselves what social group is represented. For instance, prestige texts such as high literature, academic articles, and press editorials arguably represent some of the linguistic experience of college graduate, middle to upper class speakers. In contrast, TV and radio transcripts, informal conversation, popular magazines and tabloids are probably closer to the day to day encounters of older working class speakers. Finally, blogs, chats and twitter postings perhaps resembles more naturally the daily experience of tech-savvy young individuals.

4. How far should an analyst rely on intuition?

If by intuition is meant intuited or invented data (instead of attested uses), then the answer should be 'never', as Sinclair (1991), Sampson (2001) and others have argued. However, if by intuition we mean the analyst's previous knowledge, experience, hunches, working hypotheses, and so on, then the answer should be 'all the time'. It is extremely important that analysts have some expectation about what they are likely to find in their corpus, either based on previous literature or because they know their corpus really well, otherwise findings become a lot harder to make sense of. When their expectations differ from the findings, then the first thing to do is to check the analysis to make sure it is correct, and if it is, then one should trust the data and not blame the corpus, again as Sinclair (1990/2004) has argued for in his work. Obviously, if analysts try to approach corpora with their minds as a blank slate, then they may be at risk of being misled by figures and patterns caused by badly formulated searches, bugs in software, or other problems that they were unaware of.

5. What kind of questions should an analyst think of?

That depends on the analyst's research aims. Typically I think these questions will include whether there are patterns in the data, and if so, what they look like, how frequent they are and what they mean in some context. These are fine, but what I would like to see is more people asking questions relating to socially relevant issues in a corpus perspective. By socially relevant, I mean research whose aim is, for example, to look at corpora and identify discourse features that would help expose prejudice, injustice, bias, racism, and sexism, among other aspects of society. One example is Coffin and O'Halloran (2006), who looked at covert evaluation in a tabloid article about the expansion of the European Union, and then substantiated their analysis by checking patterns found in the article against two other large newspaper corpora. They found subtle but recurrent patterns that suggest prejudice against migrants out of the new member countries. We need more cooperation with practitioners in areas such as social psychology, anthropology, education, and sociology, among others, in order to advance some of these research lines. Cooperation is not necessarily easy, but it is possible. I notice that some researchers in critical linguistics who I have been in contact with have reservations about Corpus Linguistics on the grounds that it was supposedly restricted to counting surface elements. Their worries generally echo those of van Dijk (2001: 360) that 'the emphasis on automated analysis usually implies a focus on (easily quantifiable) lexical analyses', as well as Fairclough's (2003: 6) criticism that 'findings [derived from corpus analysis] are of value, though their value is limited, and they need to be complemented by more intensive and detailed qualitative textual analysis'. However, we have to show them that lexical patterning could help them unearth regularities in discourse that could then be interpreted with their theories, and this may persuade them to try corpus techniques and software on their data. I like to believe that corpus linguistic theories or methods, when coupled with social disciplines, may advance important issues in those fields. Although limited, our current instruments and techniques do enable us to shed light on some social issues in a discourse perspective. For instance, the frequency and distribution of lexical patterns drawn from corpora allow us to map what van Dijk (1995) calls 'lexical style', that is, the choice of linguistic items to label political groups, such as 'terrorists' vs. 'freedom fighters', 'progressive' vs. 'liberal', 'right-wing' vs. 'neo-con', which in turn may reveal aspects of their ideology. At least some of this 'social corpus analysis' can already be done through collocation, but if Corpus Linguistics is to make a bigger impact on social research and stimulate cooperation with practitioners in those fields, we need to develop specific methods and software to identify socially relevant features in corpora.

6. What are the strengths and weaknesses of corpus analysis?

The main strengths of corpus analysis have to do with its ability to present evidence of use, by showing repeated occurrences of patterns, and in many cases, whenever large corpora are involved, with its power to generalise the findings to other similar contexts not present in the corpus. The main weakness, in my view, is related to the difficulty in analysing meaning with current corpus inspection methods. Typically, approaches to corpus analysis start with orthographic words, but going from them to units of meaning is a giant leap. Current software generally does a good job of extracting frequencies of words, collocations and other similar features based on orthographic boundaries, but it is less successful in retrieving elements that go beyond them, such as text topic, staging, author stance, evaluation, metaphor, etc. As Matthiessen (2006: 109) puts it, corpus techniques can adequately automate analysis at the level of graphology, but less so as we move to lexicogrammar and discourse semantics. I think that by going to so-called higher levels of linguistic analysis, we will inevitably have to see language as discourse and work our way toward corpus-aided discourse analysis. There is research into ways of finding some of these units of meaning in corpora, but much more is needed. One very interesting method is the one detailed in Biber, Csomay, Jones and Keck (2007), a bottom-up description of discourse units which combines automatic analysis of text segmentation, grammatical tagging, clustering and functional interpretation. The results are units of meaning that resemble rhetorical moves, but are lexicogrammatically formulated. One of the difficulties in researching units of meaning has to do with a shortage of methods, which derives to some degree from the historical reliance on the orthographic word. Yet another difficulty has to do with the shortage of corpus-friendly theories of meaning, such as Appraisal (Martin & White 2005) and Critical Discourse Analysis (Fairclough

1995). These are hard to implement on the computer, since their descriptive categories are not primarily lexically based and therefore cannot be retrieved automatically in non-annotated corpora by string matching.

7. What is the future of Corpus Linguistics?

I think Corpus Linguistics will continue to grow and become a more attractive field for more researchers and students. On the level of technology, what we might see in the future is the collection and availability of increasingly larger more diversified corpora, the development of better tools for corpus analysis, the use of multimedia corpora and a growing importance of the web in a number of ways, for instance as a source of data for corpus collection, as a corpus itself, and also as a platform for making corpora and tools available to the research community.

All of these are very exciting, but they also bring about challenges. Larger corpora will provide data as we have never seen before (recently a 20-billion-word corpus of Usenet postings was announced!), but these data will put pressure on corpus developers to come up with fast and accurate search engines. Retrieval speed is very important because users may approach corpus analysis tools expecting them to be as fast as their Internet counterparts, which is not normally possible because Internet companies have a better network infrastructure than corpus linguists normally have at their disposal.

As far as tools are concerned, one of the challenges is for them to do part of the work that we currently do manually beyond the initial stages of counting word frequencies, running concordances, and tagging texts for part of speech. We need better software to help us do bottom-up analyses of corpora more efficiently. For instance, in the field of metaphor analysis, the most widely used instrument is the concordancer, but most of the work preceding and following running concordances is done by hand and eye (choosing which words to look for in the corpus, looking for patterns in concordances, deciding which patterns are signalling metaphor use, and so on). Some of these tasks could be automated, though, by specialised software geared toward the needs of metaphor analysts. In a way, what we need is more specialised yet simple tools designed for specific kinds of corpus analysis. Our software scene is dominated by user-friendly programmes that are either too general to enable researchers to identify theoretically relevant units of meaning (e.g. concordance packages) or too technical for most users to come to grips with (parsers, sense taggers, etc.). In the future, I would like to see particularly more software with simple interfaces available free of charge that enables researchers and students to do some of the different kinds of analyses reported in our literature. Multi-Dimensional Analysis (Biber 1988), for instance, is a very interesting and powerful framework for corpus analysis; but it is a very complex method (Xiao & McEnery 2005: 63). In addition, its learning curve is very steep, in part because it demands familiarity with a range of computer programmes such as part of speech taggers, parsers and statistical packages. The technical side of it at least could be facilitated by integrating some of the different pieces of software needed. Such software would be particularly helpful for students to learn corpus linguistic methods and to attract partnerships with researchers in other areas. The same applies to other methods used in the field.

In relation to multimedia corpora, the challenges are evident: how to obtain reliable automatic transcriptions of audio and video recordings, how to align video, soundtrack and text, how to annotate sound and video enabling them to be searchable, how to compress video down to manageable sizes, how to display sound and image results in an efficient way, etc.

As far as approaching the web as a corpus, the challenges are many, such as how to determine, keep track and enable fast queries of its contents, among others. There are interesting projects that deal with such issues, such as WaCky, which aim at amassing very large amounts (up to 2 billion words) of textual material downloaded off the Internet; and online resources such as COCA (Corpus of Contemporary American English, 380+ million words) and *Corpus Brasileiro* (1 billion words), which, through their relational database architectures, allow users to query vast amounts of data very quickly.

On a professional level, what I would like to see is more jobs for corpus linguists, both in academic departments and in the business sector. One recent business job announcement in the Linguist List was for a corpus linguist among whose duties was analysing large bodies of conversation data to help the company and its medical clients 'share information, enhance disease understanding and participate in medical marketing research'. As our field becomes better known in the private sector, more such job openings may come along. Corpus linguists may also take programming jobs in the private sector, developing a range of language applications. This will depend on a large number of factors, such as the state of the world economy and personal qualifications (knowledge of computer programming, and experience in different language-related fields – e.g. discourse analysis and conceptual metaphor have both been listed in a job announcement with a technology company), but I am hopeful there will be more employment opportunities for corpus linguists around the world in the future than there are now.

8. What are the limits and possibilities of carrying out corpora studies in developing countries?

I cannot claim to speak for all developing countries, and so I will attempt to restrict myself to the situation in Brazil, which may or may not be similar to other so-called developing countries. Some of the limitations are:

1. Lack of mother tongue corpora: Most of the corpora readily available are of foreign languages, mainly English. There are notable exceptions, though, and in the case of Portuguese, these are *O Corpus do Português* (45 million words, at BYU, USA), *Lácio-Web* (10 million words), compiled by the Interinstitutional Centre for Research and Development in Computational Linguistics (NILC, Brazil), the *CETEM-Público* (180 million words), gathered at Linguateca (Portugal). There are also two corpora I have been involved in: the *Banco de Português* (750 million words), compiled as a reference corpus by members of the project 'Development of International Research in English for Commerce and Technology' (DIRECT), and the *Corpus Brasileiro* (1 billion words), being developed by the members of GELC (Corpus Linguistics Research Group), both at São Paulo Catholic University (Brazil).

2. Lack of literature in the mother tongue: Most of the Corpus Linguistics books and articles are written in English, but readers in many developing countries are not necessarily proficient in English. Fortunately, we have seen the publication of books and articles in Corpus Linguistics in Portuguese, which has helped bring Corpus Linguistics closer to a large number of L1 readers, disseminating the area among students and researchers in several fields.

3. Poor research infrastructure: This includes a lack of good computer labs, libraries and limited research funding. The price of hardware and software is generally very high, and having a fast reliable Internet connection at home is usually costly, beyond the reach of many. The price of imported books and journals is prohibitive, and so there are few titles available in libraries. Foreign literature circulates largely in photocopy and/or via pirate websites infringing copyright laws. Luckily, there are some tools that help remedy this situation. One of them is John Benjamins' Ebrary, which allows anyone to read on their computer screen, for free, a large portion of their

Corpus Linguistics catalogue. The others are institutional subscriptions to online academic journals; in the case of Brazil, the Brazilian Education Ministry has a programme that offers online subscriptions to international journals to universities across the country. Even though the premier journals in our field are not subscribed to (despite our continuous effort to persuade authorities), other journals which publish Corpus Linguistics research papers are available through these online subscriptions.

4. Lack of software in the mother tongue: A problem with Corpus Linguistics software is that most tools have interfaces in English, which makes it harder to use them in contexts where proficiency in English cannot be taken for granted. Thankfully, developers have made available software with interfaces in other languages. With interfaces in Portuguese, for example, there are tools such as those provided by research teams such as GELC (Corpus Linguistics Research Group, São Paulo, Brazil), Linguateca (Portugal), NILC (Interinstitutional Centre for Computational Linguistics, São Carlos, Brazil), and CEPRIL (São Paulo, Brazil).

At the same time, the possibilities are plentiful as well:

1. Opportunity for innovation: Corpus Linguistics is a novelty in many developing nations; in Brazil, the first major scholarly meetings were held in 1999 (at São Paulo Catholic University and the University of São Paulo), and the first book published in the country in Portuguese came out in 2004 (Berber Sardinha 2004). This gives researchers freedom to innovate and build local versions of CL from the ground up.

2. Interdisciplinarity: Corpus Linguistics can make connections with themes and research traditions that are typical of the academic landscape of developing countries, giving rise to different flavours of the discipline. For example, my own local version of CL is influenced by a rich array of disciplines, thinkers and researchers I encountered over the years in our Graduate Programme in Applied Linguistics (LAEL) and in meetings around the country. The major areas which have shaped my work are Applied Linguistics, Systemic Functional Linguistics, Natural Language Processing, Sociocultural Theory, British and French Discourse Analysis, Portuguese as a Mother Tongue and as a Foreign Language, Spanish and English as Foreign Languages, Social-Discursive Interactionism, Critical Discourse Analysis, Languages for Specific Purposes, and Metaphor Studies. Of course, this kind of multidisciplinary interaction is by no means

a feature of developing countries, and does indeed happen regardless of the country one is in. But my point is that some of these influences are perhaps more likely to exist in certain contexts, due to the complex ways in which academic disciplines put down roots over time in particular places. For instance, areas such as French Discourse Analysis are perhaps more influential in Brazil than in Britain or the US, and so corpus linguists are perhaps more likely to envision possible connections with it if they are working in Brazil than in other places where it is not so influential.

3. Creating a research community in the mother tongue: A growing number of researchers and students have been engaged in several projects looking at a wide range of issues in languages other than English. Wilson et al. (2006) present corpus-based research in a range of different languages. For Portuguese, see Berber Sardinha (2005) for an overview of corpus research in Brazil and other countries. Communicating research in the mother tongue is also extremely important as a means for scaffolding the development of the discipline. As mentioned above, the number of publications on Corpus Linguistics written in Portuguese has grown over the years, and our local CL meeting is already in its 10th edition in 2011.

4. Exploring the local context: The particular socio-economic conditions of developing countries provide ample opportunity for exploring issues relevant to society from a corpus perspective. For instance, in my own recent research, I have been looking at a corpus of oral narratives told by poor people who collect recyclable trash off the streets for a living, who are part of the social landscape of large Brazilian cities. I find that analysing this corpus provides interesting insights not just into these individuals' lives but also into the broader socio-historical context of the country, enabling us to better understand the social networks developing in particular communities. The results of this and other similar projects are not meant primarily as instruments for intervention in society, because like most applied linguistic research it 'is interested in language problems for what they reveal about the role of language in people's daily lives' (Elder & Davies 2004: 11–12), hence findings have not contributed directly to improving living conditions. However, understanding and trying to explain social problems can educate the public and may be an important first step in ameliorating inequality and injustice, which unfortunately plague developing countries. I wish more corpus linguists were actively engaged in these issues.

9. How feasible is it to map metaphors by means of corpus techniques?

There are roughly two kinds of metaphor: linguistic and conceptual. The former are actual expressions occurring in language that are interpreted metaphorically, such as 'our relationship has reached a dead-end'. The latter are mappings between two domains of experience, such as love and journey, which result in metaphors like love is a journey, which are very rarely expressed in text or speech, thus having to be inferred from the language that was actually uttered. People will not normally say 'love is a journey', but it is claimed they will normally think of love in terms of a journey, and as a result they will conceptualise, for instance, lovers as travellers, the couple's life as a path, problems as bumps on the road, their future as a destination, and so on.

Linguistic metaphors, on the other hand, get expressed in text and talk, and come about as a result of the tension between the basic or concrete meaning of a word or sequence of words and their meaning in a given context. For example, 'we are getting nowhere', if spoken by a husband or wife in the context of a discussion with his/her spouse, would be seen as a linguistic metaphor because the basic or concrete meaning of 'getting nowhere' usually refers to travelling, whereas the intended meaning in that context does not. In that conversation, the intended meaning would be related to problems in their relationship and their inability to solve them. Hence, there is tension between the meaning of 'travelling' and 'relationship problems', which signals that 'we are getting nowhere' is used metaphorically to refer to their relationship and not to an actual trip they were taking together.

As regards identification, there are no known methods for directly retrieving conceptual metaphors in corpora, because this involves finding domains of experience such as love and journey, which are close but not the same as semantic fields. One approximation would be to use a semantic tagger for mapping word senses and then retrieve words and expressions belonging to individual word fields, which may help find possible instances of particular domains (e.g. 'dead-end' may be assigned a label for 'travelling', flagging it as a possible realisation of the journey domain). Wmatrix (Rayson 2008) may be exploited for that purpose.

The situation with respect to linguistic metaphors is very different, since we can identify them in corpora by searching for particular lexical patterns. The problem is knowing the right patterns to look for. Researchers have used a range of strategies for predicting metaphor patterns in corpora, including reading part of the corpus, using intuition and drawing on previous research.

I have taken a corpus-driven approach to this issue and coded a large number of concordance lines (over 20,000 for Portuguese and 5,000 for English) for metaphor and then extracted the patterns associated with figurative versus literal (or basic) meanings. This later enabled me to write software to automate the task of finding metaphors in corpora; the software, called MCI (Metaphor Candidate Identifier; available for free on the web), 'learned' the patterns that typically cue metaphoric expressions and can now trawl through a corpus and spot metaphor candidates based on the patterns surrounding them. The ultimate decision on calling a stretch of language a linguistic metaphor rests with the researcher, as the programme can only go as far as pointing out likely expressions.

I assessed the programme by comparing its analysis of five texts against my own judgement of the same texts; whenever its analysis agreed with mine, a successful guess was tallied. The success of this approach ranges from 12% to 78% precision (the percentage of right 'guesses'), depending on individual texts and on the amount of predictions the programme is allowed to make (the more guesses, the more chance for errors, hence lower precision). The average success rate is 30%, based on a listing of 30 candidates. Its performance may also be influenced by the degree of specialisation of the corpus. In specialised corpora, the probability of individual words taking on both a metaphorical and non-metaphorical meaning seems to be lower than in general language. For instance, in a register diversified corpus, Portuguese words such as 'loteria' (lottery), 'fotografia' (snapshot) and 'atingidos' (hit, verb) have less than 1% chance of being used metaphorically (that is, they are mostly used in their literal senses), whereas in investment banking they all typically have a nearly 100% likelihood of being metaphors. We may see this as instance of lexical priming (Hoey 2005) as some words are primed for metaphor in particular genres. This is also evidence of upward probability resetting (Halliday 1993): the linguistic system of metaphor resets its probabilities of occurrence upwardly in specialised corpora as compared to general language corpora.

What this means in terms of automatic metaphor retrieval with the MCI is that the programme will probably work more satisfactorily if it encounters texts of the similar topics or genres to those it was trained on, as its probabilities will reflect those of the training texts. Currently, the programme has been trained on both a banking corpus and a general corpus, and so it should perform better on texts related to banking, investments and the economy, since words in these domains are more likely to be used metaphorically than otherwise. The test corpus used in this particular assessment was topic diversified, with newspaper and science texts referring to politics, health, the environment and the human body, and so this may have hindered the programme performance.

We must bear in mind, though, when evaluating the programme, that rater agreement in metaphor identification tasks is low; in Cameron (2003: 169), 25 different raters analysing a single text agreed on two metaphors only out of 14 (14%), and in Beigman Klebanov, Beigman and Diermeier (2008), nine analysts agreed on 1.7% to 4% of their judgements. Agreement tends to rise after discussions among the raters take place, because they have a chance to make identification criteria more explicit and revise their decisions. In view of these figures, a precision of more than 30% as achieved by the MCI (meaning the degree of agreement between its analysis and mine) is less disappointing than at first sight.

To conclude, I think an approach such as this, which brings together ideas from Corpus Linguistics (patterning, collocation, repetition, frequency, etc.), systemic functional linguistics (probability as an aspect of meaning, resetting, etc.), and an applied linguistic approach to metaphor (ascertaining the primacy of linguistic metaphor as opposed to conceptual metaphor, acknowledging the vital role of context in giving rise to metaphor, etc.) can prove valuable in our quest for ways of automatically finding metaphor in corpora.

10. In what ways can corpora be exploited in order to design and evaluate language teaching materials for students of English or Spanish as a foreign language (EFL/SFL)?

As we can see in the literature, corpora can be exploited in the classroom in many different ways: we can prepare concordances and lists of word frequency, chunks or keywords; we can have students work directly with corpora, searching them and obtaining different kinds of statistics for collocations, bundles, fixed expressions, individual words; we can help students become aware of typical characteristics of particular genres by showing them frequencies of use of words, collocations, textual primings, among many other applications. These are all exciting ways of bringing corpus linguistic techniques and instruments to the classroom, but I will argue these are all 'mainstream' corpus approaches for the EFL/ESL classroom. In a sense, these are attempts to transfer corpus methods more or less wholesale to the classroom.

What I would like to see is the development of other ways to connect with Corpus Linguistics that did not rely so heavily on transferring research methods (such as reading concordances and interpreting word frequency information) to the classroom, but rather that took as their starting point teachers' current practices, student needs and wants, as well as theories that are relevant for EFL/ESL practitioners. In short, it is time to go beyond the concordance (without abandoning it). For example, one of the current themes in EFL pedagogy is task-based learning (Estaire & Zanon 1994). The question that arises immediately is then how can we design materials for the task-based classroom from a corpus perspective? In my view, one of the ways to do that is to start with the task and not with the corpus, and then gradually incorporate insights, instruments, and findings from Corpus Linguistics, that is, to build the material around a task and not solely around corpus output. This means that concordances and wordlists are used, but they are not the centrepiece of the teaching unit or activity. As a matter of fact, they are a means by which we enable students to accomplish the task, the ultimate goal of which is to prepare them to deal with real language situations outside the classroom. For instance, let's suppose we are designing a task-based unit whose aim is to have students prepare a school newsletter. Typically, in this kind of project, students would divide themselves into teams, each with a specific task (editors, reporters, secretaries, etc.), as in a real newsletter/newspaper, schedule meetings, hold meetings, set agendas, interview people, write stories, lay out the typed texts, and so on, until they produce a final hard copy of the newsletter. Language practice comes in as a by-product of the interaction, and not as the main goal of the class. Here, corpora may be used meaningfully in a range of ways, from providing examples of chunks that occur frequently in newspaper/newsletter discourse, to helping make decisions about the most idiomatic way to say something in the foreign language, among many others. Corpora can be accessed directly by either teachers or students, through a range of instruments, such as concordances, lists of bundles/chunks, word frequency and keyword lists, or any other corpus mediation instrument that is available to teachers or students. The main point here is to think of corpora as resources that students should learn how to tap into in order to complete the task, and not as resources that they must use for their own sake. The manner in which corpora will be brought to the classroom will vary according to a number of factors, such as students' level in the foreign language, their skills, time, independence, school facilities, linguistic learning outcomes set for the task, and so on, but corpora may be brought to the classroom in traditional ways such as concordances teachers prepare ahead of time, student-generated word lists, as well as more innovative ways such as by having students search online corpora either in the classroom/lab or at home as an assignment and bring their findings to the classroom for discussion. What matters most is to keep the focus on the task and not on corpus exploration *per se*.

In relation to evaluating materials, corpora can be used as a yardstick for measuring the authenticity of reading and listening passages, for instance. By comparing the chunks (formed by three, four and five words, for instance) found in a text to those found in a reference corpus, we may determine which ones in the target text are frequent/infrequent/non-existent in the reference corpus, and then draw conclusions about whether the text is idiomatic (i.e. conforms to the typical ways in which words co-occur in the target language), and then decide whether it is suitable for inclusion in the material under consideration. The rationale behind this is that being an authentic text is not enough; the authentic text must contain material that is idiomatic as well. This principle could be used in material design as well if it is used as one of the criteria (but not the sole one) to guide the selection of texts.

One of my concerns about the use of corpora in the classroom is the insane amount of work and time that is involved in preparing teaching materials with corpora! There are so many different steps involved in the process, and each one requires a lot of time and expertise. These are just a few of them: deciding which items to teach, choosing/collecting a corpus, running concordances for those items, finding patterns in the concordances, studying these patterns and drawing some inferences, and writing questions or tasks for students to explore these patterns. We need more research to address this issue. One of the solutions lies in designing software specifically for teachers, as opposed to general corpus research software such as the concordance packages available at the moment. Such software would not require familiarity with corpus analysis techniques, and it would run word frequency and keyword lists, as well as concordances for a set of teacher-defined or software-defined (for instance, the top five keywords) in a text or texts that the teacher is willing to bring to the classroom. One former student of mine (José Lopes Moreira Filho) wrote some software (available at our GELC website) that does all these things and in addition outputs a handout with an activity that is basically ready for use but can be customised by the teacher (Moreira Filho & Berber Sardinha 2008). Without software such as this, I think most teachers will simply not have enough time or energy to prepare their own corpus-based materials as often as they would like. If we can empower teachers to use corpora so much the better, but realistically to a large number of them, given their normal workload, doing time-consuming corpus research is just not feasible.

Despite all the work that has been done in material design and evaluation from a corpus perspective (coming under labels such as corpus-based, -driven, -informed, -inspired, etc.), there are many questions that are left unanswered. One of these is what kinds of interaction take place among students and between teacher and students when corpus-based materials are being used in class? Does corpus-based work give rise to specific patterns of interaction, and if so, are these patterns conducive to learner-centredness, learner autonomy, collaboration with peers and mutual support or do they reinforce individual language study and/or teacher-centredness? Another set of questions is motivated by how little we know about the way students process concordances. For instance, what strategies do students employ in order to cope with the typical features of concordances, such as broken sentences/utterances, restricted context, centred alignment, huge numbers of lines, and so on? How do they perceive patterns and how do they make the leap from pattern to meaning? Yet another centres around the selection of lines for inclusion in a concordance: is it best to provide full concordances or should teachers keep certain lines only, and if so, how many and which ones? These are just some of the burning questions regarding the use of corpora in the classroom at this time in my view. Many more need to be asked, and both more research and practical experimentation are necessary to enable us to exploit corpora more fully in language teaching.

References

Beigman Klebanov, B., Beigman, E. & Diermeier, D. 2008. Analysing disagreements. In *Proceedings of the Workshop on Human Judgements in Computational Linguistics, Coling 2008*, R. Artstein, G. Boleda, F. Weller & S. Schulte im Walde (eds), 2–7, Manchester.

Berber Sardinha, T. 2004. *Lingüística de Corpus. São* Paulo: Manole.

Berber Sardinha, T. (ed.). 2005. *A Língua Portuguesa no Computador*. Campinas & São Paulo: Mercado de Letras & FAPESP.

Biber, D. 1988. *Variation Across Speech and Writing*. Cambridge: CUP.

Biber, D., Conrad, S. & Reppen, R. 1998. *Corpus Linguistics – Investigating Language Structure and Use*. Cambridge: CUP.

Biber, D., Csomay, E., Jones, J. K. & Keck, C. 2007. Introduction to the identification and analysis of vocabulary-based discourse units. In *Discourse on the Move: Using Corpus Analysis to Describe Discourse Structure* [Studies in Corpus Linguistics 28], D. Biber, U. Connor & T. A. Upton (eds), 155–174. Amsterdam: John Benjamins.

Bronckart, J.-P. 2008. Sobre linguagem, ação-trabalho e formação: As contribuições da démarche ISD. Entrevista com Jean-Paul Bronckart (About language, action-work and education: The contributions of 'demarche ISD'). Interview with Jean-Paul Bronckart. Educação em Revista 47: 273–286.

Brown, J. D. 2004. Research methods for Applied Linguistics: Scope, characteristics, and standards. In *The Handbook of Applied Linguistics*, E. Catherine & A. Davies (eds), 476–500. Oxford: Blackwell.

Cameron, L. 2003. *Metaphor in Educational Discourse*. London: Continuum.

Coffin, C. & O'Halloran, K. 2006. The role of appraisal and corpora in detecting covert evaluation. *Functions of Language* 13(1): 77–110.

Elder, C. & Davies, A. 2004. *The Handbook of Applied Linguistics*. Oxford: Blackwell.

Estaire, S. & Zanon, J. 1994. *Planning Classwork: A Task-Based Approach*. Oxford: Heinemann.

Fairclough, N. 1995. *Critical Discourse Analysis: The Critical Study of Language*. London: Longman.

Fairclough, N. 2003. *Analysing Discourse: Textual Analysis for Social Research*. London: Routledge.

Halliday, M. A. K. 1992/2001. Systemic grammar and the concept of a 'science of language'. In *On Language and Linguistics*, J. J. Webster (ed.), 199–212. London: Continuum.

Halliday, M. A. K. 1993. Quantitative studies and probabilities in grammar. In *Data Description Discourse. Papers on the English Language in Honour of John McH. Sinclair on his Sixtieth Birthday*, M. Hoey (ed.), 1–25. London: HarperCollins.

Hoey, M. 2005. *Lexical Priming: A New Theory of Words and Language*. London: Routledge.

Kennedy, G. 1998. *An Introduction to Corpus Linguistics*. London: Longman.

Leech, G. 1992. Corpora and theories of linguistic performance. In *Directions in Corpus Linguistics. Proceedings of Nobel Symposium 82, Stockholm, 4–8 August 1991*, J. Svartvik (ed.), 105–127. Berlin: De Gruyter.

Martin, J. R. & White, P. 2005. *The Language of Evaluation: Appraisal in English*. Basingstoke: Palgrave Macmillan.

Matthiessen, C. M. I. M. 2006. Frequency profiles of some basic grammatical systems: An interim report. In *System and Corpus*, G. Thompson & S. Hunston (eds), 103–142. London: Equinox.

McEnery, T. & Wilson, A. 1996. *Corpus Linguistics*. Edinburgh: EUP.

McEnery, T., Xiao, R. & Tono, Y. 2006. *Corpus-Based Language Studies: An Advanced Resource Book*. London: Routledge.

Moreira Filho, J. L. & Berber Sardinha, T. 2008. The Reading Class Builder: A tool for creating corpus-based teaching materials. Paper presented at the American Association for Corpus Linguistics 2008 Conference, BYU, Provo UT.

Rayson, P. 2008. *Wmatrix: A Web-Based Corpus Processing Environment*. Lancaster: Computing Dept., Lancaster University.

Sampson, G. 2001. *Empirical Linguistics*. London: Continuum.

Sampson, G. & McCarthy, D. 2004. *Corpus Linguistics: Readings in a Widening Discipline*. London: Continuum.

Scott, M. 1997. *WordSmith Tools*. Version 3. Computer Software. Oxford: OUP.

Scott, M. & Thompson, G. 2000. *Patterns of Text – In Honour of Michael Hoey*. Amsterdam: John Benjamins.

Sinclair, J. M. 1990/2004. Trust the text. In *Trust the Text: Language, Corpus and Discourse*, R. Carter (ed.), 9–23. London: Routledge.

Sinclair, J. M. 1991. *Corpus, Concordance, Collocation*. Oxford, New York: Oxford University Press.

Stubbs, M. 2009. Technology and phraseology: With notes on the history of Corpus Linguistics. In *Exploring the Lexis-Grammar Interface* [Studies in Corpus Linguistics 35], R. Schulze & U. Römer (eds), 15–32. Amsterdam: John Benjamins.

van Dijk, T. A. 1995. Ideological discourse analysis. *New Courant* 4: 135–161.

van Dijk, T. A. 2001. Critical Discourse Analysis. In *Handbook of Discourse Analysis,* D. Tannen, D. Schiffrin & H. Hamilton (eds), 352–371. Oxford: Blackwell.

Wilson, A., Archer, D. & Rayson, P. 2006. *Corpus Linguistics Around the World*. Amsterdam: Rodopi.

Xiao, R. & McEnery, T. 2005. Two approaches to Genre Analysis: Three genres in modern American English. *Journal of English Linguistics* 33(1): 62–82.

Variation in corpora and its pedagogical implications

In the opening of her interview, Susan Conrad, Professor of Applied Linguistics at Portland State University (United States), comments on the role of Corpus Linguistics in a country where language research has differed substantially from that of the European tradition. Conrad discusses the concept of variation – a major concern of hers – in terms of language, dialect, knowledge areas and speakers, to cite just some examples. When considering the notion of registers, she holds that their study can be greatly enhanced by corpora and their probing tools. Conrad, however, does not restrict herself to research considerations: she also writes about the role of Corpus Linguistics in teaching – including applications for specialised fields such as civil engineering, as illustrated in her interview.

1. Where do you place the roots of Corpus Linguistics? And to what do you attribute the growth of interest in the area?

Let me address the second part of this question first. I believe Corpus Linguistics has become popular because it provides a very different perspective on language than was previously available. Specifically, Corpus Linguistics techniques make it possible to describe patterns in how language is used in different contexts – that is, to describe the choices that speakers and writers tend to make in different situational and discourse conditions. This perspective is far different from the best known, traditional views of language study. Especially in the United States, where Chomskyan perspectives have been dominant, linguistics was usually thought to be the description of what was grammatical or ungrammatical in a language. Language teachers taught accurate grammatical structures and corrected ungrammatical structures that their students produced. That more traditional perspective is useful for describing what human language consists of and what sort of language capacity humans are born with, but it cannot account for variation that exists in language as it is used in naturally-occurring communication. There is always more than one grammatically accurate way to encode a message; therefore, a description that focuses only on accuracy – rather than also on appropriateness for different contexts – is an incomplete description and cannot help language learners develop judgement about appropriate forms for different situations.

Rather than focusing on issues of accuracy, corpus-based work investigates common and uncommon choices in particular circumstances. To give a simple example, all proficient speakers of English know that it is grammatical to say either 'all speakers know *that* there is variation in language' or 'all speakers know there is variation in language.' Very traditional grammar books will simply say the use of 'that' is optional and both choices are grammatical. Others will note that omitting 'that' is more common in casual speech than in writing. Corpus-based work, such as in the *Longman Grammar of Spoken and Written English* (Biber et al. 1999: 680–683), shows that the omission of *that* is associated with several factors simultaneously, including the verb in the main clause, features of the subject (personal pronoun vs. full noun; co-referential subjects in the main and complement clauses), the register (conversation vs. academic prose being a large contrast), and whether there are coordinated complement clauses. Such descriptions of what is typical or unusual in different contexts provide for a much different understanding of language than just a focus on accuracy. For many language teachers, it allows them to give far more satisfying answers to student questions about choosing between different language forms or for explaining why something a student says is grammatical but 'sounds funny'.

In terms of the historical roots of corpus work, interest in language patterns and the functions that different language choices play is most associated with the work of J. R. Firth (Firth 1957; Palmer 1968). I think Stubbs (1993) does a good job of describing factors that Firth (1957) emphasised and that are apparent today in Corpus Linguistics work. Perhaps most important is Firth's (1957) belief that language study is an empirical endeavour: that researchers need to make systematic analyses of text samples and not rely on intuition (as in a more traditional view of linguistic enquiry). The systematic, empirical analysis of text is obvious in Corpus Linguistics work.

In a general way, the historical roots of Corpus Linguistics trace to the field of sociolinguistics. This area of knowledge has always included interest in the ways that language use varies in different circumstances (e.g. see Hymes 1974). However, sociolinguistics research became most associated with dialect variation. Its typical studies emphasised variables such as different pronunciations that caused no change in the meaning of a word but reflected social class or ethnic group differences. In contrast, corpus-based analyses of variation include investigations that do have functional consequences. For example, differences between a sample of speech and writing on the same topic correspond to different concerns in regulating face-to-face interaction and in packaging information more concisely (see further discussion in Biber & Conrad 2009). Such variation is often not covered in sociolinguistics textbooks, but it certainly can be considered one way that language use and social factors are inter-connected.

2. Is Corpus Linguistics a science or a methodology? Where would you situate Corpus Linguistics in the scientific or methodological panorama?

I usually refer to Corpus Linguistics as 'an approach to studying language' because I cannot find a more specific term that seems accurate. I use 'approach' to convey that all corpus work shares certain general characteristics and a certain research philosophy. At the same time, however, Corpus Linguistics encompasses great diversity in research purposes and particular methods, so the more specific term 'methodology' seems misleading. Since corpus analyses investigate issues of interest to other linguists, I believe calling Corpus Linguistics a separate 'science' or even a subfield of linguistics is also misleading. Let me expand on each of these points in turn.

First, all Corpus Linguistics work shares certain characteristics. These include the empirical analysis of texts (spoken or written) that were produced in naturally-occurring communication situations, the use of a principled collection of texts (the corpus), the use of computer-assisted analysis techniques, and the incorporation of quantitative analysis with more qualitative, functional interpretations of language use. Some authors have argued that Corpus Linguistics is 'essentially a technology' (Simpson & Swales 2001: 1), and it is true that many of the shared characteristics involve computer use. However, behind these characteristics lies an identifiable philosophy. As I noted above, the philosophy follows from a Firthian tradition, with an emphasis on language description and theory based on systematic observations of language behaviour, not on native speaker intuition, and on language variation as an appropriate focus for linguistic research. Calling Corpus Linguistics 'a technology' recognises its superficial characteristics but hides the fact that there is a philosophical foundation behind the use of technology. 'Approach' – though admittedly vague – implies more than superficial similarities.

While it has some shared characteristics, Corpus Linguistics work is also extremely diverse. For example, suppose a student asks a teacher about the difference between 'refuse' and 'reject', and the teacher uses a concordancer and a corpus to investigate the different lexicogrammatical patterns associated with the two words (see further Conrad 2006). Alternatively, suppose a researcher uses the multi-dimensional analysis methodology to compare different registers (see, e.g. Biber 1988; Conrad & Biber 2001), using factor analysis to investigate the associations between over 50 linguistic features in hundreds of texts. In these two projects, the goals of the research are quite different (determining the difference between specific constructions vs. characterising registers with respect to numerous linguistic features), the statistics that are employed vary from none to very complex, the computer tools that are required vary from a publicly available concordancer to individually written computer programmes. However, both projects fit within Corpus Linguistics. If we call Corpus Linguistics a methodology, we minimise the diversity that exists within it.

Other terms that have been applied to Corpus Linguistics include 'sub-field of linguistics' (e.g. in the 2005 ICAME/AAACL joint annual meeting panel discussion on *Corpus Linguistics: Methodology or Sub-Field?*) or even 'a science'. In my view, these are the most problematic terms because they make Corpus Linguistics sound exclusive of other areas in linguistics. In reality, corpus analyses address research questions that are already of interest in linguistics, and interpretations of corpus findings regularly incorporate principles from other linguistics work. Corpus-based research can be part of sociolinguistics, language acquisition, stylistics, discourse analysis, historical linguistics, and World Englishes, to name just a few areas. Making Corpus Linguistics sound too distinct is a danger to its further development, I believe. Instead, I encourage corpus linguists to interact with language professionals who do not do corpus work, to publish in journals read by a variety of audiences, and to make clear how corpus techniques can address issues that are of interest throughout linguistics and language teaching.

3. How representative can a corpus be?

There is no single answer to this question since how easy it is to represent a variety of language depends on what variety of language you are trying to represent. The more tightly focused a corpus is – with fewer varieties being included and less variation existing within the varieties – the easier it is to be representative. For example, if I wanted a corpus to represent sports reports in my local newspaper over the last decade, that would be far easier to achieve than a corpus to represent all parts of all newspapers in the United States, where there are far more different sections, topics, authors, editorial policies, regions, etc., that would have to be sampled.

Numerous publications cover issues in corpus design far more thoroughly than is possible here. Readers might want to consult general overviews of considerations (e.g. Biber, Conrad & Reppen 1998, Methodology Box 1; Clancy 2010; Meyer 2002, Chapter 2; Reppen 2010); descriptions of the principles followed in compiling specific corpora (e.g. Aston & Burnard 1998; Granger, Dagneaux & Meunier 2002; Simpson-Vlach & Leicher 2006); or discussions of issues for specialised types of corpora (e.g. Bowker & Pearson 2002, Part II; Koester 2010; Thompson 2010). Here I will note just three points that are often not appreciated by newcomers to Corpus Linguistics.

A first important point concerns the need for more empirical analyses that will help corpus linguists understand the most efficient way to design corpora in order to achieve the best possible representativeness. We know that differences in situational factors (such as audience, purpose, writer/speaker, etc.) have associated linguistic differences, and corpora are generally designed to capture the situational variables in the belief that the linguistic variation will also be captured. However, most corpus compilation projects are limited by time, energy, and cost, and more information about how best to spend the limited resources would be a useful contribution to the field. We need more information about the minimum number of samples to represent different kinds of text categories, the number of samples needed from individual texts, the optimum length of samples, and numerous other decisions that must be made for corpus design. Studies by Biber (1990, 1993) and Kilgarriff (2001) started such work, but far more work is needed.

A second point is that, in considering representativeness, most people immediately think of obvious external variables such as different types of discourse and individual speaker/writer styles. These are indeed important, but it is also necessary to consider more subtle internal variation in a single type of discourse. McCarthy and Carter (2001) make a relevant point about fine-grained distinctions that need to be made in spoken corpora in order to describe the circumstances associated with certain language features. For example, they find ellipsis to be rare in narratives but common in many other types of talk; thus, a corpus that did not include different types of talk would have more limited usefulness. The same is likely to be true of any kind of discourse. For example, college textbooks tend to have different types of sections: summaries, boxed sections with special information, descriptions, summaries of research projects, etc. Fully representing such textbooks would require purposeful sampling of the different internal sub-sections.

A third point worth mentioning is that sometimes a corpus is criticised because it does not include an expression that a user knows to be grammatical and has heard occasionally used. Such a criticism reflects a misunderstanding of the usefulness of corpora. Even a very principled corpus that represents a variety of language well will not include every utterance that has ever been produced in that variety. Rather, corpora can show us what is common and uncommon, what is typical and what is rare. In other words, new users of corpora sometimes forget that the focus of Corpus Linguistics is not on what is grammatical and ungrammatical in a language, but what is common and uncommon.

4. How far should an analyst rely on intuition?

In Corpus Linguistics, the most important role that intuition plays is in helping analysts develop research questions. Your intuitions about how you use language can lead to many useful corpus investigations, as can disagreements in speakers' intuitions. For example, in a grammar class I recently taught for ESL teacher trainees, my students held very strong, opposite intuitions about which verb form is most common in American English conversation – simple present or present progressive. Since they were training to teach ESL, the question had important implications for them (Which form would their students be likely to hear more in casual conversations? Which form should they give students extra practice with in order to help with interactions outside of class?). In this case, the corpus investigations had already been done. Even though many textbooks introduce present progressive first, corpus-based studies have found that simple present is far more common (see, e.g. Biber et al. 1999: 461). Intuition in combination with anecdotal evidence can also spur research. For instance, noticing that the clerk at the post office asks you 'Did you need anything else?' might lead you to reflect on how you think past tense is used in polite offers, which might then lead to a corpus-based study of the contexts in which they are used (see Conrad & Biber 2009).

In my experience, some people conflate intuition with all interpretations made in corpus-based research; that is, they consider all subjective, human interpretation to be part of 'intuition'. However, that description misrepresents the research process. All research – whether corpus-based or any other kind – requires interpretation. In Corpus Linguistics, interpretations always need to be made for quantitative results, to give plausible explanations for speakers' and writers' choices or at least to discuss the impact of those choices. Interpretations can be based on a variety of sources. They might refer to cognitive principles such as the principle of end weight (placing heavy, long constituents, which are harder to process than short constituents, at the ends of clauses) or information ordering (placing already-known information before new information); to aspects of linguistic theory, such as principles defined in Systemic Functional Linguistics (e.g. see Hunston 2002: 177, on how the classification of verb types facilitates the interpretation of otherwise confusing corpus findings); to the historical development of the language; or any of numerous other principles or a logically developed argument. The presentation of evidence, application of theoretical principles, and development of an argument make interpretation in research studies different from intuition.

5. What kind of questions should an analyst think of?

Corpus Linguistics is useful for questions about language use and variation. It is not well suited to questions about what is grammatical or acceptable in a language. A feature may be grammatical but very rare and thus it may not be attested except in an extremely large corpus. Corpora also contain non-standard forms and production errors, and grammaticality judgements are not part of the data of a corpus.

Questions about language use and varieties can be asked on many different levels and for different purposes. For example, Biber et al. (1999) has a very large scope, describing English grammar and the distribution and use of numerous grammatical features in conversation, fiction writing, newspaper writing and academic prose, while a study like Barbieri (2005) has a very narrow focus on new quotatives in American English speech (e.g. 'be like', 'go', 'be all'). Studies address concerns as diverse as second language acquisition, author style, and historical linguistics. Because corpora and methodological techniques are diverse, research in Corpus Linguistics is equally varied.

Certain areas are well known in Corpus Linguistics. One of these is lexicography and especially the lexicogrammatical patterns of language, due largely to pioneering publications by the COBUILD project team and its director, John Sinclair (see, e.g. Sinclair 1991; Hunston & Francis 2000). Another area concerns register variation, which was spurred by the research carried out by Biber (especially with his 1988 book analysing multiple registers of writing and speech). Conversation features and the differences between conversation and written discourse became well known with the publication of Carter and McCarthy (1995) and McCarthy and Carter (1995). Work in these and numerous other fields has continued, but that does not mean that questions in other areas are not appropriate. New research foci are constantly developing, including the incorporation of prosodic analysis in the analysis of lexical bundles (Pickering & Byrd 2008), corpus-based studies of World Englishes (e.g. de Klerk 2006; Nelson 2006) and English as a Lingua Franca (e.g. Prodromou 2008), and formulaic language use by language learners (Ellis, Simpson-Vlach & Maynard 2008).

I am most interested in studies related to grammar and register analysis, especially those with applications for ESL or for university-level education. Although many corpus studies have been conducted in these areas, much remains to be investigated. For example, we still know relatively little about the overall patterns of speech and writing in different academic disciplines. Any research about disciplinary differences and similarities is likely to be useful for English for Academic Purposes instruction. Perhaps even more importantly, few corpus studies have addressed the differences between the academic writing that students are asked to do and the writing they must do in the workplace. In many places in the world, much is said about helping students develop better writing skills – but there is little recognition of how language varies across registers or of the need to prepare students to handle different registers. Corpus-based research can help identify the challenges and can be used in the development of teaching materials. In the future, I also hope to see more integration of corpus analysis with other subjective analyses of effectiveness – for example, to move beyond descriptions of academic writing and to combine corpus research with experts' judgements of the best writing to see if there are linguistic patterns that distinguish it. Overall, however, I do not believe there are particular kinds of questions that analysts *should* think of. One of the joys of working in Corpus Linguistics is the diversity of issues that can be addressed, and analysts can pursue what is interesting and useful for their own contexts.

6. What are the strengths and weaknesses of corpus analysis?

In general, I think the greatest strength of Corpus Linguistics is that it increases our ability to systematically study variation in a large collection of texts. We can investigate texts produced by far more speakers and writers, and we can examine a greater number of words than could be analysed by hand. Corpus Linguistics techniques therefore allow us to see what is typical or untypical in particular contexts. For example, in the study of grammar, the patterns might show the correspondence between the use of a grammatical feature and some other factor in the discourse or situational context – e.g. the use of 'though' turns out to be more common as a linking adverbial in American and British conversation, especially as a speaker disagrees with or adds a contrast to a previous statement, but 'though' is more common as a subordinator in academic prose (see Conrad & Biber 2009: 82). This finding does not mean that every speaker of English uses 'though' when disagreeing with someone or that no writers use 'though' as a linking adverbial, but rather that there is variation in its use. With Corpus Linguistics techniques, we can characterise the most common choices for a large number of people, rather than basing generalisations on a small set of data or anecdotal evidence.

Identifying patterns relies on quantitative analysis. Therefore, I would suggest that much of the strength of Corpus Linguistics comes from the role of quantitative analysis. There is quite a bit of variation in the emphasis given to the reporting of quantitative results (see contrasting views by Biber & Conrad 2001; and McCarthy & Carter 2001); however, virtually all corpus work includes quantitative assessments, even if they are expressed only by noting that a feature is 'common' or 'typical,' or occurs 'more often' than something else. Of course, frequency counts are not enough for describing a language or interpreting the patterns. As Biber, Conrad and Cortes (2004) explain, ' … we do not regard frequency data as explanatory. In fact we would argue for the opposite: frequency data identifies patterns that must be explained. The usefulness of frequency data (and corpus analysis generally) is that it identifies patterns of use that otherwise often go unnoticed by researchers' (p. 376).

I believe the greatest weakness of corpus analysis is that it is, by nature, bottom-up. By this I mean that analysis has to start with identifiable lexical or grammatical features. As researchers conduct analyses, they always connect the language features to their functions and contexts, but a search in a corpus has to start with a word or grammatical feature – not with a function or context. Suppose, for example, a researcher reads about the use of 'though' and wants to examine disagreements in a corpus of conversation to more thoroughly describe where 'though' does and does not occur. It is easy to find the occurrences of this word, but there is no easy way to identify all instances of the functional category 'disagreement.' Such identification is possible with a preliminary step of reading through the corpus transcripts and making judgements about where disagreements occur, but it is time-consuming and often limits the data that can be analysed. Instead, many researchers will choose to limit their analysis to features known to occur for certain functions (e.g. comparing the use of 'but', 'however', and 'though' rather than doing a more open-ended investigation of language in disagreements).

Because they start with searches on specific linguistic features, corpus techniques are also harder to apply to investigating rhetorical issues such as the effectiveness of argument development or the hierarchical structure of texts. This is not to say that there are no discourse-level corpus analyses. For example, Biber, Connor and Upton (2007) use the analysis of vocabulary to identify discourse segments in texts. Other researchers combine a more rhetorical analysis with a corpus analysis, such as Flowerdew's (2003) analysis of problem-solution text structure and associated language features used by professionals and students. In fact, there are a number of corpus analysis techniques that have been used to investigate discourse-level features (for a review, see Conrad 2002). However, especially for analysts who use readily available computer softwares such as concordancers, discourse-level issues are the most challenging to study and require incorporating other analytical approaches.

An associated weakness concerns the difficulty of applying corpus techniques to investigating interpersonal dynamics. Kachru (2008) points out that roles and relationships are negotiated throughout a social interaction, and thus far, corpus techniques have not often been applied to studying these interpersonal dynamics. Such work would require a combination of computational analysis and intensive conversational analysis. In addition, corpora for such work would likely need to have more finely grained descriptions of the relationships and social positions of the participants than most corpora currently have.

7. What is the future of Corpus Linguistics?

I think we are at a point where Corpus Linguistics is going to become more widely known, especially among language teachers, and will be considered more mainstream rather than a specialised area.

The further spread of Corpus Linguistics will likely be due to the increasing presence of corpus-related materials that are published commercially. Many teachers have expressed an interest in corpus findings, but do not have the time to figure out how to incorporate new information from corpus studies into their teaching. In the best case scenario, new textbooks will make corpus-based findings accessible to a larger audience of teachers and students, and have them packaged with effective pedagogical activities. A variety of books are already appearing, with the role of Corpus Linguistics varying dramatically. To take just two examples, consider the *Touchstone* series books (e.g. McCarthy, McCarten & Sandiford 2006) and *Real Grammar: A Corpus-Based Approach to English* (Conrad & Biber 2009). *Touchstone* is an integrated skills coursebook series in which frequency information and spoken language tips from corpus analysis are integrated into the units. *Real Grammar*, on the other hand, is a supplement meant to be used in conjunction with a grammar textbook; each unit focuses exclusively on information from corpus analysis. The books are designed for very different audiences and purposes, and present and use corpus information differently. Such variation, I expect, will continue and even increase as more books incorporate aspects of Corpus Linguistics. In the future, as with any approach that is becoming commercially popular, teachers and students will do well to ask discerning questions to learn exactly how a corpus was used in any book's development.

A second development that I expect is that Corpus Linguistics will become more mainstream among both language teachers and language researchers. By this I mean that there will be less distinction among people who are corpus linguists and those who are not, with a growing group of teachers and researchers sometimes using corpus techniques and sometimes other tools. I already see this development among students in the applied linguistics programmes at Portland State University. More and more of them consider corpus analysis one tool they have at their disposal to answer language-related questions or to teach a word or grammatical feature to ESL students. The accessibility of searches with American English in the Michigan Corpus of Academic Spoken English (MICASE) and the Corpus of Contemporary American English (COCA) has facilitated this development. In fact, when they go to teach in a new programme, our graduates are often shocked to learn that their new colleagues do not do their own corpus searches.

8. How can corpus analysis inform our understanding of registers?

The term 'register' sometimes is used in different ways, so let me first clarify the term. I consider registers to be varieties of language that can be described with reference to their typical situational contexts and their linguistic features (cf. Biber & Conrad 2009). Situational context includes characteristics such as whether the register is spoken or written, whether it is interactive, what the purpose of the communication is and numerous others (see Table 2.1 in Biber & Conrad 2009). Members of a discourse community can easily identify the situational characteristics of a named register; for example, if I say 'research article in applied linguistics,' you probably can immediately predict a written document published in a journal, no direct interaction with the author as you read the article, a purpose of introducing some new knowledge into the field, and a host of other characteristics.

I think the most important contribution of corpus analysis to this area of investigation is the realisation that describing the linguistic features of a register requires examining the *pervasive* lexical and grammatical features in the variety (Biber & Conrad 2009). By 'pervasive' features I mean those that are more common in the register being examined even though they occur in many other registers as well. The features will be more common in a particular register because they play important functions for that register – functions shaped by the situational context. For example, consider a comparison of the nominals in conversation and newspaper writing. Conversation uses many more personal pronouns, and newspaper writing uses more nouns. The personal pronouns in conversation reflect the face-to-face context and the typical communicative functions of conversation (establishing and maintaining relationships, conveying information about oneself, asking about the other participants). However, it is not the case that conversation uses exclusively pronouns and never any nouns, or newspaper writing uses only nouns and no personal pronouns. The difference concerns the relative distribution of the features.[1]

Registers have been included in corpus-based analyses from a number of perspectives. One approach is to consider as many different linguistic features as possible and compare multiple registers; the purpose here is to characterise

---

1 An alternative perspective is a genre analysis, which focuses more on identifiable textual features that characterise the variety and on organisational structure; see further Biber & Conrad (2009).

different registers and to describe the similarities and differences among them (e.g. studies using a multi-dimensional analysis fit in this category, see Biber 1988; Conrad & Biber 2001; Biber 2006). Another approach is to consider the frequency and use of a particular function in various registers; for example, metadiscourse has been found to be realised differently in different registers (Hyland 1999; Mauranen 2003; Mauranen & Bondi 2003). In this approach, the focus is on the discourse function, but the studies contribute to our understanding of the different registers in which the discourse function is studied. A third approach is to describe characteristics of a single register. Unplanned spoken discourse has received a great deal of attention in recent years (see the summary of factors and features in Biber et al. 1999, Chapter 14; and Carter & McCarthy 2006: 163-175). Comparisons are often made with other well known registers; to take one example, my TESOL students are often surprised to discover from corpus-based work that, while expository writing tends to have complex noun phrases, conversation actually has more complexity at a clausal level.

9. In what way(s) may corpus findings inform the professional practice?

The impact of Corpus Linguistics has been biggest in the field of language teaching (although applications in other fields such as lexicography, forensic linguistics, translation, and many others are also notable). In language teaching, there are numerous applications that could be discussed, including the importance of considering lexicogrammatical relationships rather than teaching vocabulary and grammar as distinct components of language (e.g. see Conrad 2000, 2010; Hunston & Francis 2000; Liu & Jiang 2009) and the need to consider frequency information in designing syllabuses and materials (e.g. see Aston 2000; Gavioli & Aston 2001; and Biber & Reppen 2002). However, I think the most important contribution of Corpus Linguistics to language teaching concerns register variation. Corpus findings consistently show that it is impossible to describe or teach a language in a generalised way. As soon as register variation is considered, it is clear that there are differences in the frequency and use of grammar and vocabulary that are important to consider in language teaching. For most teachers, many differences seem obvious when they consider teaching a language for conversation vs. the same language for academic writing. However, corpus studies show that even in describing the basic use of grammatical features, register differences matter. For example, consider explaining the use of the definite article in English. In conversation, the most common reason for use of the definite article is due to a referent being part of the shared context of the speakers (e.g. in an utterance such as 'Bob, put the dog out, would you please?' the definite article is used because the participants both know the family dog). About 55% of the occurrences of definite articles in conversation are due to shared contexts. In newspaper and academic writing, the most common use of the definite article is due to the noun having modifiers (e.g. 'The introduction of technology into teaching ... ' uses the definite article because the prepositional phrase of 'technology into teaching' specifies the noun). Modifiers account for about 30–40% of all occurrences of the definite article in informational writing, but only about 5% of the occurrences in conversation. Thus, corpus studies show that – even for explaining the use of a specific grammatical feature – register differences are important (see more on the definite article in Biber & Conrad 2010).

Findings of Corpus Linguistics are also applicable to teaching in fields that are not language-related. For example, I am currently working on a corpus-based project concerned with writing in civil engineering (Conrad, Dusicka & Pfeiffer 2010; Conrad & Pfeiffer 2011). A common complaint in this field is that students are not well prepared for writing in the workplace and they need more writing practice in school. However, rather than showing the students just to be inexperienced writers, patterns in the corpus findings suggest that some of the language differences between students and practitioners reflect different values in academia vs. business practice. For example, practitioners use more first person pronouns and active voice verbs, while students tend to rely on passives. Many faculty members have been surprised at this finding; in their view, first person pronouns are inappropriate for professional documents and they recommend passive voice. In the practitioner view, in contrast, first person pronouns and active voice verbs are often the clearest way to describe actions and make recommendations. They tend to believe that active voice makes the ideas more accessible to their clients and has less potential for ambiguity concerning which firms were responsible for which decisions. Students' use of passive voice does, in fact, often leave agents unclear, and in a business context, this could result in serious liability problems. Thus, our corpus analysis is revealing that the writing problem in this field is not simply a matter of lack of practice, but of students and even faculty often not being aware of practitioner concerns.

10. When and how should teachers (or teachers-to-be) be introduced to corpus techniques?

The short answer to this question is: the earlier, the better. As long as teachers or teachers-in-training are introduced to techniques in a logical sequence that gradually builds their skills and autonomy, Corpus Linguistics can be introduced at any level.

To take a specific example, in our TESOL MA programme we are finding that gradually introducing students to aspects of Corpus Linguistics can have a positive effect. Our students are exposed to Corpus Linguistics in a class required in their first term, working with findings from corpus-based studies to analyse reporting verbs in literature reviews in research articles and practise writing their own literature reviews. In a later term, in a teaching methods course, the students are introduced to doing their own basic searches on corpus websites to gather data that is useful for the kinds of questions that ESL students often ask. In a pedagogical grammar class, the students receive much more exposure to corpus findings and to ideas for using them with ESL students. Finally, students who choose to take a Corpus Linguistics in Language Teaching elective course practise many different functions with concordancers and web-based interfaces, do their own research, and design corpus-based teaching materials.

In my opinion, the most important outcome for our students is not that they do corpus analyses in the future; some do, and some do not. More important is that the corpus work helps change their view of language and their view of themselves as researchers of language. They come to see that there are strong patterns in the way that humans use language, and that different choices are typical in different contexts – rather than viewing language as simply grammatical or ungrammatical. They soon realise that they do not have to accept claims in a textbook or from intuition or anecdotal evidence. They recognise that, with a principled corpus, they can do their own analyses and check those claims and intuitions with empirical evidence. Some people worry about teacher trainees (or any students) feeling overwhelmed by Corpus Linguistics. Instead, I find that, presented with the right guidance to build skills, corpus work increases their feelings of self-confidence and empowerment, because they do not have to rely on experts; they can research language for themselves.

References

Aston, G. 2000. Corpora and language teaching. In *Rethinking Language Pedagogy from a Corpus Perspective*, L. Burnard & T. McEnery (eds), 7–17. Frankfurt: Peter Lang.

Aston, G. & Burnard, L. 1998. *The BNC Handbook*. Edinburgh: EUP.

Barbieri, F. 2005. Quotative use in American English: A corpus-based, cross-register comparison. *Journal of English Linguistics* 33: 222–256.

Biber, D. 1988. *Variation across Speech and Writing*. Cambridge: CUP.

Biber, D. 1990. Methodological issues regarding corpus-based analyses of linguistic variation. *Literary and Linguistic Computing* 5: 257–269.

Biber, D. 1993. Representativeness in corpus design. *Literary and Linguistic Computing* 8: 243–257.

Biber, D. 2006. *University Language: A Corpus-Based Study of Spoken and Written Registers* [Studies in Corpus Linguistics 23]. Amsterdam: John Benjamins.

Biber, D., Connor, U. & Upton, T. 2007. *Discourse on the Move: Using Corpus Analysis to Describe Discourse Structure* [Studies in Corpus Linguistics 28]. Amsterdam: John Benjamins.

Biber, D. & Conrad, S. 2001. Quantitative corpus-based research: Much more than just bean counting. *TESOL Quarterly* 35: 331–336.

Biber, D. & Conrad, S. 2009. *Register, Genre, and Style*. Cambridge: CUP.

Biber, D. & Conrad, S. 2010. *Corpus Linguistics and Grammar Teaching* [Pearson Education Monograph Series]. White Plains NY: Pearson Education. <http://www.longmanhomeusa.com/content/pl_biber_conrad_monograph_lo_3.pdf>

Biber, D., Conrad, S. & Cortes, V. 2004. 'If you look at … ': Lexical bundles in university teaching and textbooks. *Applied Linguistics* 25: 371–405.

Biber, D., Conrad, S. & Reppen, R. 1998. *Corpus Linguistics: Investigating Language Structure and Use*. Cambridge: CUP.

Biber, D., Johansson, S., Leech, G., Conrad, S. & Finegan, E. 1999. *The Longman Grammar of Spoken and Written English*. Harlow: Pearson Education.

Biber, D. & Reppen, R. 2002. What does frequency have to do with grammar teaching? *Studies in Second Language Acquisition* 24: 199–208.

Bowker, L. & Pearson, J. 2002. *Working with Specialised Language: A Practical Guide to Using Corpora*. London: Routledge.

Carter, R. & McCarthy, M. 1995. Grammar and the spoken language. *Applied Linguistics* 16: 141–158.

Carter, R. & McCarthy, M. 2006. *Cambridge Grammar of English*. Cambridge: CUP.

Clancy, B. 2010. Building a corpus to represent a variety of language. In *The*

Routledge Handbook of Corpus Linguistics, A. O'Keeffe & M. McCarthy (eds), 80–92. London: Routledge.

Conrad, S. 2000. Will Corpus Linguistics revolutionise grammar teaching in the 21st century? *TESOL Quarterly* 34: 548–560.

Conrad, S. 2002. Corpus linguistic approaches for discourse analysis. *Annual Review of Applied Linguistics (Discourse and Dialogue)* 22: 75–95.

Conrad, S. 2006. What can Corpus Linguistics offer business English teachers? *IATEFL Business Issues* 1: 2–5.

Conrad, S. 2010. What can a corpus tell us about grammar? In *The Routledge handbook of Corpus Linguistics,* A. O'Keeffe & M. McCarthy (eds), 227–240. London: Routledge.

Conrad, S. & Biber, D. (eds). 2001. *Multi-Dimensional Studies of Register Variation in English.* Harlow: Pearson Education.

Conrad, S. & Biber, D. 2009. *Real Grammar: A Corpus-Based Approach to English.* White Plains NY: Pearson Longman.

Conrad, S., Dusicka, P. & Pfeiffer, T. 2010. Work in progress – Understanding student and workplace writing in engineering. *Proceedings of the American Society for Engineering Education Zone IV Conference, 2010.* <http://web.me.unr.edu/asee2010/Proceedings.pdf>

Conrad, S. & Pfeiffer, T. 2011. Preliminary analysis of student and workplace writing in civil engineering. *Proceedings of the 2011 American Society for Engineering Education Conference.* <http://www.asee.org/search/proceedings>

de Klerk, V. 2006. *Corpus Linguistics and World Englishes: An Analysis of Xhosa English.* London: Continuum.

Ellis, N., Simpson-Vlach, R. & Maynard, C. 2008. Formulaic language in native and second language speakers: Psycholinguistics, Corpus Linguistics, and TESOL. *TESOL Quarterly* 42: 375–396.

Firth, J. R. 1957. *Papers in Linguistics.* Oxford: OUP.

Flowerdew, L. 2003. A combined corpus and systemic-functional analysis of the problem-solution pattern in a student and professional corpus of technical writing. *TESOL Quarterly* 37: 489–511.

Gavioli, L. & Aston, G. 2001. Enriching reality: Language corpora in language pedagogy. *ELT Journal* 55: 238–246.

Granger, S., Dagneaux, E. & Meunier, F. (eds). 2002. *International Corpus of Learner English.* Louvain: Presses Universitaires de Louvain.

Hyland, K. 1999. Talking to students: Metadiscourse in introductory coursebooks. *English for Specific Purposes* 18: 3–26.

Hymes, D. 1974. *Foundations in Sociolinguistics: An Ethnographic Approach.* Philadelphia PA: University of Pennsylvania Press.

Hunston, S. 2002. *Corpora in Applied Linguistics.* Cambridge: CUP.

Hunston, S. & Francis, G. 2000. *Pattern Grammar: A Corpus-Driven Approach to the Lexical Grammar of English* [Studies in Corpus Linguistics 4]. Amsterdam: John Benjamins.

Kachru, Y. 2008. Language variation and Corpus Linguistics. *World Englishes* 27: 1–8.

Kilgarriff, A. 2001. Comparing corpora. *International Journal of Corpus Linguistics* 6: 1–37.

Koester, A. 2010. Building small specialised corpora. In *The Routledge Handbook of Corpus Linguistics,* A. O'Keeffe & M. McCarthy (eds), 66–79. London: Routledge.

Liu, D. & Jiang, P. 2009. Using a corpus-based lexicogrammatical approach to grammar instruction in EFL and ESL contexts. *Modern Language Journal* 93: 61–78.

Mauranen, A. 2003. 'But here's a flawed argument': Socialisation into and through metadiscourse. In *Corpus Analysis: Language Structure and Language Use*, P. Leistyna & C. Meyer (eds), 19–34. Amsterdam: Rodopi.

Mauranen, A. & Bondi, M. 2003. Evaluative language use in academic discourse. *Journal of English for Academic Purposes* 2: 269–271.

McCarthy, M. & Carter, R. 1995. Spoken grammar: What is it and how do we teach it? *ELT Journal* 49: 207–218.

McCarthy, M. & Carter, R. 2001. Size isn't everything: Spoken English, corpus, and the classroom. *TESOL Quarterly* 35: 337–340.

McCarthy, M., McCarten, J. & Sandiford, H. 2006. *Touchstone 3*. Cambridge: CUP.

Meyer, C. 2002. *English Corpus Linguistics*. Cambridge: CUP.

Nelson, G. 2006. The core and periphery of world English: A corpus-based exploration. *World Englishes* 25: 115–129.

Palmer, F. (ed.). 1968. *Selected Papers of J. R. Firth 1952–1959*. London: Longman.

Pickering, L. & Byrd, P. 2008. An investigation of relationships between spoken and written academic English: Lexical bundles in the AWL and in MICASE. In *The Oral/literate Connection: Perspectives on L2 Speaking, Writing and Other Media Interactions*, D. Belcher & A. Hirvela (eds), 110–132. Ann Arbor MI: University of Michigan Press.

Prodromou, L. 2008. *English as a Lingua Franca: A Corpus-Based Analysis*. London: Continuum.

Reppen, R. 2010. Building a corpus: What are the key considerations? In *The Routledge Handbook of Corpus Linguistics,* A. O'Keeffe & M. McCarthy (eds), 31–37. London: Routledge.

Simpson, R. & Swales, J. (eds). 2001. *Corpus Linguistics in North America:*

Selections from the 1999 Symposium. Ann Arbor MI: University of Michigan Press.

Simpson-Vlach, R. & Leicher, S. 2006. *The MICASE Handbook*. Ann Arbor MI: University of Michigan Press.

Sinclair, J. M. 1991. *Corpus, Concordance, and Collocation*. Oxford: OUP.

Stubbs, M. 1993. British traditions in text analysis: From Firth to Sinclair. In *Text and Technology*, M. Baker, G. Francis & E. Tognini-Bonelli (eds), 1–33. Amsterdam: John Benjamins.

Thompson, P. 2010. Building a specialised audiovisual corpus. In *The Routledge Handbook of Corpus Linguistics*, A. O'Keeffe & M. McCarthy (eds), 93–103. London: Routledge.

Synchronic and diachronic
uses of corpora

In this interview, Mark Davies, Professor of (Corpus) Linguistics at Brigham Young University (United States), shows his interest in languages such as English, Spanish and Portuguese. This interest is revealed in his involvement with corpora compilation (Corpus of Contemporary American English, Corpus of Historical American English, *Corpus del Español,* and *Corpus do Português*, to name four instances). From his practical experience, Davies comments on the constraints one may find when trying to make a corpus available on the Internet and on what kind of technological knowledge is expected of corpus linguists. In line with the practice in this field, the author makes use of data to show us the role that intuition should play in linguistic analysis and generalisations. In terms of approach, he stresses that corpora may be used for both synchronic and diachronic purposes – the latter being discussed in more detail in one of his specific questions.

1. Where do you place the roots of Corpus Linguistics? And to what do you attribute the growth of interest in the area?

The roots of Corpus Linguistics are likely to be found in the emphasis on empiricism that is found in the Western scientific and philosophical tradition generally. Beyond that, however, linguistics as a field had a fairly pronounced empirical orientation from the early 1900s until the 1950s. Part of this had to do with the fact that in the United States, at least, linguists often worked on languages (such as the Amerinidian languages) for which they had no native speaker intuitions. The only way to deal with these 'unknown' languages was to gather and organise large amounts of data from native speakers. A similar situation held in the 1940s, as researchers scrambled to develop training materials in (often) non-Indo-European languages for use by forces in World War II. A second factor (at least in some countries) was the strongly behaviourist orientation of many linguists from at least the 1930s until the 1950s. This approach was also highly empirical, as it attempted to gather large amounts of data on both input and output, to study the relationship between the two.

Chomsky and his followers changed all of this in the 1950s, particularly in the United States. As many others have shown (cf. McEnery & Wilson 2001), Chomsky's methodological orientation dealt a severe blow to empirically-oriented research. He argued, for example, that it was a waste of time to spend so much time and money gathering data from native speakers, when it would be sufficient to just rely on their intuitions. Second, he suggested that although data might show that a particular syntactic construction was 'frequent', it could not explain why other constructions were unacceptable. Third, he said that the data from corpora often told us more about the 'real world' (e.g. that *sand* and *waves* are collocates of *beach*) than about our supposedly native linguistic faculty. Fourth, he argued that corpora at that time were too small, at any rate, to provide meaningful data.

Although some research on corpus-based linguistics continued in the 1960s and 1970s (such as the development of the Brown and LOB corpora), there was a real resurgence starting in the 1980s. There are at least four reasons for this, and they relate to the four arguments against corpus-based research that had been raised by Chomsky previously.

First, by the 1970s, researchers had to admit that there were serious methodological problems with so much reliance on linguistic 'intuition'. 'Data' was often produced that served to support a particular linguistic theory, but which was very much at odds with other native speakers, with no way to reconcile the competing sets of 'intuition'. Second, during the 1970s and into the 1980s, there was a resurgence of interest and work on 'functional' (and typological) linguistics, which helped to address Chomsky's concerns about why certain constructions did exist (and were frequent), while others were not. Third, the argument that corpus data taught us more about the real world than about the linguistic faculty was more or less a straw man argument. Corpora could (and did) produce some fairly trivial data (*beaches, sand,* and *waves*), but they also produced an incredible amount of data that was linguistically insightful.

Perhaps the major factor in the resurgence of interest and work in Corpus Linguistics in the 1980s and the 1990s, however, was technology. It is true that small 1-million-word corpora often produced too little data to be of real interest (a fact that some in the Corpus Linguistics community still find hard to accept, as they continue to focus on the creation of small, overly-narrow, 'boutique' corpora). But advances in computers in the 1980s and into the 1990s made possible the creation of large corpora such as the Bank of English and the British National Corpus. Finally, this data was robust enough to shed real insight into many issues that had been puzzling until that time. In the 2000s, this trend towards even larger (and yet still well-balanced) corpora has only accelerated, with the introduction of corpora such as the 425-million-word Corpus of Contemporary American English (see Davies 2009).

In the 2000s, there have been two other technological advances as well. First, not only do we have large, well-balanced corpora, but because of advances in software and architectures, we have better means of efficiently searching these corpora. Second, rather than having (often expensive) software that access the corpora locally on an individual machine, or which uses a complex client/server architecture, many of the large, representative corpora are now available (often for free) via the Web, and can be accessed very easily by means of a web browser. Finally, the power of corpora is available to the masses.

2. Is Corpus Linguistics a science or a methodology? Where would you situate Corpus Linguistics in the scientific or methodological panorama?

I would argue that Corpus Linguistics is definitely a methodology, rather than a 'science' or even a separate field of linguistics. At a general, philosophical level, Corpus Linguistics argues for the importance of data, and a frequency-based approach to linguistic phenomena. At a more specific level, it deals with the way in which data is obtained and organised. Finally, in concert with the insights of other approaches to language (particularly a functional approach), it often has something to say about what this data 'means'. But the orientation is a highly empirical one, and this empirical approach is relevant to research in a number of different 'fields' of linguistics, such as morphology, syntax, semantics, the lexicon, pragmatics, and historical linguistics.

In this sense, Corpus Linguistics is analogous to particular methodological approaches in other academic fields. To take just one example, in macroeconomics one can focus on which data are the most useful to predicting future economic activity (such as unemployment rates, savings rates, or government spending), and what is the most accurate way to obtain that data. This would contrast with a more theoretical approach, which proposed extremely abstract models for economic activity. In this case, Corpus

Linguistics would of course be analogous to the first approach, where the emphasis is on acquiring, organising, and correct interpreting the primary data – rather than overly-abstract theory that may or may not be based on accurate data.

Although Corpus Linguistics is a methodology, and although it does relate to the importance of the empirical approach to data, its results are the most meaningful when they are combined with the insights from other approaches to language. To take a simple example, consider the issue of the 'to infinitive' versus the 'bare infinitive' as a complement of *help*: *Mary helped John (to) clean the room*. The data from the 100-million-word TIME Corpus of American English (1920s–2000s) provides clear data for a shift from [+to] to [−to] over time. From a strictly Corpus Linguistics point of view, we might ask questions like: is the corpus representative, does it matter if it is (i.e. can 100 million words from just one source in just one genre provide the needed data, or do we need a more 'balanced' corpus in this case), is the corpus tagged correctly, did we use the right query string to find all relevant tokens, and so on.

But if all we do is show the shift from constructions like [*Mary helped John to clean the room*] to [*Mary helped John clean the room*] and we leave it at that, that is a fairly meaningless and sterile investigation. We probably want to know *how* and *why* the change occurred. In terms of 'how', we might ask whether it occurred with all subordinate clause verbs at the same rate, or whether it was a function of the animacy of the matrix clause subject. These questions in turn lead us into the 'why' questions, perhaps the primary one being 'Why the shift in the first place?'

To answer this question, we certainly would need to venture outside of Corpus Linguistics *per se*, to use the insights from other approaches to language. In this case, the answer probably has to do with iconicity, and the fact that in the 'real world' the linkage between 'Mary helping' and 'John cleaning' is fairly strong (as it is also with *Mary let/made/saw John clean the room*), and this is signalled iconically by the absence of [to] as a separator between the two clauses. This contrasts with *Mary asked/wanted/expected John to clean the room*, where the linkage between Mary 'asking/wanting/ expecting' and 'John cleaning' is more distant and tenuous, and the language marks with iconicity by using an intervening [to].

So, in this case, insights from Corpus Linguistics help us to acquire and organise the data ('what happened' and perhaps 'how did it happen'), but the insights from functional/typological/cognitive linguistics provides the explanation ('why did it happen'). In my opinion, it is when we have this interplay of Corpus Linguistics and other approaches to language that the contributions of Corpus Linguistics are the most meaningful.

3. How representative can a corpus be?

Ideally, of course, the data from a general corpus [such as the British National Corpus (BNC), the Corpus de Referencia del Español Actual (CREA), or the Corpus of Contemporary American English (COCA)] will represent perfectly what one would find in the 'real world'. But this is problematic in several ways. One of the most serious problems is the ratio of what we would encounter in daily life and what we find in a corpus. For example, in the BNC only 10% of the corpus is spoken, but presumably more than 10% of the linguistic input for an average speaker in a given day is spoken. Because spoken corpora are difficult and expensive to create, however, virtually every corpus has less spoken than a truly representative corpus would have. The same could be said for 'ephemera' like billboards, advertisements, instructions on packages, and so on. No corpus is a 100% mirror of what we encounter in real life.

Even with 'standard' genres such as spoken, fiction, newspapers, and academic (cf. Biber et al. 1999), the answer is not so easy. There are many different factors that we could or should consider in creating a corpus of, for instance, popular magazines: sub-genre of the magazine (sports, religion, finance, parenting, etc.), specific subject matter of the article, the author's gender, age and place of origin, the target audience, the year of publication, and so on. And each of these can be subdivided in turn. For example, with sub-genre of 'sports magazines', we can have topics like football, basketball, and golf. And within basketball, we can have a focus on individual players, teams, strategy, etc. This can go on *ad infinitum*. And we can always come back to the relationship of the corpus to the 'real world'. Do more people read articles on basketball than golf, or are there more articles published on individual players than on strategy?

As most corpus linguists will admit, no corpus will ever be truly representative. All we can do is identify that handful of features that we believe are the most important, and attempt to design the corpus accordingly. In the section that follows, rather than focusing on more abstract theorising, I will provide some concrete examples from the design and construction of the Corpus of Contemporary American English (COCA; 425 million words, 1990–present; cf. Davies 2009) and the Corpus of Historical American English (COHA; 400 million words, 1810–present).

The Corpus of Contemporary American English (COCA) is almost equally divided each year (and therefore overall as well) between the five genres of spoken, fiction, popular magazine, newspaper, and academic. Within each of these genres, there is an attempt at good balance as well. For example, in popular magazines we identified about 16 different sub-genres (sports, religion, finance, parenting, etc.), and from year to year we have roughly the same number of words in each sub-genre. Likewise, for academic articles we created about 25 categories (based on the Library of Congress classification: D = history, T = technology, etc.), and each category has roughly the same number of words from year to year. Similar care was taken with the sub-genres in fiction (novels, short stories, science fiction, juvenile fiction, etc.) and newspapers (editorial, sports, finance, 'life', national news, etc.).

The most problematic category was spoken. We wanted about 20% of the corpus to be from spoken (thus about 80 million words). But of course it would be impossible (with a corpus creation team of one person and a budget of $0) to get 80 million words of conversation. We were able, however, to acquire 80 million words of unscripted conversation from TV and radio programmes like The Oprah Winfrey Show, Good Morning America, The Today Show, Geraldo, and so on. Of course with transcripts of 'media language' there are issues relating to accuracy, naturalness, and so on. These are considered in some detail at the corpus website. However, by looking at many different linguistic features where we expect spoken English to 'behave' a certain way (based on data from studies like Biber et al. 1999), these 80 million words of spoken English pattern extremely well after what we would expect. Thus the 'proof of the pudding is in the eating'.

Historical corpora present even more complications. Perhaps the most serious issue is that most genres do not exist at the same ratio across time periods. For example, there are very few newspapers before the 1700s and virtually no 'authentic' spoken transcripts before the mid-1900s. Yet if we do not maintain the same mix of genres across time periods, how do we know that supposed linguistic changes really occurred at certain points? How can we be sure that it is not just a result of the different content included in the corpus between those two periods? As a practical example with the Corpus of Historical American English (COHA), there is very little fiction in American

English before the early 1800s. Do we just have less fiction (or no fiction) from the 1700s than in the 1800s? Or do we cut the time period of the corpus to not include anything previous to the 1800s, so that we can maintain the same mix across time periods? We have chosen the latter option (since maintaining the same composition in different time periods is the most important principle for us), but again, these are questions without easy answers.

4. How far should an analyst rely on intuition?

Perhaps the best way to answer this question is to have you take a short six question quiz. Make sure you cover the answers below until you are done.

A. (SYNTAX/GENRES) In which genre (spoken, fiction, newspaper, academic) is *shall* used most and in which the least, compared to *will*? (Note: the answer is the same for both British and American English.)
B. (SYNTAX/HISTORICAL) Which of the following two constructions is increasing at the expense of the other: *I started to walk away/I started walking away* ?
C. (MORPHOLOGY) Assume that you are reading a newspaper. Which of the following would you expect to see as a past participle (e.g. have + seen): proven/proved, shown/showed, sewn/sewed, swollen/swelled, pled/pleaded, dreamt/dreamed?
D. (WORD FREQUENCY 1) Put the following verbs in order of frequency (high to low): *promise, shine, finish, enable, jump.*
E. (WORD FREQUENCY 2) Put the following adjectives in order of frequency (high to low): *cleanable, unfurled, worry-free, fluttery.*
F. (SEMANTIC/COLLOCATES) Which of the following would occur more frequently with *little*, and which with *small*: *success, plate, hill, baby, impact, pieces, wonder, distance.*

Let's see how you did:

A. In both British (BNC) and American (COCA) corpora, *shall* is found most in fiction, and least in newspaper (possibly a surprise for those who expected that it would be spoken).
B. In the TIME Corpus (100 million words, 1920s–2000s), the V-ing construction (*I started walking away*) has been increasing slowly since the 1980s.
C. Raw frequencies in British English (BNC): proved (441 to 17), shown

(939/7), sewn (27/1), swelled (15/12), pleaded (85/11) and dreamed (22/13). Raw frequencies in American English (COCA): proved (897 to 697), shown (4228/85), sewn (125/4), swelled (100/57), pleaded (241/2) and dreamed (204/6).

D. Raw frequencies in British English: finish (11520), enable (10022), promise (6110), jump (4995) and shine (2117). Raw frequencies in American English: finish (41663), jump (27433), promise (24799), enable (15762) and shine (8617).

E. From COCA (American data): fluttery (82 tokens), worry-free (41), unfurled (20) and cleanable (10). For the smaller BNC (British data), the numbers are much lower: fluttery (9), unfurled (4), worry-free (1) and cleanable (1).

F. From COCA (American English):
   little: success, baby, impact and distance;
   small: plate, hill, pieces and wonder.

What can we learn from a simple experiment like this?

i.   Perhaps the most important point is that (as is the case with just about every other cognitive function) the accuracy of linguistic intuition varies from one person to the next. For example, my intuition tends to be much better on syntax and linguistic change (questions like A–B) than that on lexical frequency (D–E). For those who are more right-brain dominant, perhaps the results will be reversed.

ii. How you did probably has to do with whether you are a native speaker of English. Non-native speakers will likely have less reliable intuitions for questions like this.

iii. Linguistic intuition is obviously a function of dialect as well. For example, if you are a speaker of British English, then (assuming that your intuitions agreed with the corpus data) your answers may have been quite different for Questions C–D from those of a speaker of American English. Intuitions may not be 'transferrable' from one dialect to another.

iv. Intuition is probably a function of frequency as well. Chances are, you did better on Question D than you did on Question E.

As we can see, it is probably impossible to give one simple answer to the blanket question of how much we should rely on intuition – it is probably a function of a number of different factors.

5. What kind of questions should an analyst think of?

Corpus data can of course be used for many different purposes. Some are more applied – data for teaching, data for materials development, and data for natural language processing. There are many different questions that researchers in each of those fields would have. Here, however, I will focus on four of them which cover 'core' linguistic issues about variation and change.

Whether or not one can easily obtain data to look at variation (genre-based, dialectal, or historical) is a function of the textual corpus, and the architecture and interface. Some (even well-known) corpora and corpus architecture are not really designed to investigate variation (by genre, dialect, or historically) in a simple way. But if they are, then questions like those posed below are among some of the most interesting ones, from a corpus-based perspective.

A. What variation exists from one genre to another (and why)?
    Very few corpus architectures or interfaces are designed to 'easily' compare across genres. If they can, however, then we naturally ask why a linguistic feature is found more in one genre than in another (which often is answered by looking at the communicative function of that genre). For example, why are passives found more in 'careful' academic writing than in spoken data? Why does the latter have more contractions than other genres? Why are certain verbs (e.g. *clatter*, *scowl*, *shriek*, *glare* and *sigh*) found more in fiction than in other genres? Assuming the corpus architecture can compare and contrast genres, there will be no end to questions like these.
B. What variation exists from one dialect to another (and why)?
    In the late 1970s and into the 1980s, there were a number of studies that used the small Brown and LOB corpora to compare British and American English. Now that we have much larger corpora for these dialects, much more detailed studies could and should be carried out. Likewise, there has been relatively little work on corpus-based studies of dialectal differences for other languages using large, representative corpora.
C. What variation is there over time (and why)?
    Many historical corpora are much too small or else are not annotated sufficiently to allow for a wide range of research questions. But to the extent that they are, then this corpus data naturally raise questions about 'how' and 'why' languages change. For example, how do new constructions enter the language? Does syntactic change occur abruptly and completely, or does it spread slowly from one lexical item to another? What is the

relationship between genre and historical change? What is the relationship between cultural and societal shifts and what we see in the corpus? Robust corpus data can help to answer these and many other questions.

D. How is variation a function of semantic contrasts?

Until recently, it was difficult to compare phenomena with two competing words or semantic classes. For example, which adjectives occur with *go* but not *come* and vice versa (e.g. *go crazy, go bankrupt; come clean, come true*). Which verbs take [*to*] complements but not [*that*] complements and vice versa? Which collocates occur with *sheer* but not *utter*, and vice versa? Until recently, researchers looking at contrasts like these would have to carry out two separate queries, and then somehow compare the entire results sets (with thousands of entries in each set). With some new corpora, however (such as BYU-BNC, Sketch Engine, and COCA), even advanced queries like these take only 2–3 seconds.

In summary, the questions that we ask are often a function of the data that we have, and especially the variation that we see in it. But this data is also a function of the corpora that we use and the architectures and interfaces that they employ. If a given corpus only contains texts from one genre (e.g. newspapers), for example, or if the corpus architecture and interface do not allow fast and easy comparisons of a wide range of phenomena in the different genres (as is the case in most of the widely-used architectures), then we are much less likely to even know what questions to ask about genre-based variation. Thus the questions we ask are often a function of the tools that we use.

6. What are the strengths and weaknesses of corpus analysis?

There are a number of strengths and weaknesses in corpus analysis. Let's be optimists and start with the advantages (there are more of them anyway).

A. Corpora provide real data, and this data can be used to test the assumptions and claims of other researchers. To give a personal example, I started using corpora as an MA student in Hispanic Linguistics, mainly because it was the only way that I could 'compete' with more experienced researchers, many of whom were native speakers of Spanish. My intuition about Spanish syntactic constructions certainly was not at the level of a native speaker, and the only way to compete was to back up my claims with tens of thousands of tokens from large, well-balanced corpora from thousands of other native speakers of Spanish. So, (publicly-available) corpora help to put people on a level playing field in terms of the data.

B. Related to this is the idea that corpora make the claims of the 'experts' subject to empirical verification. No more is it sufficient (or safe) to hide behind the facade of 'authority'. Anyone who has access to the same (or better) data can (and should) use this data to replicate and test the previous claims, or to challenge conventional wisdom. Again, on a personal level, after coming to Corpus Linguistics from another field of linguistics where 'authority' is more important than actual 'data', I can say that corpus linguists are – on the whole much more open to change and much more open to alternate points of view, than in many other fields of study – and this is due in large part to the strongly empirical orientation of our field.

C. Corpora are great for language learners (even if they are not 'taking on the experts', as in the two previous points). Suppose that a learner of English wants to know what the difference is between *utterly*, *completely*, and *totally*. Chances are that even the best bilingual dictionary will not explain the difference (well). Or assume that a non-native speaker wants to know which of the following synonyms of *walk* are the most common: *saunter, stroll, trudge, stride, perambulate*. That information would not be found in even the best thesaurus. Or perhaps the non-native speaker wants to know how frequent preposition stranding is in academic journals. Very few grammar books would provide information like that. However, with the right corpus, all of these questions could be answered in just a few seconds.

D. Even for native speakers, corpora help provide us with a never-ending string of 'ah-hah' moments and valuable insight into our own language. Each one of us who is a teacher can probably think of moments where students have asked us a question, we have not had a good answer, and then we plunge into some corpus data. After a bit of working with the data, we then see patterns emerge that we had never been aware of before. And then once we see the data, there is a discovery moment. But without the corpus data, chances are that would have never come.

E. It is probably a small point, but as a teacher I find that the 'millennial generation' loves to use corpora. It is much more interactive than the traditional methods. We explain, they search, we discuss, they search some more – it is a model of 'active learning' that is much more meaningful for them than the 'walk through the textbook' or 'chalk and talk' presentations of days gone by.

This is just a handful of the advantages of a corpus-based approach to language, and many more could be given. What about the downside (if any) to using corpora? I will just briefly mention a few possible issues.

A. Corpus-based data can sometimes make things more complicated. All of a sudden, that simple 'rule' we had always heard does not seem so simple once we start looking at genre-based variation, dialectal differences, or competing historical trajectories.

B. Because the amount of data can sometimes be overwhelming and because creating corpora from scratch can be very time-consuming, sometimes researchers take unwise 'short-cuts'. For example, they might make and use a corpus made up entirely of web-accessible newspapers, and then assume that one genre is representative of the language as a whole.

C. As others have mentioned, there is a possible problem with 'pseudo-prescriptivism'. If an ESL student from Africa uses a word or a construction that does not exist in large mega-corpora of British and American English, her teacher may consider it 'wrong' – even though it is common in her dialect of English (which may not have a large corpus available).

D. Because Corpus Linguistics is heavily dependent on technology, and because new tools and new corpora are always being developed and there is always a learning curve, there is sometimes resistance to using new corpora and new tools. Luckily, this is always less of a problem for the younger generation.

Overall, though, as nearly everyone who has used corpora can attest, the advantages of corpus-based research far outweigh the disadvantages.

7. What is the future of Corpus Linguistics?

In terms of the direction that Corpus Linguistics is going, it is encouraging to see the number of new corpora that have become available in the past 3–4 years. We now have several different architectures and interfaces for the British National Corpus, each with their own particular strengths and advantages. With the 425-million-word Corpus of Contemporary American English (see Davies 2009), we finally have a large, well-balanced corpus of American English, to be followed by the 400-million-word Corpus of Historical American English, presumably the first large, structured historical corpus of English (or any language). 'National corpora' of other languages are also underway. Many of these are also publicly-available and free of charge. If the availability of corpora is considered, it is a good time to be doing research.

As regards tools, however, we could and should be doing better. Many of the 'stand-alone' programmes to analyse corpora are not scalable enough to handle new, 'super-sized' corpora. Too many web interfaces for corpora work and act like the interfaces from the late 1990s, where users are presented with thousands of KWIC entries, and the interface does little to help organise or make sense of the entries. Too many people continue to use the same tools they were using ten years ago, without realising that there are much better options now. But many younger researchers, especially, seem to be more open to new tools, new corpora, and new ways of doing things.

A huge challenge facing the field in the next few years is dealing successfully with increasingly large 'unstructured corpora' and 'text archives'. Some examples concern the Web (via Google and other search engines), Google Books, the Internet Archive, collections of historical texts with hundreds of millions of words of text (e.g. Literature Online or the Early English Books Online), and data repositories (e.g. Lexis-Nexis, ProQuest Research Library, and EBSCO Academic Search Premier), which have tens of thousands of magazines, newspapers, and academic journals and many billions of words of text.

There are many problems with these unstructured corpora, of course. They are not annotated (lemmatisation and part of speech tagging), they do not form a 'representative' 'corpus', and the interfaces are overly simplistic. They typically only allow for searching by word or phrase, and they often present the results in a very corpus-unfriendly manner. They often require clicking sequentially on thousands of results to see the context, and there is little if any summarisation of the data (by year, genre, source, etc.). And yet they are so appealing, simply because of their size; our traditional 50- to 100-million-word corpora look very small by comparison.

The best 'future', I think, is to 'mine' these text archives to obtain the texts to create balanced, representative corpora, with architectures and interfaces that facilitate our needs as corpus linguists. But as of yet, there are precious few of these corpora, mainly because most of the older architectures are not scalable enough to handle them. So we hobble along on with a split personality – using large text archives for some types of research, and small(er) 'boutique' corpora for others, with little connection between the two.

When I think of the most promising trends in the next few years, most of them have to do with possible collaboration with those outside of the Corpus Linguistics community *per se*. (When I speak of the 'Corpus' Linguistics community, I think of those who might be at one of the major conferences in the field – Corpus Linguistics, ICAME, or TALC.)

There are hundreds or thousands of researchers who use corpora to do research on a wide variety of languages, involving history, gender studies, formal syntax, political discourse, and a thousand other fields – but who do not consider themselves 'corpus linguists' and who do not regularly attend 'our' conferences. How well are we reaching out to those in other fields of linguistics, much less other fields of academic study, much less those outside of academia? Do our corpora meet their needs? Does our methodology inform their research?

At a recent meeting of the conference for the American Association for Corpus Linguistics (BYU 2008), Tony McEnery gave a fascinating keynote address that showed how some corpora are now being used to help inform important research by historians, anthropologists, and political scientists who are looking at 17th-century England. But much more can and should be done to create links with researchers in other fields.

In terms of the widest outreach possible, I think of famous historians, political scientists, physicists, or economists whose research is read by the 'lay public', and whose research does inform newspaper and magazines articles that reach the 'common people'. How well does our research do the same? For example, during this past political campaign in the United States (2008), I saw many 'informal' newspaper articles with colorful charts and graphs that attempted to compare the candidates based on word frequency, keyword analysis, content analysis – the kind of thing that we do day in and day out. Some of these were fairly insightful; most were rather naïve. But do these reporters and pundits have any sense of how our research could improve theirs?

When the day comes that there is convergence between what we do (as a Corpus-Linguistics-internal community) and what is being done in other communities (inside and outside of academia), and what is of interest to even non-academic communities, then we will really see the fruits of our efforts.

8. How far should tools and corpora become public domain?

In terms of tools, I would just briefly note that the Corpus Linguistics community should be grateful for those which – although they were initially created in the cocoon of well-funded universities – are now maintained and distributed as open-source materials. Perhaps the two most widely-known and used resources of this type are the Natural Language Toolkit (NLTK) and the IMS Open Corpus Workbench (CWB).

In what follows, I would like to focus more on the development of publicly available corpora. The two fundamental problems with it are (a) who is going to fund the corpus, and (b) who is going to provide the texts. In the examples below, I provide three different ways in which things can play out. I do so with the goal of showing real-world approaches to creating public domain resources. This will enable us to move beyond vague generalities about 'public domain' and beyond the overly-simplistic mantra of 'make it all available, and completely for free'.

The first scenario in corpus creation is that there is generous 'seed money' from a sponsoring institution. We might consider the British National Corpus (which received millions of dollars in seed money from the Oxford University Press) or the Bank of English (which received millions of dollars in support from Collins-COBUILD). Publishers are enticed to be part of a consortium (in the case of the BNC), or the consortium is one large publisher. These publishers participate because of the commercial value that they see in such an arrangement, and they provide the texts and the copyright permission to use the texts in the corpus.

The second way things can play out is what happened with the American National Corpus. There was no rich institution to provide seed money. Attempts were made to form a consortium, but this failed. Very few texts became available, what is there is not balanced in terms of sources or genres, and the corpus has not been completed.

The third approach is the one that we have taken in the creation of several other large corpora (see the corpora available at Brigham Young University). Because we knew that we did not have the millions of dollars that were used to create the BNC and the Bank of English, and wanting to avoid the fate of the ANC, we opted for a different plan. Copyrighted texts would be used as the basis of the corpus, but no copyright permission was requested or obtained from the copyright holders.

Without copyright permission, however, we cannot ever release the full-text version of the corpus into the public domain. It is available, however, to search and access the corpus via a web-based interface that allows for an extremely wide range of queries. KWIC displays are limited to more or less what one sees on Google or in Google Books – the node word(s) surrounded by 40-60 words. US copyright law does allow for the use of copyrighted material, as long as (among other conditions) the end user does not have access to more than a certain percentage of the original text, and cannot 're-create' the original text by stringing together different pieces of the text. We have been criticised by some for not allowing full-text access to these corpora, but there simply is no legal alternative – none whatsoever.

We have dwelt on this final approach at some length because this is probably the most realistic scenario of the three for others contemplating the creation of corpora. Well-funded corpora like the BNC or the Bank of English are the exception, not the rule. Some other lucky individuals may be part of some large government-funded plan to create a 'national corpus' of a given language. But by and large, there is little if any money available to obtain copyright permissions, or to entice publishers to be part of a consortium. In this case, the only option is to use copyrighted materials, and then restrict access to the end users in some way.

9. How much technology should an analyst master? What are the minimum requirements to develop corpus work?

The question of how much technical expertise a researcher needs depends entirely on the research question. If the researcher wants to examine metaphor in 25-50 poems by several 18th-century female Scottish poets, then probably relatively little. On the other hand, if one wants to compile a 30-million-word corpus of children's fiction or compile a frequency dictionary of a given language, then obviously it will be somewhat more.

Regardless of the project or the resources being used, however, researchers should attempt to understand (a) the limitations of the tools they are using and (b) what the alternatives are. Some researchers (even advanced ones) are technologically-wedded to stand-alone programmes that are well-designed for beginning students, and which do work well for small 1- to 10-million-word corpora. As even their creators would admit, however, they are quite inadequate for advanced queries on 50-100+ million word corpora. For advanced research on corpora of this size, researchers will probably need to use another programme, and they need to be aware of the alternatives.

These concerns extend to web-based corpora as well. To take the concrete example of the BNC, there are several very good interfaces and architectures available – each with its own particular strengths and weaknesses. With so many possibilities, it is sad to see researchers who are unaware of alternatives that might meet their needs much better. And the same extends to entirely different corpora, but that is a separate matter.

Perhaps the real concern, however, should be the stand-alone programmes and web-based architectures that claim to work with large corpora – and in fact do in PowerPoint slides at conferences – but which are not scalable in the real world. In summary, though, one needs to be savvy enough to be aware of limitations, and of alternatives.

Another issue is whether corpus linguists need to know how to programme to do meaningful research. Here, I think, we must divide researchers into two camps – corpus users and corpus creators. Corpus users can often get by with stand-alone tools or web-based corpora – interfaces created by others – as long as they understand the limitations of these architectures and interfaces. However, assuming that the users have access to full-text versions of the corpora, even a little knowledge of regular expressions will go a long way in helping with more complex queries.

For corpus creators, however, I would say that some experience with programming is a necessity. In more simple cases (1- to 10-million-word corpora, limited annotation etc.), then perhaps regular expressions and a simple knowledge of semi-automated file handling (e.g. simple batch file operations) would be sufficient. With these, one could process text downloaded from the web to strip out headers, footers, and other unwanted material. But for more complex corpus creation, one would benefit greatly from knowing a programming language.

In terms of the number of users, Perl and Python are probably the main languages. Because it has been around longer, Perl has a wider range of NLP and corpus-useful modules. But Python integrates better with NLTK (the Natural Language Toolkit), which is a very useful array of tools for corpus and computational linguistics. As an aside, I would also mention that knowing how to use at least one good tagger (and/or parser) – some of which are included in the NLTK – is invaluable to corpus creation.

Whatever language is chosen by corpus creators, however, they will want to make sure that the language has modules or objects to download and efficiently process large amounts of web-based text, and not just long lists of static URLs. In the creation of several 100+ million-word corpora, I have used VB.NET. This is a useful language because it integrates well with

Internet Explorer – to use information from a database to decide what content to download, to fill out forms, to parse the text in a web page (using regular expressions) to dynamically create URLs to download other pages, and then to store and organise the data in other databases. This type of corpus creation would have been completely impossible without a robust programming language.

Finally, I would argue that relational databases and advanced SQL queries can be used in a very powerful way as the basis for the architecture of large corpora, and that this approach lends itself to corpora that are large, very fast, and which allow almost unlimited annotation (via links between different data sources and lexicons). But this pertains only to corpus creators (not users), and is probably the topic for a separate question in any case.

10. In what ways have corpus studies impacted historical linguistics?

There are several different ways in which the use of corpora has impacted historical linguistics. Before considering these, however, we should first make a few introductory comments about the current state of historical corpora.

Virtually all historical corpora to date suffer from one of two shortcomings. First, many are far too small to be of much help for most types of linguistic research, except for high-frequency phenomena like modals, pronouns, or word order. A look at corpus-based studies of historical English during the past 15–20 years, for example, shows that the research agenda is clearly driven by whatever phenomena one can extract from small 1- to 2-million-word corpora. Second, virtually no historical corpora are annotated at the word level – lemmatisation and part of speech tagging (although see the Penn Parsed Corpora of Historical English). The main reason for poor word-level annotation is the extreme difficulty in dealing with spelling variation in older texts. Without word-level annotation, researchers are often left just looking for exact words and phrases, as with Google or with text archives. Perhaps the only large, well-annotated historical corpora currently in existence are the 45-million-word *Corpus do Português*, the 100-million-word *Corpus del Español*, and the 100-million-word TIME Corpus of American English.

Lexical and semantic change

Historical linguists have traditionally been fixated on the first occurrence of a word and they have then left it at that, because most corpora were too small to look at lexical change in a meaningful way, and corpus architectures were not designed to show frequency over time. With the free corpora mentioned above, researchers can easily see the frequency of any word, phrase, morpheme, or construction by century or decade. In terms of semantic change, rather than having to look at occurrences of a word one-by-one (as with the regular Oxford English Dictionary or the CORDE Corpus from the Real Academia Española, for example), the architecture for these corpora allows one to see and compare (by frequency) the collocates of that word, where a change in collocates can often indicate change in meaning. As a final example, with a typical corpus one has to specify exactly which word or phrase one wants to examine. With the architecture for these corpora, however, one can specify the frequency in different historical periods (e.g. ten tokens or more in the 1700s, but less frequent in the 1800s), and the corpus architecture will generate and display a list of matching words.

Syntactic change

Robust corpus data has fundamentally altered our perception of how syntactic change occurs. First, some formalist models of syntax hypothesise that there are abrupt shifts in grammar, based on abrupt changes in the 'parametric settings' for those languages (cf. Lightfoot 2003). Actual data from corpora, however, show that this is rarely the case. This syntactic process often takes place over several centuries (see, for example, Bybee 2003 for English modals and Davies 1995 and 1996 for Spanish and Portuguese causatives). Corpus data show that part of the reason for such long periods of time is that this type of change typically 'spreads' from one lexical item to another (as with 'lexical diffusion' in terms of sound).

Finally, robust corpus data can also provide valuable insight into the way in which new constructions arise and how they spread. For example, Rudanko (2010) uses data from the 100-million-word TIME Corpus (1920s–2000s) to show how English moved from 'to INF' complements to 'V-ING' complements (*accustomed to watch* > *accustomed to watching*) precisely at the point where the older construction was functionally most vulnerable, and Davies (1997, 1999) finds the same thing for the origin of the subject raising construction in Old Spanish and in Old Portuguese.

The important point here is that only corpus data can provide us with the crucial data that shows (a) that change often occurs slowly over time, (b) that it typically spreads from one lexical item to another, and (c) that it is functionally-motivated, especially in terms of the beginning stages of a construction. Without corpus data, we might be more inclined to accept alternate models, which have limited support from actual empirical data.

References

Biber, D., Johansson, S., Leech, G., Conrad, S. & Finegan, E. 1999. *Longman Grammar of Spoken and Written English*. London: Longman.

Bybee, J. 2003. Mechanisms of change in grammaticalisation: The role of frequency. In *The Handbook of Historical Linguistics*, B. Joseph & R. Janda (eds), 602–623. Oxford: Blackwell.

Davies, M. 1995. The evolution of the Spanish causative construction. *Hispanic Review* 63: 57–77.

Davies, M. 1996. The diachronic evolution of the causative construction in Portuguese. *Journal of Hispanic Philology* 17: 261–292.

Davies, M. 1997. The history of subject raising in Spanish. *Bulletin of Hispanic Studies* 74: 399–411.

Davies, M. 1999. The historical development of subject raising in Portuguese: A corpus-based approach. *Neuphilologische Mitteilungen* 100: 95–110.

Davies, M. 2009. The 385+ million word corpus of contemporary American English (1990–2008+): Design, architecture, and linguistic insights. *International Journal of Corpus Linguistics* 14: 159–190.

Lightfoot, D. 2003. Grammatical approaches to syntactic change. In *The Handbook of Historical Linguistics*, B. Joseph & R. Janda (eds). Oxford: Blackwell.

McEnery, T. & Wilson, A. 2001. *Corpus Linguistics*. Edinburgh: EUP.

Rudanko, J. 2010. Exploring grammatical change in recent American English, with evidence from the *TIME* magazine corpus. *Journal of English Linguistics* 38(1): 4–24.

Methodological and interdisciplinary stance in Corpus Linguistics

Stefan Th. Gries, Professor of Linguistics at the University of California, Santa Barbara (United States), brings out a challenging notion of Corpus Linguistics. He proposes its understanding should be merged with psycholinguistic and cognitive concerns. Gries has no qualms in classifying Corpus Linguistics as a methodology. This explains his many references to methodological issues, ranging from the design of corpora to their comparison and/or analysis. In addition, Gries extensively discusses statistical issues, including how much knowledge a corpus analyst needs to have in order to embark on such an investigation. This sharp methodological concern is also expressed in his prospects for the practice in Corpus Linguistics, which, according to him, needs to develop from a statistical standpoint.

1. Where do you place the roots of Corpus Linguistics? And to what do you attribute the growth of interest in the area?

As to the first question, I am not sure the roots of Corpus Linguistics can be placed any particular place and/or time. As so often in science, related ideas emerge and develop in different places and then over time converge to give rise to a more coherent-seeming framework. It seems to me that the following are the most prominent early examples of what from today's perspective looks like corpus-linguistic work: bible concordances, Käding's (1897) work at the end of the 19th century, Firth's (1951) bearing on collocation, the Survey of English Usage as well as the Brown and LOB corpora, and all these are without doubt some extremely important milestones. Since it seems to me as corpus linguists are still more widespread or vocal in Europe, it may not come as a surprise that this list of highlights is very Euro-centric, so I would just like to add three American strands or approaches that I think should be included just as much.

First, there is the work of early American linguists. Not only did early

Americanists such as Sapir rely on collections of utterances for their work, but so did American structuralists. For example, here is how Randy Harris (1993: 27) describes Bloomfield's approach: 'The approach [...] began with a large collection of recorded utterances from some language, a corpus. The corpus was subjected to a clear, stepwise, bottom-up strategy of analysis.' Second, there is Charles C. Fries's compilation and analysis of a corpus to discover features of spoken American English (cf. Fries 1952), which was one of the first rigorously bottom-up, or corpus-driven approach to the structure of (conversational) English. Finally, there is Zellig Harris's (1970: 785f.) statement on distributional analysis which states more clearly than any other source I have ever seen the logic underlying most corpus- or computational-linguistic approaches involving co-occurrence data, i.e. concordances and collocations:

> [i]f we consider words or morphemes A and B to be more different in meaning than A and C, then we will often find that the distributions of A and B are more different than the distributions of A and C. In other words, difference of meaning correlates with difference of distribution.

As to the second question, there is again not one single reason for the growth of interest. This growth has to do with several developments, again from different perspectives and at slightly different times. For example, there are logistic/structural reasons such that more and more corpora covering different languages, registers, etc. are becoming available, and the WWW is at our fingertips, so researchers can ask more and more diverse questions. Also, the field is maturing methodologically and conceptually: Corpus Linguistics was seen by many as consisting of little more than descriptive papers listing frequencies of occurrences of linguistic elements, but it is difficult for such onlookers to uphold that frame of mind. Not only do many corpus linguists use more and more sophisticated methods (for both retrieval and statistical analysis), but many corpus linguists are (finally ...) beginning to look beyond the confines of the texts or discourses and contribute to, and interface with, neighbouring fields such as cognitive linguistics/science, psycholinguistics, etc. Many of these fields also undergo a development towards more empirical/ quantitative methods, which makes them compatible with corpus-based work. In a nutshell, they benefit from the data and methods we are dealing with all the time, and we benefit from them injecting a healthy dose of explanatory approaches and theoretical connections into our still too often merely descriptive discipline.

2. Is Corpus Linguistics a science or a methodology? Where would you situate Corpus Linguistics in the scientific or methodological panorama?

I have thought a lot about this question, especially since August 13, 2008. On that day, I received a first response to a call for enrollment for a quantitative Corpus Linguistics bootcamp that I was going to teach at my university, which triggered a discussion that is now sometimes referred to as 'the bootcamp discourse' and that was, among other things, also concerned with that question. I think I advocate my position on this most clearly in my statement in the special bootcamp issue of the *International Journal of Corpus Linguistics* 15.3 (Gries 2010), but I will summarise it here very briefly while also taking up another related issue.

As for the first question, I think Corpus Linguistics is definitely a method(ology) or a 'methodological paradigm', no more but also no less. More specifically, to me *Corpus Linguistics* refers to (i) the study of the properties of corpora or (ii) the study of language on the basis of corpus data. I am making this difference here because I think as a corpus linguist, e.g. a corpus compiler, one can restrict one's attention to describing the frequency of linguistic phenomena in some corpora, the statistical properties of corpora, or even just methodological corpus issues (e.g. comparing how efficient different approaches to tagging a corpus are, or determining which kind of clustering algorithm best distinguishes different registers on the basis of n-gram frequencies) without necessarily being interested in a genuinely *linguistic* question, e.g. what the register differences actually reflect. Ultimately, I find the second type of study – addressing genuinely linguistic questions – more interesting, but investigations of the first type are still very important: Corpus Linguistics needs corpora and has not come up with many proven methods so compilation/sampling and methodological analyses are needed to prepare us for the second type of study.

I think the above distinction also bears on another way to situate Corpus Linguistics, namely with regard to the field of computational linguistics. While *computational linguistics* is only one of several terms to refer to a huge (and increasingly diverse) field – with *natural language processing* being one of the most widely used terms – some areas of computational linguistics of course border on, or overlap with, Corpus Linguistics. When asked where I see the (main) difference between these fields, I usually say (a bit polemically and simplistically) that some areas of computational linguistics are in fact mislabelled: taking the notion of head-modifier structure very literally, I think there are many areas that should be labelled *linguistic computing* as opposed to computational linguistics, and this distinction also relates to Corpus Linguistics. My take on this is that I want to call something *linguistics*, if its ultimate goal is to increase our understanding of (the use of) human language, or even the linguistic system's place in the larger domain of human cognition, and I want to call something *computing* if its ultimate goal is not concerned with *understanding* (the use of) human language but its computational application or implementation. For example, for me, developing a talking ticketing machine for the airport parking lot falls under the heading of *natural language processing*, but I would not call it *linguistics* (even if frequency data from corpora are used to tweak how the machine parses its input), but, if pressed, would call it *linguistic computing*. (Of course, there are cases where such a forced binary decision is difficult to make.)

As for the second question, as I have argued in Gries (2010), Corpus Linguistics should be 'a psycholinguistically informed, (cognitively-inspired) usage-based linguistics which should be located, firmly and deliberately, in the social/behavioural sciences.' As mentioned above, it is time for more of the field to move beyond the purely descriptive and sometimes ostrich-like we-must-not-look-beyond-the-texts approach and assume (proudly, I might add) the position that our discipline deserves: we are looking at complex behavioural data typically arising from social settings, which means we should describe what the data look like with decent quantitative methods and explain their nature with reference to findings from relevant fields, and fields that are obviously relevant for a discipline studying *behavioural* data from *social settings* are cognitive science/linguistics, psychology/-linguistics, and sociology/-linguistics plus their respective neighbouring fields.

3. How representative can a corpus be?

The answer to this question obviously depends on one's definition of *representative* so let me first clarify how I understand *representative*; not everybody uses it to refer to the same thing. I would call a corpus representative if it contains samples of all the different parts of the linguistic population that the corpus is supposed to represent. I would call a corpus also balanced if the sizes of the samples of the linguistic population it contains are proportional to the proportions these parts make up in the population that is supposedly represented in the corpus.

With these definitions in mind, my assessment is rather pessimistic: I think a corpus can be somewhat representative *on some level* largely by virtue of its design, but balanced probably only largely by virtue of sampling luck, but even this statement needs to be qualified some more for two reasons. First, because I think the degree to which a corpus can be representative and balanced is correlated with its position on the general-special continuum of corpora: given a particular amount of resources, the more specific the corpus is intended to be, the more representative and balanced it can be; and the more general it is supposed to be, the less representative and balanced it will be.

Second and more importantly, this statement needs to be qualified because, as with all corpus work, there are innumerable nested levels of granularity that can be considered. Theoretically, sampling for corpus compilation is a multi-dimensional enterprise even though, for obvious and reasonable practical purposes, only a small number of dimensions can be chosen. For instance, as I understand it, corpus compilers usually (and reasonably so) select a sampling scheme whose units involve modes (spoken vs. written or a more fine-grained version of this) and, within the modes, registers. The design of the ICE-GB, for example, involves three different levels of hierarchical (sampling) organisation, as indicated in the columns of Table 1 (cf. <http://www.ucl.ac.uk/english-usage/projects/ice-gb/design.htm>).

Table 1. The hierarchical organisation of the ICE-GB

Mode	*Register*	*Sub-register*
Spoken	Dialogue	Private vs. public
	Monologue	Scripted vs. non-scripted
	Mixed	Broadcast
Written	Printed	Academic vs. creative vs. instructional vs. non-academic vs. persuasive vs. reportage
	Non-printed	Letters vs. non-professional

All of this raises three problems that can decrease the representativity of a given corpus and, hence, its balancedness. A corpus will be representative and balanced to the degree that the corpus compilers succeed in

- identifying the relevant levels of corpus organisation, i.e. the adequate columns in Table 1 and their right number;
- identifying the relevant distinctions within each column of corpus

organisation, i.e. the distinctions indicated in the column-specific rows of Table 1;
- determining the sizes of each of the samples that result from the different levels and their within-level distinctions.

As for the first two problems, even if corpus compilers managed to identify all the right registers – i.e. made the corpus representative on the level of register – this does not guarantee that the way they would sample the registers does not make the corpus *un*representative on the level of the sub-register and/or, even worse, on many other levels. Strictly speaking, even if corpus compilers succeeded in choosing the right modes, registers, and sub-registers, then it is strictly speaking still possible that the way they sample from texts on the level of the sub-register was unrepresentative. For instance, if one chose only the first and the last sentence of each text/conversation or if the texts from which one sampled exhibited untypically large sentence lengths or a near complete absence of a particular construction C, then the corpus would be representative down to the level of the sub-register, but unrepresentative with regard to discourse features, sentence lengths, or the frequency of C. (Of course, corpus compilers would not just choose the first and/or last sentence, this is just a hypothetical example: any one linguistic variable could be used as an example.)

As for the third problem, even if the corpus compilers managed to make the corpus representative on many levels, they could still make it very unbalanced because they might not succeed in getting the sample sizes right. And how would they get them right anyway, how do we determine the proportional sizes of the samples – in terms of speaking time, in terms of utterances, sentences or words?

In sum, I think it is possible to achieve some degree of representativeness and balancedness when compiling a general corpus, but only on some level(s) of corpus granularity. A corpus that is perfectly representative and balanced on one level can be completely unrepresentative in terms of the frequency distribution of some specific pattern. Strictly speaking, it is therefore necessary to sample as widely as possible and explore for each phenomenon of interest how it is distributed over multiple levels of corpus divisions especially since the most meaningful division of a corpus into parts may be different for each phenomenon and may not coincide with linguists' favoured register distinctions.

4. How far should an analyst rely on intuition?

My take on this is that intuition can play a role on nearly all levels of corpus-linguistic analysis, and it often has to, but of course to varying degrees, and the following comments adopt a broad notion of intuition (itself a fuzzy word), one that involves all sorts of subjective decisions. In general, there is a subjective decision that is sometimes overlooked when the subjectivity of an analysis is evaluated, and that is which corpus or which genre/register to study. In addition, intuitive/subjective decisions come into play at different points of time.

First, the identification of a topic or problem typically involves a lot of intuition such as when a researcher finds that the explanation of phenomenon *P* does not appear satisfactorily given what else is known about *P*. A little less intuition would be involved when a researcher finds that the explanation of *P* is unsatisfactory given a new set of data.

Second, the retrieval of data may involve very little intuition as when no decision for a particular corpus has to be made (because, say, only one is available) and one looks for a uniquely identifiable word form. More intuition is needed when a decision for some corpus (or other database) has to be made, but also when one looks for partially lexically-filled constructions such as the *into*-causative (NP_{SUBJ} V NP_{DO} *into* V-*ing* as in *He tricked her into marrying him*) where one might decide to search a corpus for '\binto [^\s]+in['g]\b'[1] and then use the linguist's 'intuition' (often called *knowledge*) to weed out false hits such as *This is how the EU came into being*. And even more intuition is needed when the linguistic phenomenon of interest does not involve anything literal to search for, i.e. no specific word and/or tag or involves an unannotated corpus.

Third and most importantly, subjective decisions will become necessary during the analysis, i.e. during, for example, the coding of data with regard to features that are not always clear-cut, and during the statistical analysis of the data. As for the former, if one wants to code lengths of utterances, one must choose between counting characters, morphemes, words, phrases, etc. If one wants to code referents of noun phrases (NPs) semantically, one may have to distinguish between concrete and abstract, but within the former one

---

1 This regular expression matches a word boundary ('\b'), followed by *into* ('into'), a space (' '), some characters that are not spaces ('[^\s]+'), *in* or *ing* ('in[g]'), and a word boundary ('\b').

can again distinguish animate and inanimate. In this case, do humans get a category on their own? Do animals, or plants? What do we do with NPs referring to actions (as in *Counting is hard*)? Do we use Vendlerian categories for that (which are in turn difficult)? In the sentence *the police came to the crime scene*, is the subject concrete/human or abstract/organisation? And what about *minefield* in *wading through the minefield of autism treatments* – is it locative, or do we code the whole thing as an idiom? Maybe just as difficult is the coding of coherence relations, or the coding of referential distances (do we include cover terms or not, part-whole relations or not, etc.). It is these kinds of tricky decisions that have resulted in more and more studies including inter-rater reliability statistics in their papers (not that these are completely unproblematic, but that is a different story).

As for the statistical analysis, one sometimes also has to make decisions regarding the method to be adopted. For example, which similarity measure and which amalgamation rule to use in a cluster analysis? Or what kind of cluster analysis to use in the first place: hierarchical or phylogenetic? For example, which method to use to predict an alternation – logistic regression, classification trees or Bayesian classifiers etc.?

In sum, it is obvious that corpus linguists need to make subjective decisions all the time, and they need to document their subjective choices very clearly in their publications. However, in spite of these undoubtedly subjective decisions, many advantages over armchair linguistics remain: the data points that are coded are not made-up, their frequency distributions are based on natural data, and these data points force us to include inconvenient or highly unlikely examples that armchair linguists may 'overlook'.

5. What kind of questions should an analyst think of?

I am not sure I am in a position to tell any researcher what one *should* think of as one's primary research question, so I will instead mention two questions one should think of which concern and/or qualify the scope of one's primary research question and findings.

The first of these questions has to do with the kinds of results reported and what the sources of their variation in corpus data are. More specifically, given that corpora only provide frequencies of (co-)occurrence, studies usually provide (conditional) frequencies, means, and averages of the phenomenon in question. However, obviously each corpus and each part of a corpus will yield different results, and these differences will sometimes reflect something linguistically interesting, and they will always also reflect random variation of sampling. I would therefore like to see more exploration of how variable and sensitive such results are. Schlüter (2006) compared the widely differing frequencies of present perfects in very different corpora, motivated me to explore how widely the frequencies of present perfects differ within (parts of) *one* corpus. The results of that exploration – the frequencies of present perfects in the ICE-GB alone were just about as variable as those in very different corpora – plus some follow-up work (in Gries 2006) provided some sort of an epiphany for me: claims about an overall frequency of (co-)occurrence, a mean, or a correlation can be useless unless they are accompanied by an exploration of the diversity of the data giving rise to the overall frequency, the mean, or the correlation. It is this kind of systematic and often bottom-up exploration of different levels of granularity that I think is essential for our understanding and validation of virtually all corpus results.

The second of these questions has to do with what corpus-based results are used for, and with the question of what Corpus Linguistics is. As mentioned above, studies that, for instance, describe the frequencies of some linguistic element(s) in one or more corpora fall under my heading of Corpus Linguistics, but I also said that I prefer studies that try to go beyond that. Put differently, I prefer studies that describe something but then also answer 'why does that happen?' questions, which try to understand the motivations and the forces driving the distributions of data, and which ideally try to do this by exploring connections to findings from *other fields* to avoid the often circular description (often not even reasoning) that arises from some gatekeepers' reluctance to admit other kinds of evidence onto the corpus linguist's desk. It may be in this regard that I disagree most strongly with some other scholars' beliefs. For example, when Teubert (2005:10) writes 'When linguists come across a sentence such as "The sweetness of this lemon is sublime", their task is […] to look to see if other testimony in the discourse does or does not provide supporting evidence', I cannot even begin to understand why that should be the task of any corpus linguist: what would be explained by this? Similarly, I cannot subscribe to his statement that '[c]orpus linguistics […] is not concerned with the psychological aspects of language' (Teubert 2005: 2f.). Although there are limits to what corpus linguists can say about the human mind and its psychology, that does not mean that distributional data from corpora cannot inform, or be meaningfully related to, data from more psychological/cognitive disciplines. For example, is it not better to be able to explain distributions in corpora – of, e.g. reduced pronunciations of words – with reference to generally-known cognitive mechanisms regarding learning, habituation, and articulatory routines than to point to other things happening in the discourse? Is it not interesting to be able to explain changes in diachronic corpora – e.g. the development of *going to* as a future marker in English – with reference to generally-known effects of automation as a result of frequency?

In sum, I do not really dare make specific research recommendations, but I would love to see corpus linguists be more aware of, and explore in a bottom-up fashion, the variability of the data they report on as well as establish more explicit (and explanatory) connections of their descriptive results to findings from other disciplines.

6. What are the strengths and weaknesses of corpus analysis?

To my mind, the two most important advantages of corpus work are the following. First, the data come from authentic settings: conversations and texts that were produced in largely natural contexts. While that makes corpus data very messy and noisy compared to experimental data (which then of course are in turn potentially more tainted by the artificiality of the experimental setting), it also enriches them and allows us to include cotextual and contextual/situational aspects of language use in our analyses.

Second, corpora only provide statistical data – even if no proper statistical analysis is conducted – and that means that statements such as 'in corpus *C*, 8.5% of X were Y, compared to 22.1% of Z' can be straightforwardly tested for replicability, compared to other corpus or experimental studies, be extended by additional data, and tested for significance, whereas armchair statements of the types 'X is rather untypical' or 'X is marginally acceptable' fare much worse in these respects.

In terms of weaknesses, or maybe risks, of corpus analysis, I see a few of those, but many of them are not peculiar to corpus analysis but apply to many empirical settings. For instance, one must bear in mind that whatever findings one reports that one can only generalise from the studied sample to a larger population to the extent that the corpus is representative with regard to the targeted population. Unfortunately, there are some authors who are quite happy to generalise more liberally.

Second and in a related manner, while corpus data are usually samples from naturally-produced texts as mentioned above, one needs to be aware of the fact that the circumstances of these texts can still be at odds with one's research question. For example, given the easy availability of large amounts of journalese data, many corpus studies use them, and often this is a good thing. However, as we argued elsewhere (cf. Gilquin & Gries 2009), even if corpora consisting of journalese data only may be large, they are still rather unsuited as a general corpus since they are a very peculiar register: they are created much more deliberately and consciously than many other texts, they often come with linguistically arbitrary restrictions regarding, say, word or character lengths, they are often not written by a single person, they may be heavily edited by editors and typesetters for reasons that again may or may not be linguistically motivated, etc. Thus, the more such characteristics can undermine one's research purpose, the more one must hedge the generalisability of one's findings or turn to additional (corpus or experimental) data for validation.

Finally, on the most fine-grained level of specific analyses, I am sometimes rather unhappy with the methodological decisions made by some analysts. On the one hand, the level of statistical sophistication of quite a few studies leaves much to be desired, with the two most pressing issues being (i) the complete lack of statistical significance testing (ignoring for now the problems that may come with significance testing) and (ii) the problem that multifactorial phenomena are studied monofactorially, disregarding the nature of often complex interactions of factors. On the other hand, there are (thankfully fewer and fewer) studies that can never be characterised better than in Pullum's (1978: 400) words: 'The fault is the procedure of attempting to establish a case on the basis of a set of data the size of a small workbook problem (though with theoretical biases of more generous proportions).' I have seen many papers which made far-reaching claims regarding a frequent phenomenon/word based on perhaps 200 examples. When I explain to my students why I hate that kind of practice, I tell them, 'How come corpus linguist X thought, "Gee, let me look at 150 examples this afternoon, surely that will be enough … " while biologists try to grow some cultures for months, archaeologists try to dig up stuff for years, etc. We look at, code/annotate, and evaluate examples and their frequencies, so how come some assume looking at 150 examples on one afternoon does the job?'

Thankfully, my perception is that the field is maturing more and more and addressing these shortcomings in various ways. Still, all of us, me included, still have a long way to go …

7. What is the future of Corpus Linguistics?

I do not think I have a good answer to that question. There are some currently hot topics but I think it is pretty much impossible to even make a reasonably precise educated guess, given that scientific disciplines do not exactly evolve nicely linearly. I will therefore only offer some brief 'guesstimates'.

In terms of areas/topics, I think corpus-based research will play an increasing role in applied linguistics, especially with the growing number of learner corpora and the ever increasing interest in second language acquisition and teaching. Similarly, I expect to see a greater degree of convergence between Corpus Linguistics and sociolinguistics, given how these disciplines share commitments to authentic data and quantitative analysis. Also, there seems to be a growing interest in corpus-based methods in the fields of language description and language documentation, which involves long-term digital archiving to store data on often endangered languages. Obviously, this ultimately raises issues of formats and annotation, but at the same time this increasing availability of such data will doubtlessly stimulate more desire to retrieve data from such databases or corpora for linguistic analysis, and I would hope that both fields can help each other evolve. On the one hand, corpus linguists have long thought about matters of corpus formats, storage, annotation, and access and have learned many lessons – especially from corpora much larger than those handled in language documentation – that documentary linguists could benefit from. On the other hand, documentary linguists routinely deal with languages whose structural complexity poses complicated but interesting annotation challenges that corpus linguists, who have mostly (but not exclusively) worked on the usual suspects from the Indo-European language family with often much more impoverished morphologies.

Second, I think that the current trend of using corpus data in psycholinguistic and cognitive approaches will become stronger. As for the former, language acquisition research has long involved corpus data, but there is also more and more work on probabilistic approaches to language production and comprehension, and much of this work is based on frequencies of words, *n*-grams, and constructions from corpora. The number of articles in the *Journal of Memory and Language* that mention corpora has risen considerably over the past few years. This trend can also be seen in cognitive-linguistic approaches. That whole field is taking the notion of usage-based approaches more and more seriously,[2] and the number of submissions to *Cognitive Linguistics* that involve corpus data has been on the rise. Since there are now also more corpus linguists talking about such issues and seeking explanations that transcend the narrow boundaries of pure corpus description, I would hope that this marks the beginning not of a convergence of these fields, but of recognition of what these fields have to offer each other as well as more fruitful mutual collaboration.

Finally, Corpus Linguistics will mature statistically. I know of maybe one multifactorial corpus-based study of a syntactic alternation from before 2000 (Gries 1999, later improved on in Gries 2003), but now binary logistic regressions, mixed-effects models, cluster analyses, etc. are not uncommon anymore and can be found in nearly every corpus-linguistic journal. Doubtlessly, and fortunately, this trend will continue.

8. What is the role of programming knowledge in undertaking corpus work?

Unfortunately, the role is rather limited, and that, together with the absence of proper statistical training, is the largest methodological problem of this discipline. Just look at the situation from an unbiased observer's perspective: why is it that corpus linguists often must retrieve complex patterns from gigabytes of messy data in various languages, encodings, forms of organisation and with widely differing forms of annotation, but most curricula do not contain even a single course on basic programming skills or relational databases (while psychologists, computational linguists, cognitive scientists etc. devote years to acquiring the required methodological skills)? It is true that there are several tools that allow users to perform a few elementary corpus-linguistic tasks with a graphical user interface but, while I am not evaluating these programmes here, let me say this quite bluntly: the superficial richness of functions and buttons is deceiving and debilitating. I know colleagues whose corpus-linguistic skills are defined by what WordSmith Tools (or AntConc, or ConcGram, etc.) or, even worse, web interfaces can do – if you take whatever resource they use away from them, they cannot pursue their corpus studies anymore. This means that if these corpus linguists' programme(s) cannot

---

2 The term *usage-based* is used in the sense of assuming that human linguistic systems are affected by the actual use of linguistic elements and structures, which makes for an obvious connection to corpus-based work.

lemmatise or use regular expressions, or compute keywords for *n*-grams (with $n \geq 2$), neither can they. If their programme does not allow them to conflate several files into one or compute particular collocational statistics, neither can they, etc. Does anyone know any other scientific discipline where this is the case, where quite a few practitioners' main methodology is opening a (corpus) website in their browser?

Thus, the field must step it up a bit and go beyond commercial software (and websites) because, first, the software many people use is severely limited in terms of

- availability: not every programme runs on every operating system and not every researcher can afford the programme(s) they would want to use;
- functionality: programmes/websites can only do what is hardwired into them so if the programme/website cannot compute collocational statistics, handle Unicode, corpora with particular tag formats, corpora with stand-off annotation or multi-tier annotation, then a (commercial) programme or website, rather than our interests/needs, dictate our research agenda!
- user-control: users are at the mercy of the developers. If, for instance, the creator of a programme updated the way keywords are computed without informing the users, then users would be clueless as to why the same data set suddenly yields different results, and with non-open source software, one cannot find out what has happened and why. Or, if the developer of 'your' programme decided to discontinue its development or a Microsoft Windows update changes a .dll so the programme stops working, then what? Or, finally, to return to the previous point: how are we even going to make any progress in the field? How would one study whether minimum sensitivity or $p_{\text{Fisher-Yates exact test}}$ or ΔP are better collocational statistics than *MI* and the loglikelihood statistic if one is utterly dependent on one tool which happens to not offer these measures? And are we happy with the fact that this situation would put the vast majority of the field under the control of two or three people who happen to develop nice-looking software? MonoConc Pro's current version – 2.2 – has been around with this version number since 2002 but I for myself am glad that my methodological knowledge has advanced a bit since then ...

Second and again quite bluntly, inflexible software creates inflexible researchers: more methodological knowledge sometimes suddenly suggests ways of analysis one would not think of, given how one's dependence on a ready-made tool can restrict one's way of thinking about a problem. Put differently, with a programming language, one does not need to think outside the box – because there is no box: everything's possible. Recently, I was involved in a project where we needed to recover sequences of two or more adjectives in a learner corpus. However, the corpus was not tagged, which for many colleagues would mean they would not be able to do the study. In our project, we used a small R script that searched the whole BNC for *all* words tagged as adjectives, saved them into a list, and then added an adjective tag to every occurrence of a word from that list in the learner corpus. Thus, we could then simply search for sequences of two words tagged as adjectives. A maybe even more telling example involves the search for ditransitive constructions, again in an untagged/unparsed learner corpus. As a heuristic, we used a script (less than 60 lines) that recovered all verb tokens tagged as used ditransitively in the ICE-GB, looked up the lemmas for these tokens in a lemma list, looked up all the forms for these lemmas in the lemma list (to get *allocating* as a search term even if only *allocated* had been used ditransitively in the ICE-GB), and then outputted a concordance of all matches of those forms in the learner corpus. This is not perfect, but it is easy to see that no ready-made programme could ever do this (especially not quickly). Thus, it is absolutely imperative for the field to further evolve in this direction, and fast, please![3]

---

3 One reviewer suggested a parallel between a linguist's computer programme and a doctor's instrument to ask whether the former would need to develop a tool of his/her own. This is wrong on so many levels that I hardly know where to start. Some of the above points should already illustrate why, but here is a different take on this. Many doctors practise medicine work in an applied field, where they use a set of finite heuristics to quickly identify a patient's illness, often out of a small and finite set of possibilities. They typically use several instruments (e.g. a stethoscope), which are often highly specialised (performing just one function), which do not differ much as to how well they perform that function, and which do not undergo developments and updates that do not allow to replicate results. If a stethoscope does not yield the desired result, the doctor uses another tool from the large set of available tools. By contrast, many corpus linguists work in a fundamental research field, where they must develop a research strategy in many different steps to describe/explain a phenomenon, usually involving an open-ended set of alternatives. Thus, the above-mentioned methodological and conceptual imprisonment caused by the few non-customisable functions of commercial software impedes the development of the research strategy *and* the procedure of arriving at, and interpreting, the results. And if the commercial software is not designed to produce the desired results, then the corpus linguist without programming experience either has to live with a potentially foul compromise or drop the project? This is not acceptable: every corpus-linguistic researcher should have some programming skills.

9. What are the issues involved in comparing corpora?

In some sense, I have already touched upon this issue in some of the above questions and, as I will argue below, I think the question should actually be asked slightly differently. By way of preface, this topic's importance is so large as to only be matched by the degree that it is understudied. The reason for why this topic is so important is twofold. First and as mentioned above, for any phenomenon every corpus and every part of a corpus will yield different results, and whatever results we report, they will come with some degree of variability. Second and as a consequence of that, we need to assess the variability of the results we obtain against differences between corpora, between parts of different corpora or of one corpus (i.e. corpus homogeneity), and between corpora and the linguistic population they are supposed to represent (i.e. we again face the problems of representativity and balancedness), which are all inextricably related. Thus, questions regarding 'the issues involved in comparing corpora' should actually *always* be phrased as regarding 'the issues involved in comparing (parts of) corpora'.

I said the topic is unbelievably under-researched, and this is so for three issues, which the present question is concerned with. The first issue is the complexity arising from the interrelations of these various kinds of differences. If a corpus yields an overall result then this result may only be really worth considering at the level of the corpus if

- the corpus parts did not yield completely different results such that the one on the level of the corpus is only an unrepresentative average of very different results from corpus parts;
- the corpus is representative (and maybe balanced) enough with regard to the language or variety or register it is supposed to represent so that we may assume the corpus result will speak to what happens in the population.

The moral therefore is to bear in mind, in corpus compilation and analysis, that there are many different levels of corpus granularity: varieties, registers, files, texts, and within- and between-corpus comparison should take all of them into consideration.

The second issue is the fact that we still do not know yet which statistics are best suited for the comparison of corpora. There are studies that have begun to address this notion by proposing, reviewing, and/or exploring a variety of statistics that could be used; other studies approach the issue with different simulation/resampling-based approaches, but this problem is far from resolved (cf., e.g. Kilgarriff 2001, 2005, who argues against significance testing, and Gries 2005, who demonstrates that some of Kilgarriff's objections are mistaken). Thus, we need more exploration of statistical methods for corpus comparison, but also – a very general problem of Corpus Linguistics – much more validation of new *and* existing methods.

The final issue is the fact that, with very few exceptions, the little work that is out there only addresses a single level of corpus granularity and corpus comparison: the word. This has to do with a general bias of corpus linguists to study words, or lexical items, and it has to do with ease of retrievability of these elements (especially in the usual suspects of Indo-European languages that most corpus linguists work with, where words can be identified more easily than in polysynthetic and fusional languages). However, since (parts of) corpora can differ on any level of linguistic granularity and, somewhat ironically, it is corpus linguists and cognitive linguists who now assume that words are not different in kind from more schematic patterns/constructions, corpora that seem very similar on the level of the word may be very different on the level of other linguistic expressions. Thus, corpus comparison has to not only take differences arising from the granularity of the corpus/corpora and its/their parts into consideration (cf. issue #1 above), but also differences arising from the (level of) linguistic phenomena whose frequencies are used for comparing corpora and/or their parts. Thus, this answer is again a plea for more systematic bottom-up exploration of where similarities reside and what their implications are.

10. How much statistics does a corpus analyst need to master?

In a sense, there are two answers to this question. Superficially, the first answer is that this of course depends on what exactly a corpus linguist's focus is on. It would seem that a corpus linguist studying a word *w* by means of a highly qualitative analysis of the contexts of *w* in a small sample of newspaper texts (e.g. two texts each from ten consecutive years) does not need statistical expertise. However, as I have argued frequently, this view is fundamentally mistaken. Again, just look at the situation from an unbiased observer's perspective: why is it that corpus linguists look at something (language) that is completely based on distributional and probabilistic data and just as complex as what psychologists, psycholinguists, cognitive scientists, sociologists, etc. look at, but most of our curricula do not contain even a single course on statistical methods (while psychologists etc. regularly have two to three basic and one or two advanced courses on such methods)?[4] To understand more concretely why this is a huge problem, let's assume a linguist finds that w appears to be used increasingly negatively over time. The questions that immediately arise from this assumption are (i) how did the linguist find that and (ii) how can or must this be interpreted.

As to the first question, it is important to realise that corpora do not provide such findings without recourse to frequencies because corpora provide nothing but frequencies of (co-)occurrence and dispersions. Thus, a corpus linguist can only infer that w is used increasingly negatively because the percentage of times w is used with negative collocates out of all uses of w is becoming larger over time. Thus, whatever pattern or function, meaning, or use is inferred from corpora, it is based on distributional data, and the science that tells us how to handle distributional data best is statistics. But while percentages are of course not exactly a most sophisticated statistic requiring expertise and training, there is still the second question, which is concerned with how the increase in relative frequency is interpreted.

As to the second question, two points must be considered. First, is the trend statistically significant, i.e. whether pronounced enough to probably not just result from random variation in data? To answer that question, one needs to decide on whether to use a correlation coefficient (and if so, which one to use), or whether to group the data into, say, two, four, or five groups of ten, five, or four percentages each and do a comparison of means (and if so, which test for means to use) or a comparison of observed frequencies (maybe with a chi-square test). Deciding which correlation coefficient to use (e.g. Pearson's

---

4 When asked about how future generations could learn statistics if it is not part of the curriculum, I have two answers to this question: one is serious, the other is serious, too, but also has a 'duh' attached to it. As to the former, the number of researchers who have realised how important statistical training is increasing and so is the number of places where statistical training is offered. Also, there are now several venues – workshops, bootcamps, etc. – in which researchers and students can begin to take their first steps under supervision, just as they can spend time as a visiting scholar/student in departments where such resources/people are available. As for the latter answer: when there are no such opportunities – which was actually the case for my own linguistic upbringing: at the time, the department from which I obtained my degrees offered no Corpus Linguistics or statistics training at all – then there is still another approach, which is somewhat old-fashioned but has worked well for me: it is called 'self-study' (books and other resources) ... Where, if not in academia, is living to be equated with learning?

r, Kendall's τ, etc.) or which test for means to use (e.g. a t-test, a U-test, a one-way ANOVA, etc.) or whether a chi-square test can be used in turn requires knowledge of notions such as normality, variance homogeneity, maybe the central limit theorem etc., so it is not clear how even something as simple as distinguishing a change of semantic connotations over time from random variation can be done without statistical knowledge. (And I do not even mention issues such as independence of data points etc. here ...)

Second, let's assume the computation of Kendall's τ shows there is a significant upwards trend. This still leaves open the possibly interesting questions what kind of trend (linear or nonlinear?) and whether that trend is specific to w or whether w's collocational behaviour is just one reflection of a more general trend. What if w is the word *Muslim*, but in the wake of 9/11, religiously-motivated conflicts throughout the world, and the recent financial and abuse scandals of the Catholic Church, words from the semantic field of religion, or even of any larger organisation or group, are reported on more negatively? Would one want to make a claim about how newspaper coverage on Muslims has become more negative over time when in fact newspaper coverage on *all* religions has become more negative? I do not think so, and thus one needs one or more additional samples of collocate frequencies on words referring to, say, a Christian religion and some other religion and then do a statistical test to see whether *Muslim* is special and worthy of much individual discussion in this context or whether *Muslim* is just one example of a general trend. Again, this cannot be done without statistical knowledge (about, here, regressions or linear models), and it has always completely escaped me how there are still people who cannot see this ...

References

Firth, J. R. 1951. *Papers in Linguistics, 1934–1951*. Oxford: OUP.

Fries, C. C. 1952. *The Structure of English: An Introduction to the Construction of English Sentences*. New York NY: Harcourt Brace.

Gilquin, G. & Gries, St. Th. 2009. Corpora and experimental methods: A state-of-the-art review. *Corpus Linguistics and Linguistic Theory* 5(1): 1–26.

Gries, St. Th. 1999. Particle movement: A cognitive and functional approach. *Cognitive Linguistics* 10(2): 105–145.

Gries, St. Th. 2003. *Multifactorial Analysis in Corpus Linguistics: A Study of Particle Placement*. London: Continuum Press.

Gries, St. Th. 2005. Null-Hypothesis significance testing of word frequencies: A follow-up on Kilgarriff. *Corpus Linguistics and Linguistic Theory* 1(2): 277–294.

Gries, St. Th. 2006. Exploring variability within and between corpora: Some methodological considerations. *Corpora* 1(2): 109–151.

Gries, St. Th. 2010. Corpus Linguistics and theoretical linguistics: A love-hate relationship? Not necessarily ... *International Journal of Corpus Linguistics* 15(3): 327–342.

Harris, R. A. 1993. *The Linguistics Wars*. Oxford: OUP.

Harris, Z. S. 1970. *Papers in Structural and Transformational Linguistics*. Dordrecht: Reidel.

Käding, F. W. 1897. *Häufigkeitswörterbuch der deutschen Sprache*. Steglitz: no publ.

Kilgarriff, A. 2001. Comparing corpora. *International Journal of Corpus Linguistics* 6(1): 1–37.

Kilgarriff, A. 2005. Language is never, ever, ever, random. *Corpus Linguistics and Linguistic Theory* 1(2): 263–276.

Pullum, G. K. 1978. Assessing linguistic arguments by Jessica R. Wirth. *Language* 54(2): 399–402.

Schlüter, N. 2006. How reliable are the results? Comparing corpus-based studies of the present perfect. *Zeitschrift für Anglistik und Amerikanistik* 54(2): 135–148.

Teubert, W. 2005. My version of Corpus Linguistics. *International Journal of Corpus Linguistics* 10(1): 1–13.

Looking through corpora into writing practices

Professor of Applied Linguistics at the University of Hong Kong, Ken Hyland focuses on what is gained when writing practices are informed by Corpus Linguistics. Based on his studies, Hyland discusses the styles of specific communities of writers. In fact, he addresses issues which lie at the heart of the university setting, such as academic literacy, social construction of knowledge, and interpersonal features. While most of his examples refer to academia, some other spheres of life also find a place in his interview. In a thought-provoking way, he offers a distinction between 'consolidating' and 'innovative' research when writing about the future of Corpus Linguistics, arguing that we have been seeing too much of the former. He holds that ground-breaking investigations are needed to make sure that the field will continue to evolve and draw the attention of newcomers.

1. Where do you place the roots of Corpus Linguistics? And to what do you attribute the growth of interest in the area?

I do not really have a clue about this question. Curious individuals have probably tried to get a purchase on their intuitions by counting features in texts since linguistics began. Certainly the anthropologist Boas (1940) was basing studies on data he gathered on poorly documented languages in the 1930s. Firth (1968) based a lot of his observations on corpus evidence in the 1950s and the American structuralists like Harris (1951) and Fries (1952) believed that linguists were virtually obliged to study authentically occurring texts to gain any understanding of the ways language worked. These researchers used simple processing methods which were restricted by the limits of the tools they had available, producing frequency counts and basic syntactic patterning, but they also showed how language varied and the meanings words took on in different contexts which led to the later explosion of interest in corpora.

My own first encounter with CL was when I came across a frequency analysis of the Brown Corpus (Kučera & Francis 1967), but I only really got excited by all this after reading Biber's (1988) work on language variation across contexts of use. The most decisive book which influenced me, however, was John Sinclair's (1991) *Corpus, Concordance, Collocation*. This is a deceptively unassuming little book with a brilliant insight on almost every page. It opened my eyes to the possibilities of basing language descriptions on quantities of data rather than picking apart individual sentences and led me to many late nights pouring over concordance lines.

We probably have Chomsky to thank, at least in part, for the growth of interest in this area, as the debates with generative linguists both hardened and clarified our thinking on the value of attested data compared with that of native speaker intuitions. In its most polar form, CL counters the idea that real language is so riddled with performance-related errors that the only way to study language is through the careful analysis of small speech samples obtained from either reflection or highly controlled laboratory settings. The arguments that CL supporters had to muster to challenge the 'competence/ performance' doctrine went a long way towards clarifying the role of CL and undermining the Chomskian orthodoxies that native speaker gut feeling was ample evidence for building theories about language. This spurred on the development of CL so that gradually the value of attested data to support descriptions of use became clearer as a result. Appeals to cognitively plausible models which relied on abstract conceptualisations were no longer acceptable as a basis for language analysis, comparative linguistics or even, eventually, pedagogy.

These debates were accompanied by the first large scale corpus developments which contributed to greater interest in the area. The Survey of English Usage, for example, was a massively ambitious project for its time. Founded in 1959 by Randolph Quirk at University College London, it involved the manual annotation of data cards with detailed grammatical and prosodic information on transcriptions of talk. Corpus searches meant a trip to London (Quirk 1960). Later, John Sinclair's COBUILD corpus-based dictionary project at Birmingham in the early 1980s and Sidney Greenbaum's International Corpus of English (ICE), representing varieties of English from around the world, captured the imagination and pushed interest in CL forward.

More generally, and perhaps more decisively, the growth of CL could not have happened without the large scale availability of computers and network technology, at first in universities then expanding to the homes of many academics and teachers around the developed world. CL could not have taken off as it has if not for the hands-on participation of thousands of applied linguists around the world doing their own searches and getting involved in interpreting KWIC concordance lines. The availability of increasingly user-friendly software interfaces such as MonoConc Pro (Barlow 2000) and WordSmith Tools (Scott 2008) together with the availability of online corpora such as the early Brown Corpus and the LOB Corpus have had a huge impact on do-it-yourself CL. More recently still, free Internet corpora and analysis software such as Mark Davies' impressive 400-million-word *Corpus of Contemporary American English* and the *Michigan Corpus of Academic Spoken English* mean that almost anyone can look up whether or how a word is used in a particular context.

2. Is Corpus Linguistics a science or a methodology?

This is a deceptively tricky question. I suppose it is essentially a methodology, a research tool which offers us perspectives on data that would be too labourious, if not actually impossible, to access by simply observational techniques. Some corpus linguists are in danger of losing perspective on this issue, though, probably because of the need to defend the approach against generativists and others, and have overstated the case for their trade.

However, on second thoughts, there is more to it. Science is a set of practices capable of resulting in reliably-predictable type of outcomes: a systematic way of gathering knowledge about the world and organising and condensing that knowledge into testable laws and theories. All the rest of it – replication, objectivity, falsifiability and such like – are the trappings of scientific methods. Therefore, science implies a perspective on reality rather than simply a way of studying it, while methods are never neutral but imply a set of assumptions or evaluations about what counts as knowledge and how the world can be known. It is not too fanciful to push CL further along the methods-science cline towards science as it makes some fairly explicit assertions about the study of language: that knowledge must be based on observable instances of use, that frequency and collocation matter, and that statements should be capable of being tested by other researchers. It suggests that how often something occurs and what it frequently occurs in the company of is important, both in terms of what has happened in the past and how people will continue to use language (at least for a while) into the future.

Not only is CL a means of opening the black box of how language is patterned to create meanings, but it is also a perspective on interpretation and what we should value about data. In fact, given that science rests on making inferences about reality from observable data with no other surer foundation, there does not actually seem to be much of a distinction that can be made between science and method.

3. How representative can a corpus be?

Representativeness refers to how far the findings can be generalised to a particular context of language use as a whole, whether the language studied represents a genre, a particular community of users, a given setting, and so on. Obviously, it is not possible to collect an entire language to test the representativeness of a corpus, so some analysts solve this problem by techniques which filter results or divide the corpus into chunks (see McEnery et al. 2006:15-16). More usually, analysts make decisions about representativeness depending on the type of corpus they are compiling, whether it is specialised, a parallel corpus, a learner corpus, a comparable corpus, and so on (e.g. Hunston 2002). A corpus is obviously always representative of itself. On this basis, I could make a reasonable claim that the frequencies and patterns of hedging I found in my study of 16 research articles in the biological sciences (Hyland 1998) characterised that feature in that collection of texts. This does not really go a long way towards answering the 'so what' question, however. It might make sense as a case study, but we generally want to say a little more about our findings, extrapolating to a wider sample of language use.

The concept of representativeness is clearly context-bound in that it depends on the date a corpus was compiled and the purpose it was intended to serve. The apparently massive corpora of a few years ago – a million words in the Brown Corpus in 1964, for example – is now seen as tiny against something like the 100 million words of the BNC or the 400-million-word Bank of English. Certainly, a larger corpus can tell you more about something, but it is also relative to the type of questions that are going to be asked of it. It is possible to get useful, and fairly representative, data from a small corpus, particularly when investigating high frequency items. So, if the researcher is interested in a commonly occurring feature like regular past tense verbs, then these are pretty plentiful in most corpora and the corpus can be smaller than if you are looking to compare 'while' and 'whilst', for instance. In fact, it might be better to do this than to be overwhelmed by too much data from a big corpus. There is not much point in having a massive corpus without the time, energy, and technical resources to examine it. Some corpus analysis programmes (especially some of those online), for example, set limits on the number of concordance output lines and stop searching when they get to these limits. Clearly, a tremendous amount can be done with small corpora, particularly in the field of language teaching (e.g. Ghadessy et al. 2001).

In general, it is important to be pragmatic in creating a corpus and to be as specific as possible in terms of the data for collection. This means, for example, if we are compiling a corpus of academic writing, we will need to recognise that differences of discipline, sub-field, genre, year of publication may influence the kind of language used, as will the fact that the text reports research findings, is a theoretical paper, or offers a state-of-the-art review. Similarly, in some cases, it is also necessary to consider characteristics of the writers themselves, so that the degree of expertise of the writers and the prior experiences with the genre can influence the text produced, while the first language, proficiency in the target language, the year of study and age of the writers have to be considered when building a learner corpus. Compiling a corpus with these factors in mind can help increase its representativeness.

4. How far should an analyst rely on intuition?

Can analysts ever not rely on intuition? We have intuitions about what to look for and then in interpreting what things mean. Obviously it is the over-reliance on intuition that has attracted criticism in the past – cases where sometimes whole theories of language were based on armchair theorising and invented examples. But while intuition is generally a poor guide to judgements about frequency, collocation, semantic meanings, phraseology, etc., interpretation is important when generalising from corpus data and understanding the numbers and patterns we find in it. Almost every corpus study teaches us something about language use that we could not find out about in any other way and often which we could not imagine without looking at lots of contextualised examples.

So, inside every corpus linguist there is an armchair theorist trying to get out, or rather, the corpus analyst is also a theorist in that the raw data of a corpus requires organising and explaining. Expertise in at least the basic functions of corpus analysis is fast becoming a requirement of the practicing applied linguist – whether he or she is conducting research or teaching students, and the ability to interpret concordances and collocations is a key aspect of this expertise.

5. What kind of questions should an analyst think of?

This really depends on the purpose of the study and the kind of analyst you are. I cannot imagine that many people just sit down and stare at frequency lists or concordance screens in the hope that they will find something interesting. While we may come across something new and surprising, we are generally looking for something more or less specific. Analysts work in different ways depending on their interests and abilities. To be honest, I see myself as less a corpus analyst than someone who uses corpora to inform my curiosity about writing. This means that *real* corpus linguists or computational people do different things and ask different questions to those that I usually do.

Essentially, I am interested in what people do when they write and why they do it, and these questions can be approached in an enormous variety of ways. For some, writing is a kind of cognitive performance which can be modelled by analogy with computer processing through observation and writers' on-task verbal reports. Others are interested in the impact of immediate local contexts of writing and observe the actions of individual writers. A third group looks to the cultural and institutional context in which communication occurs to explore the ideologies and power relations which writing expresses and maintains. All methods, in other words, are inseparable from theories: we look for answers in the places that will best inform our views of what writing is. As a socially-oriented applied linguist, I prefer to start with texts and look for community preferences in the rhetorical practices of groups of writers.

I study corpora because corpus data represent a speaker's experience of language in a restricted domain, offering evidence of typical choices in that domain. This moves us away from individual texts, or the preferences of individual writers or speakers, to focus on community practices, revealing interaction as a collection of rhetorical choices rather than as specific acts of writing. It is a method which highlights representativeness rather than the uniqueness of texts, approaching them as a package of specific linguistic features employed by specific groups of users. In other words, because every act of writing is embedded in wider social and discursive practices, texts carry assumptions about participant relationships and how these should be structured and negotiated. The ways that information is structured, arguments made, relationships established with readers, opinions expressed, and so on are shaped by the writer's experience and perception of audience and membership of a given community.

The kinds of questions I ask when analyse a corpus are sketched below, together with a brief illustration from a paper of mine a few years ago on the role of the first person in student and professional academic genres (Hyland 2002).

a. What is this feature doing?

   In the self-mention study, the main functions used by Hong Kong students in their final-year projects theses were to state a discoursal goal and explain a methodological approach. More argumentative functions, such as presenting and justifying claims, were more commonly expressed without direct reference to the author.

b. How many instances are there and how can we account for them?

   The frequency counts indicated relatively low uses and the reasons for this were explored through interviews with writers and through study of the advice given to students in textbooks and by supervisors.

c. Why is a form seen consistently with another form (or not seen)?

   Concordances indicated regularities in the texts. In a third of all cases, for example, students used authorial pronouns to signal their intentions in the text and to provide an overt structure for their texts. Forms such as 'I am going to' and 'I will' were frequent.

d. How is it used in another context and does this tell us anything about its use in this one?

   Comparison of the student reports with published research articles shows that the professional writers were *four times* more likely to explicitly intervene with the first person, with figures higher for the soft disciplines than the hard ones.

e. Is this meaning expressed in any other way and what is the difference in those meanings?

   Passive and dummy subjects were widely used by students to avoid authorial self-mention.

f. What do text users say about all this?

   Interviews with student writers showed that they deliberately avoided the most authoritative functions of the first person and sought to deny ownership and responsibility for their views. They did this to minimise the communicative risks and because they saw this form as closely linked to a subjectivity which they considered inappropriate for academic discourse.

Asking these questions of a corpus of L2 undergraduate writing showed that these students tended to see self-reference as a marker of self-assurance and individuality, which they did not feel when composing, preferring to take refuge in the anonymity of passive forms.

6. What are the strengths and weaknesses of corpus analysis?

These arguments have been rehearsed elsewhere on many occasions, so I will be brief. Essentially, corpus analysis is a method that gives access to information about language use that cannot be obtained in any other way, and certainly not by native-speaker intuition. Corpus studies can tell us how frequent something is, which can be an indication of importance or salience to users, and how words combine in particular ways or the meanings they carry for them. This obviously does not tell us whether something is possible or not – our corpora can never be large enough for that – but this limitation is probably a good thing since it helps us to avoid prescriptivism.

Corpus analysis does offer insights into interaction, argument, cultural and community preferences, identity construction, political manipulation, translation, language teaching, and a whole range of areas related to the ways we go about our daily lives. One important field of research opened up by this method is comparison – between languages, genres, communities, and so on – revealing the specificity of language use and opening up the possibility of studying aspects of social life such as expertise and communicative competence. Among the many other advantages, it is a method that can tell us about cultural attitudes and the ways media, advertising, politicians and institutions seek to influence opinion and behaviour.

In some circumstances, and with a certain amount of computational power and methodological expertise, it might even be possible to fully describe a particular text or specific genre. Biber (1996: 173), for example, argues that:

> Using computational techniques, it is feasible to entertain the possibility of a comprehensive linguistic characterisation of a text, analysing a wide range of linguistic features (rather than being restricted to a few selected features); further, computational techniques can be used to analyse the complex ways in which linguistic features interact within texts.

Related to this point is the fact that CL enables a scope and reliability of analysis not otherwise possible as it allows subsequent studies to test the results of previous research on a corpus and for findings to be compared across studies, so building a cumulative linguistic description of the language. In other words, corpus analysis is closely related to the more general issue concerning the importance of empirical data. It enables the linguist to make statements which are objective and based on language as it really is rather than statements which are subjective and based upon the individual's own internalised cognitive perception of the language.

Additionally, CL has paved the way for new understandings and theories of language, such as Sinclair's (1991) observations about the primacy of lexis in language organisation, Hoey's (2005) lexical priming, the study of bundles and collocations (Hyland 2008), and the systematic relations between patterns and meaning (see Hunston 2002). Corpus-based techniques also enable investigations of research questions that were previously disregarded because they were considered intractable. In particular, the corpus-based approach makes it possible to identify and analyse complex 'association patterns': the systematic ways in which linguistic features are used in association with other linguistic and non-linguistic features.

I suppose a weakness might be the representative issue: generalising from a corpus will always be an extrapolation – it gives evidence of something but not real information about it. That is the work of the analyst as it involves deduction rather than statements of actual fact of how language works in the real world.

Corpus studies also treat language as an artifact. It is language outside of its real context and so is essentially one dimensional. This data therefore requires a focus on 'action' to balance the focus on 'language', which means 'rematerialising' the features that have been studied to understand how and why language users make the choices they do when they speak/write. It is then needed to go to text users and try to interrogate them on their use and understanding of features. Interviews help ground patterns of text meanings in the conscious choices of writers and readers.

7. What is the future of Corpus Linguistics?

This is another difficult question. Probably ten years ago we could say that it was the most interesting and fastest growing area of linguistics and the future looked rosy. The emergence of new tools, and of large, publically available, online corpora all contributed to an explosion of interest and activity across a range of areas of applied linguistics. Now, I am not so sure. In fact, I think it might be worth taking a collective pause to reflect on Fillmore's (1992: 35) comment that while corpus data may give you information about language that is true, it might well be information that is not very interesting. The problem seems to be that a great deal of CL research is disappointing and simply repeats what we already know. While I do not want to make too wide a claim for this, certainly in my field of English for Academic Purposes, we are seeing a plethora of replications, 'preliminary', and small-scale studies on the same features and genres and while these may well be useful, they do not really push the field forward very far or very fast.

While exciting 'innovative' work continues to be done, there is a danger that there is too much 'consolidating' research being published, particularly using very small corpora. While many researchers defend small corpora – and they certainly have their uses in pedagogic contexts – in many situations, they are simply more limited versions of larger corpora. Bigger corpora are particularly important in studies of features such as multi-word combinations or infrequent items, which require large amounts of text to generate examples. So, while CL will no doubt continue to grow and attract new users and converts, only by continuing to ask interesting questions, being innovative in our studies and striving to make the most of large corpora, can we make the most of the tools we have at our disposal and learn more about language use.

8. What have corpus studies revealed about academic literacy at the university?

Studies of academic corpora have enormously increased our understanding of academic discourse, disciplines, student and expert communication practices, and the ways persuasion is accomplished and knowledge constructed in different fields. Essentially, corpora bring evidence of typical patterning to discourse studies, providing language data which represent a speaker's experience of language in a restricted domain. In other words, it is a method which moves away from individual preferences to focus on community practices, dematerialising texts and approaching them as a package of specific linguistic features employed by a group of users. As a result, it is particularly valuable in research into academic discourse as Biber (2006), Swales (2004), Hyland (2004, 2009) and others have shown.

First, I think perhaps the main insight is that how authors are everywhere built into texts, how they insinuate themselves into their writing to present a stance towards what they say and how they relate to readers. This contrasts with earlier and more traditional 'author-evacuated' conceptions of academic writing which emphasised the predominance of passive voice and nominalisation and underplayed the presence of writers. Instead, we see that academic writing carries the author's stance and that this projects both an individual and disciplinary identity, what I have called proximity and positioning (Hyland 2011). *Proximity* refers to the relationship between the self and community, and *positioning* to the relationship between the speaker and what is being said. Stance can thus be seen as how academics relate to their communities and the topics of their texts. Corpus studies help show how proximity and positioning are expressed and how language works to both shape decision-making and constrain the options that writers have in crafting a professional self, while at the same time *how authors work* with these resources to them to carve out a distinctive space for a personal self.

A second, related aspect of this is that corpus studies reveal every act of academic writing to be an act of identity because identity has come to be seen as what the writer *does* in a text. It is implicated in the texts we engage in and the linguistic choices we make in creating them on a moment-by-moment basis. What and how we write articulate a performance which says something about how we want to be seen by others. In writing, we not only convey topic 'content' – what we are writing about – but also both give and 'give off' information about ourselves as we relate to a community of readers. Corpus analyses can help illuminate this process and underline the idea that language offers us a system of choices for representing ourselves, our allegiances, and our ideas in various ways so that the constraints of genre and disciplinary conventions are also the raw materials which facilitate conformity and idiosyncrasy. This is because corpus studies offer evidence of typical choices in a particular domain. By mapping typicality, they show what is usual and what is deviant in collections of texts and so help to reveal both underlying discourses (or ideologies and values) and individual preferences. An example of how this works is in a recent paper of mine (Hyland 2010) which compares the writing of two celebrated applied linguists, John Swales and Deborah Cameron, with a corpus of academic writing in applied linguistics more generally. The study reveals how these two individuals, repeatedly and routinely, position themselves in relation to their readers so that in constructing knowledge and social relationships they also construct themselves.

Third, corpus studies help us to see disciplines as language using groups as texts function to join writers, readers and communities together. The analysis of corpora moves us away from individual texts, or the preferences of individual writers or speakers, to focus on community practices. It is a method which highlights representativeness rather than the uniqueness of texts, approaching them as a collection of specific linguistic features employed by particular groups of users. It illuminates what Bourdieu (1990) referred to as 'habitus' and Foucault (1981) as our 'archive': the partially visible discursive systems which we take for granted and operate within. This is because it enables us to see that successful academic writing does not occur in an institutional vacuum. Instead, it largely depends on the individual writer's projection of a shared professional context as writers seek to embed their writing in a particular social world which they reflect and conjure up through approved discourses. For this reason, corpora have proved particularly valuable in how we understand communities of language users and in demonstrating language variation across disciplines, genres, and languages.

Fourth, studies show us also that discoursal conventions are persuasive because they are significant carriers of the epistemological and social beliefs of community members. They have made it possible to link regularities in rhetorical and language conventions to the knowledge constructing practices that broadly reflect the types of intellectual enquiry and cognitive understandings of the hard and soft knowledge domains. Simply, different social and language communities organise texts and construct arguments in different ways which are related to their beliefs about knowledge and how it can be authorised by others.

9. In what way(s) may Corpus Linguistics account for the social construction of knowledge?

We have tended to treat science's opinion of itself with some respect and see academic discourse as a unique form of argument which depends on the demonstration of absolute truth, empirical evidence or flawless logic. Its persuasive potency has been regarded as grounded in rationality and based on exacting methodologies, dispassionate observation and informed reflection. Academic writing, in other words, represents what Lemke (1995: 178) called the discourse of 'Truth'. It provides an objective description of what the natural and human world is actually like and this, in turn, gives it a cultural authority which distinguishes it from the partisan rhetoric of politics and commerce.

Those working in the sociology of science, however, have always argued that there is an intimate connection between knowledge and the social practices of academic communities. Corpus studies help show how this connection is made – how writing constructs knowledge through acts of persuasion which appeal to community expectations. Basically, academic texts do more than report research that plausibly represents an external world. They work to transform findings or reflections into academic knowledge using accepted patterns of argument and representation. A corpus of 240 research articles of 1.5 million words, for example, shows that some 75% of all features marking author visibility, such as self-mention, personal evaluation, hedges, and explicit interaction with readers, occur in the humanities and social sciences (Hyland 2005a). This should not, perhaps, surprise us. After all, empiricism finds its truths by observing the world and so needs a language that represents real events without the mediation of rhetoric.

In the sciences, new knowledge is accepted by experimental proof. Science writing reinforces this by highlighting a gap in knowledge, presenting a hypothesis related to this gap, and then reporting experimental findings to support this. Positivist epistemologies therefore mean that the authority of the individual is subordinated to the authority of the text and facts are meant to 'speak for themselves'. Writers seek to disguise their interpretative activities behind linguistic objectivity as they downplay their personal role to suggest that results would be the same whoever conducted the research. The less frequent use of hedges, boosters, self-mention and explicit markers of attitude is one way of minimising the researcher's role, as is the preference for modal verbs over cognitive verbs in science writing as modals can more easily combine with inanimate subjects to downplay the person making the evaluation and 'objectify' the research.

In the humanities and social sciences, on the other hand, claims are accepted on the strength of argument. Clearly argument relies more on recognising alternative voices. The fact that there is less control of variables than in the sciences, more diversity of research outcomes, and fewer clear bases for accepting claims means that writers cannot report research with the same confidence of shared assumptions. Arguments have to be expressed more cautiously by using more hedges such as 'possibly', 'might' and 'perhaps' (Hyland 2005a). Similarly, the fact that corpus analysis shows that citation is significantly heavier in the hard sciences suggests different knowledge constructing practices and reflects the extent to which writers can assume a shared context with readers. This is because natural scientists produce knowledge through cumulative growth where problems tend to emerge on the back of earlier problems as results throw up further questions to be followed up with further research. Readers therefore tend to be familiar with the earlier work on a topic as they are often working on the same problems and are reading the research for insights into their own experimental work. As a result, writers do not need to report research with extensive referencing. In the humanities and social sciences, on the other hand, the literature is more dispersed and the readership more heterogeneous, so writers cannot presuppose a shared context but have to build one far more through citation (Hyland 1999).

The conventions of impersonality in science writing thus play an important role in reinforcing an objective ideology by portraying the legitimacy of hard science knowledge as built on socially invariant criteria. Corpus analyses can help us unpack this ideology to reveal the social basis of persuasion and how it is located in rhetorical practices.

10. How may the corpus approach enhance our understanding of interpersonal features in writing?

To see writing as interpersonal and interactive means examining discourse in terms of the writer's projection of the perceptions, interests, and needs of a potential audience. Here corpora help us see that every text carries traces of how writers view their readers and how they understand the evaluations, values and expectations of a particular reader as a member of a language-using community. Corpus studies have enabled us to identify patterns in the choices of interactive features, such as evaluative terms, attitude markers and personal pronouns. Research into stance and engagement features (Hyland 2005a), appraisal (Martin & White 2005) and metadiscourse (Hyland 2005b) has been particularly productive.

It is often difficult to see how writing can be interactive, so let me start with an example. This is from a hiking guide and while this is a highly informative text, we can see here that the writer is not simply giving changes of direction for a route, but taking the trouble to see the walk from the reader's perspective:

There is a *fine prospect* of Penshurst Place as *you* cross the field and the walk takes *you* directly to the stone wall surrounding it. *Go along* this wall and in 200 metres *cross* the style into the churchyard of St John the Baptist church. *Walk through* the churchyard – *the church is well worth visiting if you have time* – and *continue out* to the road where *you turn left, your* direction 110 degrees.

(Time Out Book of Country Walks)

The use of imperatives, second person pronouns, and evaluative commentary puts the writer into the text – not just to convey information more clearly, but to present an identity and to engage the reader as a fellow enthusiast. These are interpersonal features, and if they are removed, then the text becomes less personal, less interesting, and less easy to follow.

We cannot, of course, simply read off interpersonal features without reference to their co-text. If we are researching hedging, for example, we find that the word 'possible' can refer to general enabling conditions ('it is possible to') rather than act as a hedge ('it is possible that'). Analyses of corpora, however, have begun to reveal the frequencies and collocations of terms which potentially carry interpersonal meanings and to show the extent to which even formal texts are 'recipient designed' to take account of readers' likely background knowledge, processing needs, potential response and rhetorical expectations. Searching for features which commonly express interpersonal meanings therefore offers a way of exploring interactions in a systematic way, revealing something of how such features are used by different individuals and communities and allowing us to make comparisons across languages, disciplines and genres.

One model of interpersonality I mentioned earlier draws on the systems of stance and engagement (Hyland 2005a). Stance refers to the writer's textual 'voice' or community recognised personality, an attitudinal, writer-oriented function which concerns the ways writers present themselves and convey their judgements, opinions, and commitments. Engagement, on the other hand, is more of an alignment function, concerning the ways that writers rhetorically recognise the presence of their readers to actively pull them along with the argument, include them as discourse participants, and guide them to interpretations (Hyland 2001). Together they recognise that statements need to both present the writer and his/her ideas as well as anticipate readers' possible objections and alternative positions, incorporating an appropriate awareness of self and audience.

Stance and engagement are two sides of the same coin because they both contribute to the interpersonal dimension of discourse. A major analytical problem is that the marking of stance and engagement is a highly contextual matter for while writers can mark their perspectives explicitly through lexical items (such as 'unfortunately', 'possible', 'interesting', etc.), they can also code them less obviously through conjunction, subordination, repetition, contrast, etc. Writers can also make evaluations through a shared attitude towards something which may be opaque to the analyst. Nor is it always marked by words at all: a writer's decision not to draw an obvious conclusion from an argument, for example, or to leave an utterance unfinished may be seen as a significant absence. It should also be recognised that many lexico-grammatical features can be used to indicate the personal stance of a writer in English, including value-laden word choice ('heavy' vs. 'well-built' for example) and paralinguistic typographical devices (such as underlining, capitalisation, scare quotes and exclamation marks in writing).

Essentially interpersonal features are key aspects of message construction as they assist readers to connect, organise and interpret material in a way preferred by the writer and with regard to the understandings and values of a particular community. By looking at the frequencies of features such as first person pronouns, directives, hedges and boosters, we can see how a writer is able to not only transform a dry, difficult text into coherent, reader-friendly prose, but also relate it to a given context and convey his or her personality, credibility, audience sensitivity and relationship to the message.

References

Barlow, M. 2000. *MonoConc Pro* Version 2.0. Houston TX: Athelstan.

Biber, D. 1988. *Variation Across Speech and Writing.* Cambridge: CUP.

Biber, D. 1996. Investigating language use through corpus-based analyses of association patterns. *International Journal of Corpus Linguistics* 1(2): 171–197.

Biber, D. 2006. *University Language: A Corpus-Based Study of Spoken and Written Registers* [Studies in Corpus Linguistics 23]. Amsterdam: John Benjamins.

Boas, F. 1940. *Race, Language and Culture.* New York NY: Macmillan.

Bourdieu, P. 1990. Structures, habitus, practices. In *The Logic of Practice*, P. Bourdieu (ed.), 52–79. Stanford CA: Stanford University Press.

Fillmore, C. 1992. 'Corpus Linguistics' or 'Computer-Aided armchair linguistics'. In *Directions in Corpus Linguistics*, J. Svartvik (ed.), 35–60. Berlin: Mouton de Gruyter.

Firth, J. R. 1968. *Selected Papers of J. R. Firth*, F. R. Palmer (ed.). London: Longman.

Foucault, M. 1981. The order of discourse. In *Untying the Text: A Post-Structuralist Reader*, R. Young (ed.), 48–78. London: Routledge.

Fries, C. 1952. *The Structure of English: An Introduction to the Construction of Sentences*. New York NY: Harcourt-Brace.

Ghadessy, N., Henry, A. & Roseberry, A. (eds). 2001. *Small Corpus Studies in ELT: Theory and Practice* [Studies in Corpus Linguistics 5]. Amsterdam: John Benjamins.

Harris, Z. 1951. *Methods in Structural Linguistics*. Chicago IL: University of Chicago Press.

Hoey, M. 2005. *Lexical Priming*. London: Routledge.

Hunston, S. 2002. *Corpora in Applied Linguistics*. Cambridge: CUP.

Hyland, K. 1998. *Hedging in Science Research Articles* [Pragmatics & Beyond New Series 54]. Amsterdam: John Benjamins.

Hyland, K. 1999. Academic attribution: Citation and the construction of disciplinary knowledge. *Applied Linguistics* 20(3): 341–367.

Hyland, K. 2001. Bringing in the reader: Addressee features in academic writing. *Written Communication* 18(4): 549–574.

Hyland, K. 2002. Authority and invisibility: Authorial identity in academic writing. *Journal of Pragmatics* 34(8): 1091–1112.

Hyland, K. 2004. *Disciplinary Discourses: Social Interactions in Academic Writing*. Ann Arbor MI: University of Michigan Press.

Hyland, K. 2005a. Stance and engagement: A model of interaction in academic discourse. *Discourse Studies* 7(2): 173–191.

Hyland, K. 2005b. *Metadiscourse*. London: Continuum.

Hyland, K. 2008. As can be seen: Lexical bundles and disciplinary variation. *English for Specific Purposes* 27(1): 4–21.

Hyland, K. 2009. *Academic Discourse*. London: Continuum.

Hyland, K. 2010. Community and individuality: Performing identity in Applied Linguistics. *Written Communication* 27(2): 159–188.

Hyland, K. 2011. *Disciplinary Identities*. Cambridge: CUP.

Kučera, H. & Francis, W. 1967. *Computational Analysis of Present-Day American English*. Providence RI: Brown University Press.

Lemke, J. 1995. *Textual Politics: Discourse and Social Dynamics*. London: Taylor and Francis.

Martin, J. & White, P. 2005. *The Language of Evaluation: Appraisal in English*. London: Palgrave MacMillan.

McEnery, T., Xiao, R. & Tono, Y. 2006. *Corpus-Based Language Studies*. Abingdon: Routledge.

Quirk, R. 1960. Towards a description of English usage. *Transactions of the Philological Society* 59: 40–61.

Scott, M. 2008. *Wordsmith Tools* Version 5. Oxford: OUP.

Sinclair, J. 1991. *Corpus, Concordance, Collocation*. Oxford: OUP.

Swales, J. 2004. *Research Genres*. Cambridge: CUP.

A multilingual outlook of corpora studies

Professor Emeritus at the University of Oslo (Norway), Stig Johansson unfortunately passed away before this book was completed, and his interview is here published posthumously. In his contribution, the wealth of languages available in the world assumes special relevance, with mentions to languages such as Dutch, German, Norwegian and Swedish, besides English. Johansson points out that these languages (as well as any other) may be studied on their own, but this is not the only possibility available to researchers. As he explains, a lot can be gained from cross-linguistic studies (i.e. contrasting any pair of languages) – whether by means of comparable or parallel corpora.

1. Where do you place the roots of Corpus Linguistics? And to what do you attribute the growth of interest in the area?

The term Corpus Linguistics first appeared in the early 1980s, but its roots go way back, unless we restrict the term to the use of texts in electronic form. For traditional language scholars, it was taken for granted that language description had to be based on a study of language data in the form of words, sentences or texts. One of the pioneers in computer Corpus Linguistics, W. Nelson Francis, discusses some well-known examples in his paper 'Language Corpora B.C.' (Francis 1992): the material used for lexicographic projects, such as Dr. Johnson's dictionary and the *Oxford English Dictionary*; corpora assembled for the purposes of dialect study; and corpora compiled for the writing of grammars, such as those by Otto Jespersen and by Randolph Quirk and his co-workers.

But there were problems with most pre-electronic corpora. As pointed out by Randolph Quirk (1960), the material used by Jespersen and other traditional grammarians was selective and did not adequately represent the full range of language use. It tended to focus on what was conspicuous at the expense of typical language use. Nor did the use of sentences in isolation allow the study of language in contextual depth. For his Survey of English Usage, Quirk stressed the importance of *total accountability* (Quirk & Svartvik 1978: 204). Texts should be selected systematically to represent the range of language use, and they should be studied fully in all relevant aspects. The extended context should be made available. The disadvantage of the Survey material (which was only later computerised) was, however, that anyone who wanted to consult it had to visit University College London. Although many scholars did so, it restricted the use of this important material.

A great advantage of electronic corpora is that the storage and analysis capacity of computers is enormous. The availability of electronic corpora and the appropriate analysis tools have made it possible to examine language on a larger scale and see new patterns which would have been beyond the capacity of the human eye. It is no longer necessary to study examples in isolation. Extended texts can be stored, and with the electronic search and analysis tools which are now available we can zoom in on and study individual examples in their context. Another great advantage is that electronic corpora are transportable and are not restricted to the original physical location, as long as access is provided by the compilers. Corpora such as Brown, LOB, and London-Lund have been put at the disposal of the international community of language researchers, and this has greatly influenced the progress of language studies. It is no longer necessary for individual researchers to start from scratch and compile their own corpora; but if they want to do so, developments in technology have made life much easier for them.

To sum up, the roots of Corpus Linguistics go far back, but the modern electronic corpora are superior in a number of respects. This has led to a growth of interest in corpus research. Underlying the development, and making it possible are the amazing technological advances we have witnessed in the last few decades. Also important is the growing concern among linguists with the study of language in use, a development which has in its turn probably been strengthened through the growth of Corpus Linguistics.

2. Is Corpus Linguistics a science or a methodology? Where would you situate Corpus Linguistics in the scientific or methodological panorama?

The wide range of corpora and the many uses to which they have been put make it hard to generalise and give a straightforward answer to these questions. Corpora are used in synchronic grammar and lexical studies, in studies of social and regional variation, in stylistics, in the study of child language, in translation studies and comparative language studies, in diachronic research, etc. In applied fields such as natural language processing and lexicography, they also play an important role. In lexicography, they have, in fact, become virtually indispensable, as they provide new evidence on an unprecedented scale.

We can distinguish between three main uses according to the role played by the corpus. There are *corpus-informed* studies, where the use of the corpus is incidental and provides exemplification or supporting evidence. Here it is doubtful whether the term Corpus Linguistics is applicable. Then, there are *corpus-based* studies, where the use of the corpus is a necessary element. Without the corpus these studies simply cannot be carried out. An example of a corpus-based study is Douglas Biber's well-known work on variation in English speech and writing (Biber 1988). The use of a corpus does not mean, however, that other means of accessing data are ruled out. Elicitation is often necessary to extend the database, and intuition is inescapable in any language study, though it is questionable as the only source of data.

The most radical use of corpora is found in *corpus-driven* studies, advocated in particular by John Sinclair and his associates (see e.g. Tognini-Bonelli 2001: 84–100). With the corpus-driven approach, the researcher examines the corpus without any prior assumptions and expectations. The idea is not to illustrate or support a pre-existing linguistic theory, but to see what patterns emerge on the basis of corpus observations. The corpus-driven approach led John Sinclair to a redefinition of the place of lexis in linguistic description and to the emphasis of extended lexical units (cf. his well-known idiom principle), with far-reaching implications for linguistic theory. It is doubtful, however, whether a study can be entirely corpus-driven. Some basic assumptions are inevitable, for example that there will be words and that these will form patterns which can be identified by corpus analysis (through concordances and other tools). In interpreting the patterns, it is also inevitable to draw on the researcher's intuitive knowledge of the language. But the hallmark of corpus-driven studies is respect for the data and the attempt to deal as fully as possible with the evidence the corpus provides.

Is Corpus Linguistics then a science or a methodology? Is it theoretical or applied? I think it would be a pity to restrict the term to a particular use or application. For most people who use corpora, the emphasis is probably on methodology, whether the study is theoretical/descriptive or serves a practical/

applied purpose. Corpora and the appropriate analysis tools provide an instrument through which we can reveal new things about language structure and use. Some of the discoveries, as in John Sinclair's work, may have such far-reaching consequences for the understanding of language that they may be used to lay the foundation for a new theory of language. We have seen a lot already, but much more can be expected if corpora are used with care and imagination. There is probably a bright future for Corpus Linguistics, however it is defined, and – more importantly – for the study of language in general.

3. How representative can a corpus be?

One of the corpus pioneers, W. Nelson Francis, defined a corpus as 'a collection of texts assumed to be representative of a given language, dialect, or other subset of the language, to be used for linguistic analysis' (Francis 1979: 110). Representativeness was crucial for the compilers of the Brown and LOB corpora. The texts to be included were restricted to printed prose published in one particular year (1961), a number of relevant text categories were defined, their size was determined, and measures were taken to ensure adequate sampling of individual texts. But these corpora are not truly representative of American and British English more generally. First of all, there is the time restriction. More importantly, many types of texts are not covered, notably all forms of speech but also many types of writing: drama, poetry, advertising, non-printed material such as letters and diaries, etc. As for the sampling of individual texts, note this comment in the manual for the LOB Corpus (Johansson et al. 1978: 14):

> The true representativeness of the present corpus arises from the deliberate attempt to include relevant categories and subcategories of texts rather than from blind statistical choice. Random sampling simply ensures that, within the stated guidelines, the selection of individual texts is free of the conscious or unconscious influence of personal taste or preference.

It is particularly problematic to compile representative general-language corpora, where it is virtually impossible to define the population from which a sample is drawn. The more limited the aim, the greater the chance of compiling a well-defined corpus and achieving a reasonable degree of representativeness.

Statistical representativeness alone is not sufficient. There will always be an element of judgement in deciding the types of texts to be included and their relative size. For Randolph Quirk, it was important to include a broad range of texts in the corpus of the Survey of English Usage, including varieties of speech as well as writing, to make sure that the main types of language variation would be included in the writing of a new English grammar. In contrast, quantity rather than range was a major consideration for John Sinclair in compiling the COBUILD corpus to be used for a new dictionary, as lexical patterns require a large quantity of material.

Representativeness remains a thorny issue, and different views have been voiced by corpus researchers. A particularly interesting example is the debate during the 'Using Corpora' conference in Oxford in 1991 on the motion 'A corpus should consist of a balanced and representative selection of texts' (see the brief report in *ICAME Journal* 16 <1992>: 113–115). After a lively debate, with Randolph Quirk and Geoffrey Leech speaking for the motion and John Sinclair and Willem Meijs against, the motion was defeated. The result is understandable, in view of the development from fairly small, carefully constructed corpora (such as the corpus of the Survey of English Usage) to the vast data collections which were becoming available at the time (such as the Bank of English). We need both types of corpus initiatives, and proponents of both approaches must admit that a corpus, however large or well-balanced, may not by itself provide sufficient evidence relevant to a particular research question.

To conclude, we cannot give a simple definition of representativeness that is valid for all kinds of projects, but this does not mean that anything goes. The corpus compiler must carefully consider the composition of the corpus, taking into account the purpose of the study. The principles of corpus compilation should be commented on in publications based on the corpus, and analysis results should be evaluated in the light of possible shortcomings of the material.

4. How far should an analyst rely on intuition?

The place of intuition has been controversial in linguistics. For the sake of clarity, I will distinguish between introspection (to provide data) and intuition in a wider sense. Many linguists in the generative school have used introspection, without the necessary caution, to provide data for linguistic analysis, e.g. concerning questions of grammaticalness or acceptability. As I have explained before, I find that introspection is questionable as the only source of data. Introspection is fallible, it easily weakens, and it can be biased by the researcher's theoretical stance.

Does the access to corpora mean that we can dispense with intuition? I think it would be a mistake to reject what we can see with our 'inner eye'. But there is a need to check intuitive judgements. Here corpora may play an important role. Corpus use and intuition do not exclude each other; they go well together. I remember hearing John Sinclair speak about 'intuition in the presence of large amounts of data'. If there is a need for caution in using introspection as a source of data, intuition is indispensable in analysing corpus data. According to John Sinclair (2004: 45), 'In the evaluation of corpus evidence the researcher has virtually no option but to yield to the organising influence of his or her intuition.'

At this point, I would like to widen the question to the role of judgement more generally. This cannot be ruled out in the study of language, not even in corpus studies. It is needed in defining research questions. It is needed in compiling the corpus. What text categories should be included? How large should they be? For those who use existing corpora, it is essential to select the most appropriate corpus for the study. Which corpus is appropriate for the particular research question the investigator has in mind?

Judgement is also necessary at the analysis stage, even in corpus-driven research. Concordances have to be interpreted. Patterns of distribution require comment, drawing on the researcher's knowledge of the language and his/her experience of corpus studies. Finally, judgement is necessary in summing up the findings of a corpus study. To what extent has the study answered the research question? Were there problems with the corpus? If so, what problems? Is there a need for further work? If so, what sort of work?

In conclusion, the corpus does not give answers automatically; they emerge in the interaction between the researcher and his/her material. In this process, judgement is inescapable, intuition is essential, and introspection may turn out to be an important supplementary source, suggesting points that need to be studied further in the corpus (or in elicitation experiments).

5. What kind of questions should an analyst think of?

It is important to stress that the questions should come first, then the choice of corpus. Where do research questions come from? They may have their root in a particular theory which the investigator wants to test. They may derive from the findings of previous research. Or they may have been stimulated by more or less incidental observations of language use. Once the questions have been defined, the next step is to compile an appropriate corpus.

With the increasing availability of ready-made corpora, we have a different situation. Many have been built to answer particular research questions, for example the relationship between British and American English in the case of the LOB Corpus as compared with the Brown Corpus, historical change in the case of the Helsinki Corpus, learner language in connection with the International Corpus of Learner English (ICLE), language comparison in the case of the Oslo Multilingual Corpus. It remains for the user to define specific research questions within the area covered by the corpus, taking into account research that has already been done on the particular corpus or in the relevant field more generally.

The types of questions have changed over time. When electronic corpora first became available, there were many quantitative studies, for the simple reason that these were new and could now be carried out in a fairly straightforward manner using computer programmes, whereas such studies required an enormous amount of manual work in the pre-computational age. In the course of the development, the range of questions has grown enormously, including both quantitative and qualitative studies. Some widely used corpora have been used in ways which the compilers may not have imagined. For example, the Brown Corpus has been used very widely: in lexical studies, variation studies, semantics, stylistics, software development, studies of graphemic patterns and punctuation practice, etc. (see the ICAME Bibliography: http://icame.uib.no/).

The appearance of a new corpus may lead to a spate of new questions. This is true of the London-Lund Corpus, the first major publicly available electronic corpus of spoken English. The consequences for our knowledge of spoken English have been far-reaching. Similarly, the ICLE corpus has greatly stimulated the study of patterns in learner English.

With the vast material that is now available on the Web, there is again a new situation. Many people these days speak of the 'Web as Corpus'. I would prefer to say that the Web is a vast archive of texts from which material can be drawn by the researcher taking into account his/her research question. It must be remembered, however, that not all types of texts are adequately represented on the Web, in particular carefully transcribed casual speech. With multilingual corpora, the available material is chiefly restricted to certain types of formal and institutional language.

The wide availability of ready-made corpora and the virtually unlimited store of texts on the Web offer great possibilities, but must not dominate the corpus researcher. Noam Chomsky once said that 'you don't take a corpus, you ask questions' (see the interview in Aarts 2000). I agree, as long as corpus use is not rejected. We should not ask: here I have a lot of material, what can I do with it? But: I have this research question. How do I find appropriate evidence? This may come from corpora, from elicitation, or from a combination of different sources of data. The challenge is to use corpora *and* ask questions.

6. What are the strengths and weaknesses of corpus analysis?

Let's compare three means of accessing data for linguistic analysis: corpus, introspection, and elicitation. The main strength of corpus data is that it represents attested language use in real communicative contexts. Unlike introspection, which may be biased by prior expectations, it is neutral with respect to the investigator's theoretical stance. Unlike elicitation, which is necessarily more or less artificial, it represents natural language use. With both introspection and elicitation, it is difficult to generalise to actual language use.

Corpus analysis is the only possible option in historical studies, where there are no informants to consult and where the investigator cannot draw on introspection to provide data. It is also indispensable in studies of synchronic language variation. If it can be difficult to introspect or elicit information on questions of grammaticalness/acceptability, the problem is compounded if the question is widened to include the range of variation across speakers and communicative contexts.

Corpora provide an almost unlimited access to data, and they allow exact quantitative studies of language variation. It is becoming increasingly recognised, e.g. in cognitive linguistics and usage-based theories, that frequency is important for understanding both language use and change. For frequency studies, corpus analysis is the only practical option.

Although corpus analysis is often associated with quantitative studies, it is just as important for qualitative studies. It is a common experience in using a corpus that the researcher will make discoveries which are unrelated to the original research question. Working with corpus data sharpens the eye and the power of observation. This is perhaps how we should best understand Randolph Quirk's notion of total accountability. The corpus may force you to see what you might otherwise overlook.

A further positive aspect of electronic corpora is their transportability.

Many researchers have been able to share a common basis of data. It has become easier to verify previous work and carry out complementary studies. Particularly for types of data which may be difficult to obtain, such as careful transcriptions of face-to-face conversation and other forms of speech, the access to publicly available corpora has greatly advanced the possibilities of research.

Corpora have weaknesses as well. They may not provide sufficient evidence on the questions the researcher has in mind. There are problems with representativeness. There is a danger that corpus analysts will be dominated by their material. There was a time when corpora were commonly rejected because they were necessarily limited and could not be expected to provide evidence on all points of interest to the researcher. As electronic corpora have grown immensely, this problem is less acute. We have also seen proposals for *monitor corpora*, first presented by John Sinclair (1982), which are non-finite collections of texts changing with the development of the language. But the more corpora have grown, the more important it has become to develop tools for accessing the relevant data.

What is important for the language researcher is not to rely exclusively on one particular method of accessing data. Depending upon the research question, it is often vital to go beyond the corpus. Introspection and elicitation are important. It would be a mistake to define Corpus Linguistics in such a way that these are ruled out. It would also be a mistake to regard Corpus Linguistics as something totally new which can afford to neglect previous research. As I put it once in a paper (Johansson 1980: 98), 'A good description derives from the fruitful combination of previous work, introspection, corpus, and experiment; or, more generally, from tradition, imagination, and observation.'

7. What is the future of Corpus Linguistics?

As I have stated before, the prospects seem good if corpora are used with care and imagination. There are some challenges, however. It is important not to be dominated by texts which are easily available. If we want to gain a full understanding of language(s), we need corpus studies for both major and minor languages (in terms of their global importance and the number of speakers) and for both common and less frequent domains of language use. An important goal for the future is to compile corpora for endangered languages, as a means of facilitating access to them, and perhaps even serving to revitalise them, thereby making sure that the linguistic and cultural heritage which they represent will not be lost.

Among types of corpora where there is a need for further work in the future are multimodal corpora (audio plus video) and multilingual corpora. We need to further explore the use of corpora in language teaching and the training of translators, although a good deal of progress has already been made in these areas. Corpora have many applications which are relevant to language teaching. They can be used in the preparation of textbooks, grammars, dictionaries, and other teaching material. They can be used in syllabus design. They can be used in the training of teachers. They can be used in testing. And they can be used in the classroom. Multilingual corpora provide good material for the training of translators.

Further work is needed on the development of learner corpora, representing a wide range of mother-tongue backgrounds, to serve as a basis for a better understanding of the processes of language learning. A particularly interesting development in this field is the Integrated Contrastive Model (Granger 1996), which combines the study of multilingual corpora and the study of learner language. Predictions based on contrastive analysis can be compared with what learners actually do. If further developed, the Integrated Contrastive Model holds a key to the understanding of foreign-language acquisition. To what extent is it guided by the mother-tongue background of the learners vs. by general learning processes?

It is not just the gathering of data that is important. We need to learn how best to use corpora in research and teaching. Mere access to corpora and computational tools is insufficient. There is a need for training to see significant patterns. There is a need for software which goes beyond an analysis of surface patterns. There is a need for a better understanding of the relationship between theory and data. A basic question which needs further exploration is the relationship between lexis and grammar. As pointed out before, the corpus-driven approach led John Sinclair to a redefinition of the place of lexis in linguistic description and to the emphasis of extended lexical units. But where do we draw the line between lexical patterns and open choice?

Lastly, it is important not to define Corpus Linguistics too narrowly, but to recognise that there is a range of uses. As far as I see, there is hardly a subdiscipline of linguistics, whether theoretical or applied, that cannot be enriched by the use of corpora. Linguistics has often been marred by sharp divisions. Noam Chomsky once said that Corpus Linguistics does not exist (see the interview in Aarts 2000). I think the development has proved him wrong. It would be equally wrong for corpus linguists to reject a type of linguistics which does not use corpora. Just as linguists are preoccupied with understanding language structure and use, they need to understand and respect each other. If so, there is a bright future not just for Corpus Linguistics, but for the study of language.

8. How would you describe the changes which have taken place in the field of Corpus Linguistics?

If by Corpus Linguistics we mean computer Corpus Linguistics, there have been great changes during the 40–50 years since the first electronic corpora were developed. Computers have become smaller, cheaper, more powerful, and more user-friendly. In the past, text input was slow and cumbersome. Now we have optical scanning of printed material, and increasing numbers of texts in electronic form can be drawn from a variety of sources, not least through the Web. The storage capacity of computers has grown far beyond what anyone could have imagined in the early days of computer corpora. When the Brown and the LOB corpora were produced, a million words seemed vast – and anyone who had to proofread a million-word corpus, as I did, can testify that this is a lot of material. Now we have corpora of a hundred million words or more, such as the British National Corpus and the Bank of English, and there seems to be virtually no limit to growth, both in terms of size and the range of texts.

In the early days, electronic corpora were difficult to use, and linguists had to rely on assistance from experts in computing or had to develop some degree of computational expertise on their own. To make the Brown and the LOB corpora easier to use for linguists without such expertise, concordances were early on prepared in the form of microfiche sets. No one would use these nowadays. We have user-friendly programmes, such as WordSmith Tools (http://www.lexically.net/wordsmith/), which the linguist can handle – without much training – in order to produce concordances, frequency lists, lists of collocations, keywords, etc.

At the outset, those using computer corpora were few and were considered to be outside the mainstream of linguistics. With the increasing availability of corpora and computational analysis tools, the number of linguists making use of these facilities has grown rapidly, the quantity and range of studies have grown, and studies linked to computer corpora have earned increasing acceptability and respect. As a pioneering corpus linguist put it in 1996, 'corpora are becoming mainstream' (Svartvik 1996). There is no sign that the development has slowed down since then.

With the increasing use of corpora, the range of research questions has grown far beyond those focused on in the early quantitative studies and encompasses virtually every aspect of language structure and use: grammar, lexis, semantics and pragmatics, metaphor, language variation and change, etc. Corpora have also turned out to have important practical applications: in natural language processing, lexicography, language teaching, translator training, etc. Change has been the keyword since the beginning and will probably remain so, as long as those who use corpora keep in mind that the essence of research is asking questions.

9. How can corpora enlighten cross-linguistic studies?

In the last couple of decades corpora have been increasingly used for cross-linguistic research. A common resource has been the Canadian Hansard, with reports in English and French from parliamentary proceedings. This is valuable for many purposes, but certainly not for all, as the reports are not strictly verbatim. Other corpora have been designed especially for cross-linguistic studies, such as the English-Norwegian Parallel Corpus.

Cross-linguistic studies in the past were often limited to a comparison of structures without considering their use in context. There were problems with comparability, and questions were raised on the basis of comparison, or *tertium comparationis*. The great advantage of multilingual corpora, provided that they have been compiled with care, is that they contain extended comparable texts, which both reduces the problem of comparability and makes possible a comparison of language use in context. We can compare not just structures, but their conditions of use.

A simple example showing how corpora can enrich cross-linguistic studies is my comparison of the English verb *spend* (in the sense of spending time) and its correspondences in German and Norwegian (Johansson 2007: 107–115). Although both German and Norwegian have corresponding verbs, German *verbringen/zubringen* and Norwegian *tilbringe*, other means are commonly used to express the notion of spending time. A particularly interesting case is the 'raising' construction which is generally preferred in rendering English *spend* plus a temporal expression and a verb in the *-ing* form. Judging by a text-based comparison, the most natural correspondence both in German and Norwegian is to 'raise' the *-ing* verb, e.g. *we spent a lot of time driving* rendered in German by *die meiste Zeit fuhren wir* and in Norwegian by *mye av tiden kjørte vi bil* (both meaning 'most of the time we drove'). Here both the German and the Norwegian translations omit the 'spending' verb.

A corpus-based study may compare not just individual items, but may establish paradigms of correspondences, as shown in Altenberg's (1999) comparison of adverbial connectors in English and Swedish. It may show not just what forms correspond cross-linguistically, but whether there are corresponding structures at all. Often we find *zero correspondence*, i.e. cases where there is no overtly corresponding form, where there is no natural match across languages, and particularly in the case of forms expressing interpersonal and textual (rather than ideational) meaning.

An interesting aspect of multilingual corpus studies is that they may make meaning visible through cross-linguistic correspondences. An example is Aijmer and Simon-Vandenbergen's (2003) study of the English discourse particle *well* and its correspondences in Swedish and Dutch. Although the meaning of *well* is often left unexpressed, there are many overt correspondences which help us build up a picture of the meaning of *well*. Using translation corpora can be regarded as a systematic way of exploiting the cross-linguistic intuition of translators.

Text-based studies may also be used to reveal discourse features of the languages compared, as in the study of information density in English, Norwegian, and German by Fabricius-Hansen (1998). The higher information density in German is shown to have important consequences for text structure in translation. Discourse comparison of this kind is comparatively new and represents an area where much more work is needed.

To sum up, there are many ways in which the use of multilingual corpora can enrich cross-linguistic studies. It is up to the user to define fruitful research questions and use the corpora creatively. In this process we learn not only about individual languages and their relationships, but also about language in general – provided that the study becomes truly multilingual. Seeing through corpora we can see through language.

10. What are the advantages and disadvantages of compiling and using parallel and/or comparable corpora?

Corpora for cross-linguistic studies must be comparable in some way, either because the texts are related by translation or because they satisfy other criteria of comparability (genre, time of composition, etc.). Unfortunately, both types have been called parallel corpora, but this term is mostly applied to corpora of texts which are in a translation relationship, and the other type is generally referred to by the term comparable corpora. Both types have their advantages and disadvantages.

Parallel corpora are probably most difficult to compile, at least if we want them to contain a variety of text types, not just political documents such as the Canadian Hansard or EU or UN texts. Permission from copyright holders must be secured for both the original and the translated texts; this is particularly difficult if several languages are involved. The texts must be aligned, so that the user can retrieve the corresponding sections from the original and the translated texts. The special advantage of parallel corpora is that they contain texts which are intended to express the same meanings and have the same discourse functions in the relevant languages. Using the source or the target language as a starting-point, we can establish paradigms of correspondences. The main problem in using parallel corpora for cross-linguistic studies is that the range of translated texts is restricted as compared with the range of original texts. In other words, we cannot generalise from translation corpora to the languages more generally. Translated texts may differ from original texts because of source language influence. There may also be general features which characterise translated texts. In using parallel corpora for contrastive studies, it is therefore important to be able to control for translation effects.

Comparable corpora have the advantage that they represent ordinary language use in each language and should allow safe conclusions on similarities and differences between the languages compared. With the increasing availability of electronic texts in many languages, there is plenty of material to select from. But it may be difficult to match texts across languages, as text types may differ. Ideally, comparable corpora should contain a range of registers. The most difficult problem in using comparable corpora is knowing what to compare, i.e. relating forms which have similar meanings and pragmatic functions. Similarities across languages are not limited to elements which belong to the corresponding levels. For example, what is expressed by a modal auxiliary in one language could correspond to a variety of forms in another language (lexical verbs, adverbs, clauses, etc.). How do we find all the relevant forms? This is where it is useful to turn to parallel corpora, where we can explore and compare whole areas of meaning.

Fortunately, it is not necessary to choose between parallel corpora and comparable corpora. Both can be combined within the same overall framework, as we have done in the English-Norwegian Parallel Corpus (ENPC) and the Oslo Multilingual Corpus (OMC); see Johansson (2007: 11–14, 18–19). Here we can make a number of types of comparison: original texts across languages, original texts and their translations, translations across languages, and original and translated texts in the same language. To take the English verb *spend* as discussed previously, we can examine both how translators have rendered the verb in German and Norwegian and the extent to which the forms selected agree with their use in original texts in the target language. We can see then that translators commonly overuse *verbringen/zubringen* and *tilbringe*, respectively. In other words, we can distinguish between language differences and translation effects.

Corpora like the ENPC are difficult to compile. The number as well as the range of texts is limited, as the text selection is restricted to text types that have been translated in both directions. It is difficult to compile very large corpora according to this model, at least for English and Norwegian, and the evidence they provide on individual points may turn out to be insufficient. If we increase the number of languages, problems are compounded. In compiling the OMC, we did not find sufficient material that had been translated across the three languages (English to German and Norwegian, German to English and Norwegian, Norwegian to English and German). Although there are many advantages with the bidirectional translation model, corpora built in this way need to be supplemented by larger corpora compiled according to the two main models presented above, as these are less constrained with respect to the types and the range of texts.

References

Aarts, B. 2000. Corpus Linguistics, Chomsky, and fuzzy tree fragments. In *Corpus Linguistics and Linguistic Theory. Papers from the Twentieth International Conference on English Language Research on Computerised Corpora*, C. Mair & M. Hundt (eds), 5–13. Amsterdam: Rodopi.

Aijmer, K. & Simon-Vandenbergen, A.-M. 2003. The discourse particle *well* and its equivalents in Swedish and Dutch. *Linguistics* 41: 1123–1161.

Altenberg, B. 1999. Adverbial connectors in English and Swedish: Semantic and lexical correspondences. In *Out of Corpora. Studies in Honour of Stig Johansson*, H. Hasselgård & S. Oksefjell (eds), 249–268. Amsterdam: Rodopi.

Biber, D. 1988. *Variation Across Speech and Writing*. Cambridge: CUP.

Fabricius-Hansen, C. 1998. Informational density and translation, with special reference to German–Norwegian–English. In *Corpora and Cross-linguistic Research. Theory, Method, and Case Studies*, S. Johansson & S. Oksefjell (eds), 197–234. Amsterdam: Rodopi.

Francis, W. N. 1979. Problems of assembling and computerising large corpora. In *Empirische Textwissenschaft: Aufbau und Auswertung von Text-Corpora*. H. Bergenholtz & B. Schaeder (eds), 110–123. Königstein im Taunus: Scriptor.

Francis, W. N. 1992. Language corpora B.C. In *Directions in Corpus Linguistics. Proceedings of Nobel Symposium 82, Stockholm, 4–8 August 1991*, J. Svartvik (ed.), 17–32. Berlin: Mouton de Gruyter.

Granger, S. 1996. From CA to CIA and back: An integrated approach to computerised bilingual and learner corpora. In *Languages in Contrast. Papers from a Symposium on Text-Based Cross-Linguistic Studies, Lund 4–5 March 1994*, K. Aijmer, B. Altenberg & M. Johansson (eds), 37–51. Lund: Lund University Press.

ICAME Journal. Bergen: Norwegian Computing Centre for the Humanities. <http://icame.uib.no>

Johansson, S. 1980. Corpus-Based studies of British and American English. In *Papers from the Scandinavian Symposium on Syntactic Variation, Stockholm, May 18–19, 1979*, S. Jacobson (ed.), 85–100. Stockholm: Almqvist & Wiksell.

Johansson, S. 2007. *Seeing Through Multilingual Corpora. On the Use of Corpora in Contrastive Studies* [Studies in Corpus Linguistics 26]. Amsterdam: John Benjamins.

Johansson, S., Leech, G. & Goodluck, H. 1978. *Manual of Information to Accompany the Lancaster-Oslo/Bergen Corpus of British English, for Use with Digital Computers*. Oslo: Department of English, Oslo University. <http://icame.uib.no>

Quirk, R. 1960. Towards a description of English usage. *Transactions of the Philological Society* 59: 40–61.

Quirk, R. & Svartvik, J. 1978. A corpus of modern English. In *Empirische Textwissenschaft. Aufbau und Auswertung von Text-Corpora*, H. Bergenholtz & B. Schaeder (eds), 204–218. Königstein im Taunus: Scriptor.

Sinclair, J. M. 1982. Reflections on computer corpora in English language research. In *Computer Corpora in English Language Research*, S. Johansson (ed.), 1–6. Bergen: Norwegian Computing Centre for the Humanities.

Sinclair, J. M. 2004. Intuition and annotation – the discussion continues. In *Advances in Corpus Linguistics. Papers from the 23rd International Conference on English Language Research on Computerised Corpora (ICAME 23),* K. Aijmer & B. Altenberg (eds), 39–60. Amsterdam: Rodopi.

Svartvik, J. 1996. Corpora are becoming mainstream. In *Using Corpora for Language Research. Studies in the Honour of Geoffrey Leech,* J. Thomas & M. Short (eds), 3–14. London: Longman.

Tognini-Bonelli, E. 2001. *Corpus Linguistics at Work* [Studies in Corpus Linguistics 6]. Amsterdam: John Benjamins.

Corpus Linguistics and translation studies

From an interdisciplinary stance, Sara Laviosa, Senior Lecturer in English and Translation Studies at the University of Bari (Italy), discusses the use of corpora in translation studies, and highlights the advantages that are opened up to translation practitioners and researchers when working with Corpus Linguistics. In addressing her specific questions, she first details the benefits that the corpus approach has brought to translation studies. From an applied perspective, she then discusses the kind of information found in corpora that is absent or lacking in traditional resources most commonly used by professionals. Finally, taking into account their practical needs, Laviosa comments on the specificities of choosing suitable corpora for translation tasks and explains important terms in corpora classification.

1. Where do you place the roots of Corpus Linguistics? And to what do you attribute the growth of interest in the area?

Scholars who privilege corpus-driven versus corpus-based approaches to the study of language[1] tend to trace the origins of Corpus Linguistics to the work of John Rupert Firth (see Tognini-Bonelli 2001: 157–164 and Stubbs 1996: 22–59). On the other hand, linguists who use the term 'corpus-based' in a broad sense, comprising both corpus-based and corpus-driven approaches (e.g.

---

1 In Tognini-Bonelli's (2001: 84–85) terminology, the term corpus-driven approach refers to an inductive methodology which consists of: (a) examining the corpus in a systematic manner; (b) accepting corpus evidence with a view to making descriptive and theoretical statements that 'reflect the evidence' (Sinclair 1991: 4). On the other hand, the term corpus-based approach 'is used to refer to a methodology that avails itself of the corpus mainly to expound, test or exemplify theories and descriptions that were formulated before large corpora became available to inform language study' (Tognini-Bonelli 2001: 65). In this paper, unless otherwise stated, the term 'corpus-based' is intended to encompass both corpus-driven and corpus-based approaches.

McEnery et al. 2006), generally place the roots of Corpus Linguistics in post-Bloomfieldian American structural linguistics (cf. Leech 2002: 85).

Firth's theoretical pronouncements connect with Corpus Linguistics in several ways. First of all, he advocates the study of authentic language use in texts when he affirms that 'the complete meaning of a word is always contextual, and no study of meaning apart from a complete context can be taken seriously' (Firth 1935: 37, cited in Stubbs 1996: 53). Secondly, Firth (1935, 1957, cited in Stubbs 1996) was one of the first to propose exploring the meaning of words through their distribution in different contexts and their habitual collocations, which 'are quite simply the mere word accompaniment' (Firth 1957: 11, cited in Stubbs 1996: 35). Thirdly, Firth's view of language is functional, since any utterance is regarded as a 'way of acting on other people and influencing one's environment' (Firth 1957: 36, cited in Tognini-Bonelli 2001: 160). From the 1960s onwards Firth's contextual theory of meaning was developed by Michael A. K. Halliday and John McH. Sinclair.

Developed in the 1940s and 1950s, post-Bloomfieldian American structural linguistics was characterised by a strict empiricism, which accepted only data that were directly observable (Malmkjaer 2002: 255). For post-Bloomfieldians, 'the corpus was not merely an indispensable practical tool, but the *sine qua non* of scientific description' (Leech 2002: 85). They focused on the study of the sounds and structures of language through bottom-up 'discovery procedures' (Malmkjaer 2002: 255).

In the 1950s and 1960s, American scholars such as Fries (1952, cited in Stubbs 1996: 28) as well as Francis and Kučera (1964) contributed significantly to corpus research. In 1964, the *Standard Sample of Present-Day American English* (the *Brown Corpus*) was made available to the scholarly community. It was the first computer corpus designed specifically for linguistic research and contained one million words of running text of English prose published in the United States in 1961 (Francis & Kučera 1964).

From 1970 to 1978, thanks to the cooperation between British and Scandinavian linguists (most notably Geoffrey N. Leech, Lancaster, Stig Johansson, Oslo and Jostein H. Hauge, Bergen), the *Lancaster-Oslo/Bergen (LOB) Corpus* was assembled so as to be a British English equivalent to the *Brown Corpus* (Johansson et al. 1978).

The 1980s represented a turning point not just because the term 'Corpus Linguistics' appeared in a book with that title (Aarts & Meijs 1984), but because they marked the beginning of the second-generation multi-million-word corpora of written and spoken English. The *Collins-Birmingham University International Language Database (COBUILD)* (Sinclair 1987) and the *Longman/Lancaster English Language Corpus (LLELC)* were both designed for the compilation of English dictionaries aimed at advanced learners (Kennedy 1998: 48). This was also the time when, in Sinclair's (1991: 1) words, processing 'texts of several million words in length [...] was considered quite possible but still lunatic'.

We had to wait till the 1990s for Corpus Linguistics to become very popular (Sinclair 1991: 1). This achievement was largely due to the refinement of text retrieval software, the increased storage and processing power of computer hardware together with the development of computer typesetting, word-processing, automatic data capture and CD-ROM optical disks (Leech 1991). This made it possible to create corpora of hundreds of millions of words and design other corpus types such as the open-ended monitor corpus, i.e. the *Bank of English*®, set up in 1990 by Collins and the University of Birmingham (Kennedy 1998: 47); the *International Corpus of English (ICE)* (Greenbaum 1991); and the interactive *Corpus of Spoken American English (CSAE)* (Chafe et al. 1991). Resources such as these permitted systematic and large scale study of written and spoken language use, which gave rise to 'a new view of language' (Sinclair 1991: 1) and 'a new way of thinking about language' (Leech 1992: 106).

Since the start of the new millennium, the technological revolution has continued to give such a powerful stimulus to Corpus Linguistics that even scholars not directly engaged with corpus research claim that the study of language through corpora has brought about a 'third perspective' [2] in the scientific study of English (Crystal 2003: 446). This new perspective is assumed 'to have far-reaching effects on the goals and methods of English language research' (Crystal 2003: 446).

The successful partnership between descriptive linguistics and technology, which has enabled scholars 'to expect answers to questions that it would have been impracticable to ask a generation ago' (Crystal 2003: 447), is in my view one of the main reasons, if not *the* main reason why Corpus Linguistics has attracted and is still attracting much scholarly attention worldwide. The corpus

---

2 The other two perspectives were provided by a tradition of historical enquiry, which prevailed in the 19th century, and a tradition of research inspired by the theories and methods of descriptive linguistics, which was dominant in the 20th century (Crystal 2003: 446).

revolution is therefore intimately linked to the computer revolution. It is spreading rapidly in descriptive linguistics and in the broader interdisciplinary field of applied linguistics, whose role has been, from the 1980s onwards, 'to address language issues and problems as they occur in the real world' (Grabe 2002: 4). Conceiving the nature of linguistics as essentially a social science and an applied science has been one of the fundamental principles inspiring the work of linguists belonging to the British tradition from Firth onwards (Stubbs 1996: 23). This tenet, central to much British linguistics, is also one of the key contributing factors to the growing interest in Corpus Linguistics.

2. Is Corpus Linguistics a science or a methodology? Where would you situate Corpus Linguistics in the scientific or methodological panorama?

Whether Corpus Linguistics is an independent branch of linguistics or a research method is still the object of ongoing debate. Tognini-Bonelli (2001: 1) argues that, unlike other subfields of Applied Linguistics, 'that start by accepting certain facts as *given*', Corpus Linguistics has a theoretical status because it defines 'its own sets of rules and pieces of knowledge *before* they are applied'. This means that Corpus Linguistics is distinctively characterised by the interrelationship among data, description, theory and methodology. These four elements take part in a continual spiraling process involving corpus creation, discovery, hypothesis formation, testing and evaluation as well as the gradual accumulation of facts about language. These are progressively accommodated in new descriptions of language use, where new parameters are used to account for the empirical evidence. It follows that Corpus Linguistics can be seen as a '*pre-application methodology*' (Tognini-Bonelli 2001: 1) as opposed to a mere methodology, defined as 'the use of a given set of rules or pieces of knowledge in a certain situation' (Tognini-Bonelli 2001: 1).

On the other hand, McEnery et al. (2006: 7–8), while agreeing with Tognini-Bonelli's (2001: 1) claim that Corpus Linguistics 'has become a new research enterprise and a new philosophical approach to linguistic enquiry', maintain that Corpus Linguistics 'should be considered as a methodology with a wide range of applications across many areas and theories of linguistics' (McEnery et al. 2006: 8). In fact, as they put it, Corpus Linguistics does not describe or explain a particular aspect of language use, as phonetics, syntax, semantics or pragmatics do, but it can be used to explore almost any area of linguistic research in addition to other non-corpus methods (McEnery et al.

2006). Moreover, although Corpus Linguistics can be assigned a theoretical status, this, in their view, cannot be equated to a fully-fledged theory. A similar position is held by Kennedy (1998: 268) when he states that 'the use of corpora does not itself constitute a new or separate branch of linguistics. Rather, corpus linguistics is essentially descriptive linguistics aided by new technology'.

I think we can reach a consensus on this issue by recognising that Corpus Linguistics is indeed a new kind of research domain, 'an immensely important development in descriptive linguistics' (Widdowson 2000: 7), and a new approach to language studies which involves methodologies as varied as word-frequency and keyword lists, monolingual and bilingual concordancing, collocational statistics, and multi-dimensional analysis. Also, it might be worth reminding ourselves of the basic tenets of Corpus Linguistics because it will help us highlight the distinctive theoretical assumptions underlying this new perspective on language and the versatility of its methods of enquiry. Adapted from Stubbs (1996: 23), the main principles underlying much corpus work today can be identified as follows:

- rejection of the Chomskian competence-performance and internalised-externalised language dualisms, which have been influential in undermining the importance of corpus evidence in linguistic research and the role of descriptive linguistics in formulating theories of language;
- language is viewed as a social phenomenon which reflects, constructs and reproduces culture;
- language in use involves both routine and creative processes, individuality and generality; typicality in language carries meaning and plays an important socialising role;
- linguistics is essentially a social science and an applied science;
- language in use is systematically heterogeneous (Halliday 1991); '[t]here is no such thing as *une langue une* and there never has been' (Firth 1957: 29); texts are therefore studied comparatively across corpora which represent different language varieties;
- language is studied empirically in large collections of authentic spoken, written, or multimodal texts because the patterning of language use is not accessible to the native speaker or linguist by introspection;
- '[t]he aim of studying language in corpora is to describe and explain the observed phenomena, not to predict what some other corpus may contain' (Sinclair 2008: 30);

- real, genuine language rules, i.e. those without which communication would break down, are recurring, subconscious patterns, which need to be distinguished from invented rules, i.e. those that are artificially imposed (Aitchison 1997: 5, 102).

3. How representative can a corpus be?

'A corpus is a collection of pieces of language text in electronic form, selected according to external criteria to represent, as far as possible, a language or language variety as a source of data for linguistic research' (Sinclair 2005: 16). This definition of a sample corpus, as opposed to a monitor corpus, which is constantly supplemented with fresh linguistic material, qualifies representativeness as a feature that cannot be achieved in absolute terms when designing a general or a specialised corpus, but only in relative terms. As Sinclair (2005: 9) observes, representativeness, like balance, is a target notion. It cannot be defined precisely nor can it be fully attained, yet it must be used to guide the corpus builder in selecting the range of text types included in the corpus. This is echoed by McEnery et al. (2006: 21) who claim that representativeness and balance should be 'considered as a statement of faith rather than as fact, as presently there is no objective way to balance a corpus or to measure its representativeness'.

I will now look more closely at this important issue in corpus design. A corpus is a sample of a language or language variety, the latter being the population that the corpus is intended to represent. Representativeness depends on two factors: balance and sampling. Balance is the extent to which a corpus includes the full range of text types that are considered to represent the population. As noted earlier, it is a *desideratum* because the text types that make up a corpus are primarily selected on the basis of external rather than internal criteria, a procedure that is agreed on by many corpus linguists (McEnery et al. 2006: 14). While external criteria concern text categories (variedly called registers, genres or text types), internal criteria concern their lexical and grammatical features. Using external criteria as primary parameters ensures that the linguistic characteristics of corpus data are independent of the selection process (Sinclair 1995, cited in McEnery et al. 2006: 14). Giving prominence to internal criteria would in fact skew the corpus and determine beforehand the very lexicogrammatical patterns that the corpus linguist aims to investigate. However, as there are no reliable ways of classifying text categories, the use of external criteria as the basis for the selection of data can only ensure relative balance. This can subsequently be improved by using the results of corpus analysis that reveal a particular distribution of words and/or grammatical features as secondary parameters for the selection of additional texts. Findings may therefore provide the only opportunity for testing the selection method adopted, hence it is advisable, as Barnbrook (1996: 24–25) suggests, 'to carry out a pilot study of an exploratory corpus to refine the basis of selection for the final corpus which will be used in the project itself'.

The other factor that impacts on representativeness is sampling, i.e. the way in which abridged or unabridged texts for each genre are selected, so that the corpus is a scaled-down version of the population it is supposed to represent. First of all, sampling involves defining: (a) the population, either in terms of language production or language reception, (b) the sampling units, e.g. book, newspaper, periodical, etc., and (c) the sampling frame, i.e. lists of sampling units, such as catalogues or bibliographies. Then, a technique is applied to select the actual texts for each genre – for instance, simple or stratified random sampling.[3] Moreover, the corpus builder has to decide whether to include full texts or text extracts, and in the latter case it is important to ensure that text segments are of constant size and there is balance as regards initial, middle and end samples. Finally, the number of texts for each genre should reflect, as far as possible, the relative frequency in the population. However, when this is unknowable, the proportion of each text category included in the sample corpus is based on guesswork (Hunston 2002: 28–30).

Representativeness in corpus design is inevitably an act of faith because 'language text is a population without limit, and a corpus is necessarily finite at any one point; a corpus, no matter how big, is not guaranteed to exemplify all the patterns of the language in roughly their normal proportions' (Sinclair 2008: 30). Corpus linguists are fully aware of this particular limitation inherent in corpus design and they should take it into account when interpreting their findings.

4. How far should an analyst rely on intuition?

An intuition-based approach to the study of language relies mainly on the introspective knowledge of the informed, educated language user who can

---

3 The method of simple random sampling numbers all sampling units and chooses them with a table of random numbers. Stratified random sampling divides the population into relatively homogenous groups (or strata) and takes random samples from each stratum.

invent examples for analysis to illustrate certain hunches about language behaviour or may explore his or her intuitions with hands-on methods using small amounts of data. Concocted examples are undoubtedly well formed, nevertheless they may be idiosyncratic and reflect the speaker's own usage, rather than what a particular speech community considers as acceptable and typical. The same criticism may be expressed in connection with the use of limited, handpicked, non-invented examples. On the contrary, the corpus-based approach enables scholars to make claims on large quantities of observable empirical data and on statistical measures of significance which enhance the reliability and validity of their research findings.

The lexical relation of collocation is a case in point. Firth (1957, cited in Sinclair & Teubert 2004: xxi) makes a distinction between significant and casual collocations. Intuitively, *dark night*, *long night*, and *previous night* are all examples of fluent collocations, but only statistical measures of significance obtained from large corpora can indicate in which examples the two words are used together more often than they would by pure chance. This type of analysis is particularly relevant when designing dictionaries of English for advanced learners, where the lexicographer lists only the most frequent significant collocations of a headword.

Despite their differences, intuition-based and corpus-based approaches are not incompatible; they complement each other in corpus studies. We may consider, for example, the procedural steps proposed by Sinclair (2003: xvi–xvii) for the analysis of an ever expanding set of KWIC concordance lines:

Step 1: Initiate	Look at the words that occur immediately to the right of the node word to note any that are repeated; do the same with the words to the left of the node and decide on the strongest pattern.
Step 2: Interpret	Look at the repeated words to form a hypothesis that may link them.
Step 3: Consolidate	Look for other evidence that can support the hypothesis formulated in Step 2.
Step 4: Report	Write out the hypothesis formulated in Step 2 and revised according to the evidence collected in Step 3 so as to have an explicit, testable version.

Step 5: Recycle	Start with the next most important pattern near the node going through the same steps as before, and then look for the strongest pattern remaining on either side, until there are no repeated patterns.
Step 6: Result	Make a final list of hypotheses linking them in a final report on the node word.
Step 7: Repeat	Gather a new selection of concordances and apply your report on this new data, going through the same steps and confirming, extending or revising the list of hypotheses drawn up in Step 6.

In this cyclical process of observation, discovery, hypothesis formation and testing, intuition plays an important role, particularly in the initial selection of suitable lexical items to explore and in the interpretation of the patterns emerging from corpus data. As John Sinclair puts it in an interview, '[n]umbers are not sensitive to meaning' (Sinclair & Teubert 2004: xxii). Therefore, analysts have to rely on their judgement to distinguish good examples of phrasal units, such as *on the verge of* or *on the basis of* or *on the strength of*, from phrases which share the same pattern *on the ... of* merely because they are composed of fairly frequent words, as is the case with *on the surface of*. As Tognini-Bonelli (2001: 85) explains with reference to the corpus-driven approach, 'this methodology is not mechanical, but mediated constantly by the linguist, who is still behaving as a linguist and applying his or her knowledge and experience and intelligence at every stage during this process'. It cannot be otherwise if it is true that since '[m]eaning is an impression in the mind of an individual, and that is impenetrable, using linguistic techniques' (Sinclair 2003: xxviii), all that corpus linguists can do is to 'search for a consensus – a very loose consensus based on just sufficient similarity of these impressions for the discourse to proceed' (Sinclair 2003: xxviii). Corpus analytical techniques combined with intuition and interpretative skills are, in my view, one of the best possible ways in which the linguist can unveil the consensus on meaning shared by a speech or discourse community.

5. What kind of questions should an analyst think of?

Whether the analyst's questions are based on a hunch, firmly grounded in theory or a mixture of the two, they should be expressed ideally in terms of operational hypotheses or at least as precise statements of objectives. This enables the researcher to think carefully about what is, and what is not worth investigating, and how the study will be carried out (Bell 1993: 19). Also, it must be possible for the results either to support or reject the initial hypotheses.

Moreover, the types of questions that the researcher should think of depend on the preferred method of investigation and the approach that lies behind it (Hunston 2002). For example, the 'category-based method', underlain by the corpus-based approach, favours the use of annotated corpora at different levels of linguistic analysis: phonological, morphological, semantic, parts of speech, types of error, lexical, syntactic, discourse, pragmatic, or stylistic (Hunston 2002; McEnery et al. 2006). Annotated corpora enable the researcher to ask questions concerning categories. For example, in a corpus annotated for parts of speech, it is much easier to extract quantitative data on the frequency of *love* as a noun and *love* as a verb, and then retrieve semantic information about each word class, which can be included in dictionaries or descriptive grammars. A category-based methodology is ideally suited to investigate language variation and linguistic borrowing beyond the word level. It has also great potential for contrastive and error analysis as well as interlanguage research. Recent studies of 'local grammar' (Hunston 2002: 90–91), which attempt to describe only one set of meanings in a language together with the associated patterns, can benefit from the annotation of selected semantic categories such as the expression of sameness and difference.

On the other hand, the 'word-based method', underlain by the corpus-driven approach, relies mainly on the use of non-annotated corpora (Hunston 2002). Plain text corpora enable the researcher to analyse raw data that have not been classified in any way beforehand. From this perspective, the research questions tend to concern the behaviour of individual words studied through KWIC concordance lines and collocational statistics, with a view to unveiling the interrelationship between lexis and grammar. The procedural steps proposed by Sinclair (1996c, cited in Tognini-Bonelli 2001: 19 and Sinclair 2003: 173–178) to describe units of meaning on the basis of the correlation between the node word and its context are as follows:

a. identify collocational profile (lexical realisations), i.e. two or more words occurring near each other in a text;
b. identify colligational patterns (lexicogrammatical realisations), i.e. the occurrence of a grammatical class or structural pattern with another one, or with a word or phrase;

c. consider common semantic field (semantic preference), i.e. a clear preference in the structure of a phrase for words of a particular meaning;

d. consider pragmatic realisations (semantic prosody), i.e. the special meaning conveyed by words grouping together, which relates not so much to their dictionary meanings as to the reasons why they were chosen together; it has been recognised in part as connotation, pragmatic meaning and attitudinal meaning.

Investigations of two main principles of the organisation of language: 'idiom principle' and 'open-choice principle' (Sinclair 1991) and 'functionally complete units of meaning' (Tognini-Bonelli 2001) are generally carried out with word-based methods. Lexical borrowing too is best studied with plain text corpora to unveil variations in the lexicogrammatical profile of loan words across donor and receptor languages (Furiassi 2008; Pulcini 2008).

Word-based and category-based methodologies are mutually enriching and can be combined with other approaches such as action research, the ethnographic style, the survey method, or the experimental style (see Bell 1993). Exemplary is Joanna Channell's (1994) study of vague language, which integrated spoken and written corpus data with invented examples, elicitation tests and introspective observations collected from test respondents and authors.

6. What are the strengths and weaknesses of corpus analysis?

The advent of corpora has enabled descriptive and applied linguists to unveil facts about natural language behaviour that are impossible to discover through introspection. A good example is Nuccorini's (2008) lexicography-oriented analysis of the phraseological differences between three pairs of English and Italian 'true friends', defined as 'semantically cognate words which are used in different syntagmatic patterns in two languages' (Nuccorini 2008: 171). The set of true friends examined were *absolutely/assolutamente*; *terrorist/terrorista*; *kamikaze/kamikaze*. In bilingual English-Italian dictionaries, these words were found to be translation equivalents of each other. However, the investigation of their lexico-grammatical profile in the press subcorpus of the *Corpus di Italiano Scritto (CORIS)* and the newspaper and magazine subcorpora of the Collins WordbanksOnline English Corpus[4] revealed that these posited direct equivalents could not be regarded as functional equivalents of each other

---

4 This corpus is part of the *Bank of English*®.

because they were not 'comparable units of meaning' (Tognini-Bonelli 2002: 80), i.e. units of language that are comparable across languages denotationally, connotationally and pragmatically. On the basis of these findings, Nuccorini (2008) proposes to include phraseological information about true friends in bilingual dictionaries.

The results obtained by corpus studies are systematically organised in new descriptions of language use which feed into linguistic theory where concepts and language models are confirmed, refined or modified to explain the phenomena empirically observed. Hypotheses are continually put forward and tested with improved tools and resources to produce robust linguistic accounts which are then further elaborated in various applied fields. Many areas of study in applied linguistics have been influenced by the insights and analytical techniques of Corpus Linguistics. Lexicographic and lexical studies, grammatical studies, register variation and genre analysis, dialectology and language variation, contrastive and interlanguage analysis, translation studies, diachronic study and language change, language learning and teaching, semantics, pragmatics, sociolinguistics, discourse analysis, stylistics and literary studies, forensic linguistics, computational linguistics, terminology, second language acquisition, language development, and clinical language studies are all experiencing significant changes in their methodological approaches thanks to the influence of Corpus Linguistics (Barnbrook 1996; McEnery & Wilson 1996; Crystal 2003; McEnery et al. 2006). The transparence of the methods developed by Corpus Linguistics enables scholars not only to replicate and refine previous studies, but also to engage in collaborative endeavours, thus enhancing cooperation and dialogue among scholars within and across disciplines.

Since the 1980s major advances have undoubtedly been made in the development of really huge databases of spoken and written language.[5] But this means that corpus research is still focusing largely on the investigation of 'the textual traces of the processes whereby meaning is achieved' rather than 'on the complex interplay of linguistic and contextual factors whereby discourse is enacted' (Widdowson 2000: 7). So the criticism expressed by

---

5 The Collins Word Web is a 2.5-billion-word analytical database, which grows by 35 million words every month, making it the largest resource of its type. Data from a trillion words from the Internet is available from the Linguistic Data Consortium. In the summer of 2006, a billion-word collection was announced by Oxford University Press (Sinclair 2008: 25).

Widdowson (2000) about the inability of corpora to provide ethnographic descriptions of language in use is still valid. Inspired by the work of Kress and van Leeuwen (1996, 2001) in multimodal communication, corpus linguists have made encouraging progress in the study of word, image and sound in different language varieties (e.g. Baldry & Thibault 2004, 2006; Carter & Adolphs 2008). However, the multimodal approach to language data has not yet entered the mainstream of corpus-based research, and this is to be hoped for in the future.

7. What is the future of Corpus Linguistics?

The progress of Corpus Linguistics in the future is linked to the electronic revolution. This has been dramatically changing the ways in which we access, represent, collect, process, and analyse language data. Corpus Linguistics has dissolved the traditional dichotomy between lexis and grammar and given rise to the new notions, such as local grammar (Gross 1993; Barnbrook & Sinclair 1995; Hunston & Sinclair 2005 – all of them as cited in Hunston 2002: 90) and pattern grammar (Hunston & Francis 1999) as well as new linguistic theories, such as lexical priming (Hoey 2005). These novel descriptions of language in use have impacted and will continue to impact many fields of research where communication plays a central role, such as the arts and humanities, computational linguistics and social sciences.

Very promising is the close collaboration between corpus linguists and computer scientists, which has recently led to 'the development of machine-based techniques that enable all visual and verbal patterns to be aligned and enable common multimodal patterns to be recognised' (Carter & Adolphs 2008: 288). Research in multimodal analysis has begun to explore approaches that permit the simultaneous analysis of video, audio and textual records of naturalistic conversation (see the *HeadTalk* project outlined in Carter & Adolphs 2008). Multimodal Corpus Linguistics will undoubtedly play an important role in the analysis of the interplay between contextual and textual data in everyday communication, thus providing a more accurate account of language use. It will also be of considerable interest to scholars engaged in the study of sign languages and audiovisual translation (cf. Díaz Cintas 2009; Kenny 2009; Leeson 2009).

The fruitful cooperation between Corpus Linguistics and computer science has also produced new types of text-retrieval software, such as ConcGram (Greaves 2009), which is designed to identify co-occurrences of two or more words fully automatically. Alongside n-grams (Furiassi & Hofland 2007), concgrams will enable linguists to achieve substantial progress in the analysis of phraseology in speech and writing. Moreover, it can be foreseen that the construction of web-derived mega corpora and standard-size corpora in an ever-increasing number of languages will foster the development of contrastive linguistics and the study of language contact (cf. de los Ángeles Gómez González et al. 2008; Siemund & Kintana 2008; Braunmüller & House 2009).

Also, the combination of corpus-linguistic methods of enquiry and those employed in adjacent fields of scholarship (e.g. psycholinguistics) will continue to provide linguistic theory with a rich variety of corpus as well as experimental and questionnaire data. In turn, this will contribute to the development of novel and robust theoretical approaches in language-based studies (cf. Gilquin & Gries 2009; Mollin 2009).

The future of Corpus Linguistics is relevant to translation since corpora, even in the words of scholars not directly engaged in corpus research, are viewed, in the wake of globalisation and the digital revolution, as 'central to the way that Translation Studies as a discipline will remain vital and move forward' (Tymoczko 1998: 652). One of the main reasons for this is that 'the modes of interrogation [of corpora] – as well as care in the encoding of metatextual information about translations and texts – allow researchers to move from text-based questions to context-based questions' so that the analyst is able 'to address not simply questions of language or linguistics, but also questions of culture, ideology, and literary criticism' (Tymoczko 1998: 653). Corpus Linguistics is also likely to affect the expanding field of interpreting studies. Current research, which is mainly based on case studies, will be further enhanced by corpora to describe prevailing norms in the interpreters' translational and interactional behaviour (cf. Shlesinger 1998).

Moreover, corpora are essential to the development of machine translation (MT) (Ping 2009), computer-aided translation (CAT) tools (e.g. translation memories) (O'Hagan 2009) and terminology management systems (TMSs) (Bowker 2009), just as they are important for making advances in computer-assisted language learning (CALL) and language technology in general (Leech 2002). It is therefore envisioned that the partnership between Corpus Linguistics, translation studies and computational linguistics will grow even stronger in the years to come.

8. In what ways can Corpus Linguistics help translation studies?

In the interdisciplinary and international field of Translation Studies, corpora are playing an important role in research, education, professional practice and technology (Granger et al. 2003; Kruger 2004; Olohan 2004; Vandeweghe et al. 2007; Anderman & Rogers 2008; Kenny 2009). Corpus-based methods of enquiry underlie studies as diverse as the quest for translation universals (Mauranen & Kujamäki 2004), the examination of translators' styles and translation shifts (see Kenny 2009 for an overview) as well as the extraction of translation equivalents in bilingual terminography and lexicography (Barnbrook et al. 2005). Moreover, the influence of English on European languages through translation (Anderman & Rogers 2005) and the linguistic features of dubbing (Freddi & Pavesi 2009) have recently been explored with the employment of corpora.

The insights gained by translation scholars into the specificity of translational language have been a source of inspiration also for researchers/teachers,[6] who have tested in the classroom environment a number of universals. Their aim has been twofold: raising students' awareness about the nature of the process and product of translation (Jääskeläinen 2004; Kujamäki 2004) and testing the usefulness of universals in translation quality assessment (TQA) (Scarpa 2008: 108–113, 314–317). Furthermore, translation teachers draw on the resources and materials developed in the neighbouring fields of foreign language learning, intercultural communication studies, information and communication technologies, machine (assisted) translation, contrastive analysis, terminology, lexicography, and LSP studies.

It is safe to say that nowadays, in postgraduate translation programmes that have an established reputation and are aimed specifically at preparing students for the profession, trainee translators use language technologies (Kelly 2005: 61–79; Ulrych 2005[7]), of which corpus-based methods are an essential

---

6 Lederer (2007: 18–19) makes a distinction between translation scholars, researchers/teachers and translators/teachers.

7 A survey carried out on a sample of 41 higher education institutions situated mainly in Europe and North America shows the following results about the types of technological/machine aids available: 'computers/word processors 100%, Internet 100%, e-mail 100%, MT (Machine Translation) tools 47%, CAT (Computer-assisted translation) tools 47% (of these: online glossaries/dictionaries 85%, terminological data banks 90%, corpora 47%, translation memory tools 52%, translators workbench 52%)' (Ulrych 2005: 17).

part[8]. Different types of corpora are employed as sources of data that enhance the acquisition of translation skills, target language competence as well as subject-specific knowledge and terminology in languages for special/specific purposes. In the corpus-based, student-centred translation classroom, corpora are usually created and investigated to extract terminology for glossary building, retrieve translation equivalents in context, improve the quality of the translation product and the efficiency of the translation process, discover the translation procedures adopted by professional translators, examine text type stylistic conventions, and gain an insight into language behaviour in general (Botley et al. 2000; Hatim 2001; Bowker & Pearson 2002; Granger et al. 2003; Zanettin et al. 2003; Gavioli 2005; Anderman & Rogers 2008).

Generally speaking, corpus-based translator education is inspired by the principles underpinning the Data-Driven Learning (DDL) approach (Johns 1991) and collaborative learning (Kiraly 2003). This composite pedagogy encourages trainee translators to become critical thinkers and researchers in their own right. In authentic collaborative translation projects and corpus building exercises, they identify problem areas, suggest descriptive hypotheses and then test them on *ad hoc* corpora created under the guidance provided by the tutor who assumes the role of facilitator. Students' evaluations of the usefulness of corpora tend to be positive (Bowker 2003). They generally perceive their learning experience as being professionally empowering, i.e. aimed at developing useful skills through 'teaching methods and techniques that reflect the translation profession as we know it today' (Kiraly 2003: 26).

---

8 Postgraduate programmes that aim to join the EMT network (European Master in Translation) are a case in point. They are required to provide training in the effective use of a range of tools and search engines, including electronic corpora, translation memories, terminology databases, voice recognition software, machine-translation systems, and the Internet so that students can acquire information mining and technological competences. These are consistent with the skills and abilities stated in job advertisements for translators in large international language service providers and in the official European Commission job profile for translators (Kelly 2005: 25–27). They also conform to the European standard *EN 15038: 2006 Translation Services – Service Requirements*, which includes technical competence as one of the five types of professional competence that translators must acquire, the others being translating, linguistic and textual, research and cultural competence (Olohan 2007: 50–51).

9. What advantages do corpora provide when compared to traditional resources used by translators?

As Vintar (2008) observes, the stereotyped image of the translator as a solitary person working at a desk and surrounded by specialised and encyclopedic dictionaries, thesauri, glossaries, technical manuals, periodicals, commercial leaflets and encyclopedias is by now a thing of the past. In the present days, the word 'translator' conjures up a vision of a professional working at a desk and glaring at a computer screen dotted with an array of desktop icons and with an Internet browser minimised on the task bar. Robinson (2003: 369) goes even further and argues that 'all translation in the world today is already "cyborg translation" – translation involving some significant interface between humans and machines'. This vision appears to be consistent with the results of a survey conducted in 2006 by Vande Walle (2007, cited in Scarpa 2008: 343) on a representative sample of 500 translators in Europe. The vast majority of respondents (88%) declared that they used only the computer in their professional work.

In the modern translation industry, traditional reference materials[9] are being gradually replaced by electronic language resources and computer applications, which can be used either as stand-alone desktop products or integrated into a commercial package[10] (Bowker 2002: 43–76; Olohan 2004: 176–189; Alcina 2008: 96–99; Scarpa 2008: 298–317). The translator's workbench (or workstation) is an example of a single integrated system made up of a translation memory, an alignment tool, a concordancer, a tag filter, electronic dictionaries, terminology databases, a terminology management system, spelling checkers and grammar checkers (Quah 2006: 93–94).

Corpora are essential for the creation of translation memories (TMs) and for carrying out monolingual and multilingual terminology research. A TM is a database consisting of source text (ST) and target text (TT) segment pairs which are aligned, in most cases, at the sentence level. These translation units (TUs) are re-used when a new ST segment matches the ST segment stored in the database. Moreover, it is possible to input whole source texts and their translations in a TM system. Therefore, a translation memory can be

---

9 Research shows that they are still used by professional translators (Jääskeläinen & Mauranen 2005; Magris and Rega 2007, cited in Scarpa 2008: 311).

10 SDL Trados Studio 2009 Service Pack 1 (SP1) is an example: it provides users with an integrated environment for translation, review, terminology and project management needs.

considered as a specific type of bilingual parallel corpus that can be searched also with a built-in concordancer to review the translation of a particular lexical item, construction or phrase (Olohan 2004: 187; O'Hagan 2009: 48–49). TMs permit to achieve a high level of terminological, lexical and syntactic consistency. This is crucially important for producing large multilingual documents that need updating regularly, such as technical and instruction manuals (Scarpa 2008: 305–306).

Computer-aided terminology research relies on the semi-automatic construction of specialised high quality corpora made up of documents available online and selected on the basis of keywords.[11] Once a customised corpus on a specific subject field has been constructed in this way, term extraction tools can be used to retrieve a list of candidate terms which are then further examined by the researcher in order to compile a glossary.[12] Moreover, bilingual term extraction tools analyse aligned bilingual parallel corpora to identify potential terms and their translations (Bowker & Pearson 2002; Bowker 2009). Compared with published materials, corpora have the distinctive advantage of providing the translator with a more reliable and up to date source of accurate terms, which can be analysed in their natural context of use (Scarpa 2008: 308–309).

As we have seen, technology, of which corpora are an integral part, enables specialised translators to meet the demands of the modern language industry that needs to process a huge amount of multilingual technical documentation rapidly, accurately and cost-effectively. It has been estimated that the use of TMs, which are at the core of the translator's toolkit, leads to an increase in translation productivity by 20% up to 80% (Poeiras 2005: 36, cited in Scarpa 2008: 305).

10. What are the criteria for selecting a suitable corpus for a translation task?

Corpus design criteria vary according to the types of questions the translation scholar, the translation teacher (in collaboration with the students) or the practising translator intends to investigate (Kenny 2009). Studies of translation

---

11 An example of computer application for the creation of a customised corpus is WebBoot-CaT, available through Sketch Engine.

12 SDL MultiTerm Extract 2009, which includes also PhraseFinder, is a term extraction tool for finding terms and creating custom glossaries.

universals, for example, are carried out with two main types of corpora. Posited universal differences between translations and comparable non-translated texts are investigated with the monolingual comparable corpus. This is made up of two subcorpora in the same language: one consists of translated texts; the other comprises non-translated texts. The two subcorpora are comparable for text genre, topic, time span, distribution of male and female authors and readership.[13] Hypotheses concerning universal differences between translations and their source texts are investigated with the unidirectional or the bidirectional bilingual parallel corpus. The former is made up of two subcorpora: one containing original texts in language A, while the other comprises their translations in language B.[14] The latter consists of four subcorpora: original texts in language A, their translations in language B, original texts in language B and their translations in language A.[15]

Unidirectional parallel corpora are used in translator education to discover norms of translational behaviour. For example, the students' analysis of the Anglicism *business* in an English-Italian parallel corpus of economics articles revealed a preference for Italian native equivalents, such as *affari*, *settore*, *industria*, *attività*, and *azienda* (Laviosa 2006). Unidirectional parallel corpora are also used to explore the procedures adopted by professional translators to deal with terminological and lexical gaps as well as mismatches at different levels of linguistic analysis. In a collaborative project with trainee translators, Gavioli and Zanettin (2000) compiled two specialised English-Italian and Italian-English parallel corpora of medical texts. They found that translators used marked paraphrases such as *pazienti con/senza esperienza di/con* to render the unmarked subject-specific collocation *patient(s) experienced*.

Bilingual and multilingual comparable corpora, i.e. collections of original texts in two or more languages, which are assembled on the basis of similar

---

13 Olohan (2004) describes a number of studies carried out with a monolingual comparable corpus comprising a 3.5-million-word subcorpus selected from the Translational English Corpus (TEC) and a subcorpus selected from the British National Corpus (BNC). Another example is the 10-million-word Corpus of Translated Finnish (Mauranen & Kujamäki 2004).

14 An example of unidirectional parallel corpus is the *German-English Parallel Corpus of Literary Texts (GEPCOLT)* (Kenny 2001, 2005).

15 Notable examples of bidirectional parallel corpora are the *English-Norwegian Parallel Corpus (ENPC)* (Øveras 1998) and the parallel corpus of English and Portuguese *COMPARA* (Frankenberg-Garcia & Santos 2003).

design criteria, e.g. subject matter, topic, communicative situation, are used in translator training to discover functional translation equivalents. The students' examination of an English-Italian comparable corpus of abstracts of research articles showed that the equivalent of *biopsia epatica* was *liver biopsy*, rather than *hepatic biopsy*, whereas *hepatic* was found to collocate with other medical terms, such as *failure* (Gavioli 2005).

The target language monolingual reference corpus is also useful, particularly in the context of teaching translation into L2. Stewart's (2000) classroom-based research into the use of the *BNC* for translating tourist brochures from Italian into English is a case in point. He shows that students are able to produce naturally sounding collocations by examining the frequency of occurrence and concordance lines of assumed target language equivalents of source language noun phrases. Two examples of corpus-derived translation equivalents were *gran giro della città* and *grand tour of the city*; *strada panoramica* and *road with panoramic views*. A reference corpus can therefore be effectively used to compensate for the translator's lack of native-speaker knowledge of target language and culture.

Corpora, as shown earlier, are an essential language resource for LSP translators. In the niche market of literary translation,[16] there is very little evidence that corpora are used for professional purposes. However, unidirectional parallel corpora can be a very useful addition to traditional resources, as is the case with Zanettin's translation of *Grimus* by Salmon Rushdie.[17] The creation of a parallel corpus consisting of five novels and one short story together with the translations of Ettore Capriolo and Vincenzo Mantovani provided Zanettin with a repository of translation strategies and linguistic equivalents. The corpus proved to be invaluable in helping the translator find his own solutions to problems encountered at the level of lexis and grammar (Zanettin 2008).

On the basis of the present overview, I can affirm with fresh confidence that, in the current digital era, corpus studies of languages and translations constitute a large scholarly, pedagogic and professional enterprise interfacing with numerous fields of scientific endeavour. This thriving and variegated research area is likely to further expand in the future by strengthening two

---

16 In 2006, literary translation represented only 0.03% of the total number of translations produced in Europe (Vande Walle 2007, cited in Scarpa 2008: 76–77).

17 Zanettin's Italian translation of *Grimus* is published as a hypertext in *IperGrimus* (© 2001 Federico Zanettin & *inTRAlinea*).

distinctive features of its emerging physiognomy: internationalism and interdisciplinarity.

Acknowledgements

I wish to thank the anonymous referees for their insightful comments on the earlier versions of this contribution.

References

Aarts, J. & Meijs, W. (eds). 1984. *Corpus Linguistics: Recent Developments in the Use of Computer Corpora in English Language Research*. Amsterdam: Rodopi.

Aitchison, J. 1997. *The Language Web: The Power and Problem of Words*. Cambridge: CUP.

Alcina, A. 2008. Translation technologies: Scope, tools and resources. *Target* 20(1): 79–102.

Anderman, G. & Rogers, M. (eds). 2005. *In and Out of English: For Better For Worse?* Clevedon: Multilingual Matters.

Anderman, G. & Rogers, M. (eds). 2008. *Incorporating Corpora: The Linguist and the Translator*. Clevedon: Multilingual Matters.

Baldry, A. & Thibault, P. 2004. *Multimodal Transcription and Text Analysis*. London: Equinox.

Baldry, A. & Thibault, P. 2006. Multimodal Corpus Linguistics. In *System and Corpus*, S. Hunston & G. Thompson (eds), 164–183. London: Equinox.

Barnbrook, G. 1996. *Language and Computers. A Practical Introduction to the Computer Analysis of Language*. Edinburgh: EUP.

Barnbrook, G., Danielsson, P. & Mahlberg, M. (eds). 2005. *Meaningful Texts: The Extraction of Semantic Information from Monolingual and Multilingual Corpora*. London: Continuum.

Bell, G. 1993. *Doing your Research Project. A Guide for First-Time Researchers in Education and Social Science*, 2nd edn. Buckingham: Open University Press.

Botley, S., McEnery, A. & Wilson, A. (eds). 2000. *Multilingual Corpora in Teaching and Research*. Amsterdam: Rodopi.

Bowker, L. 2002. *Computer-Aided Translation Technology: A Practical Introduction*. Ottawa: University of Ottawa Press.

Bowker, L. 2003. Towards a collaborative approach to corpus building in the translation classroom. In *Beyond the Ivory Tower: Rethinking Translation Pedagogy* [ATA Scholarly Monograph Series XII], B. J. Baer & G. S. Koby (eds), 193–210. Amsterdam: John Benjamins.

Bowker, L. 2009. Terminology. In *Routledge Encyclopedia of Translation Studies*, 2nd edn, M. Baker & G. Saldanha (eds), 286–290. London: Routledge.

Bowker, L. & Pearson, J. 2002. *Working with Specialised Language. A Practical Guide to Using Corpora.* London: Routledge.

Braunmüller, K. & House, J. (eds). 2009. *Convergence and Divergence in Language Contact Situations* [Hamburg Studies in Multilingualism 8]. Amsterdam: John Benjamins.

Carter, R. & Adolphs, S. 2008. Linking the verbal and visual: New directions for Corpus Linguistics. In *Language, People, Numbers: Corpus Linguistics and Society.* A. Gerbig & O. Mason (eds), 275–291. Amsterdam: Rodopi.

Chafe, W., Dubois, J. & Thompson, S. A. 1991. Towards a new corpus of spoken American English. In *English Corpus Linguistics. Studies in Honour of Jan Svartvik,* K. Aijmer & B. Altenberg (eds), 64–82. London: Longman.

Channell, J. 1994. *Vague Language.* Oxford: OUP.

Crystal, D. 2003. *The Cambridge Encyclopedia of the English Language,* 2nd edn. Cambridge: CUP.

de los Ángeles Gómez González, M., Mackenzie, J. L. & González Álvarez, E. M. (eds). 2008. *Current Trends in Contrastive Linguistics: Functional and Cognitive Perspectives* [Studies in Functional and Structural Linguistics 60]. Amsterdam: John Benjamins.

Díaz Cintas, J. (ed.). 2009. *New Trends in Audiovisual Translation.* Bristol: Multilingual Matters.

Firth, J. R. 1957. *Papers in Linguistics 1934–1951.* London: OUP.

Francis, W. N. & Kučera, H. 1964. *Manual of Information to Accompany A Standard Sample of Present-Day Edited American English, for Use with Digital Computers* (revised and amplified 1979). Providence RD: Department of Linguistics, Brown University. <http://khnt.hit.uib.no/icame/manuals/brown/index.htm> (20 May, 2009).

Frankenberg-Garcia, A. & Santos, D. 2003. Introducing *COMPARA* the Portuguese-English Parallel Corpus. In *Corpora in Translator Education,* S. Bernardini, D. Stewart & F. Zanettin (eds), 71–88. Manchester: St. Jerome.

Freddi, M. & Pavesi, M. (eds). 2009. *Analysing Audiovisual Dialogue: Linguistic and Translational Insights.* Bologna: Clueb.

Furiassi, C. 2008. What dictionaries leave out. In *Investigating English with Corpora: Studies in Honour of Maria Teresa Prat,* A. Martelli & V. Pulcini (eds), 153–169. Milano: Polimetrica.

Furiassi, C. & Hofland, K. 2007. The retrieval of false Anglicisms in newspaper texts. In *Corpus Linguistics 25 Years On,* R. Facchinetti (ed.), 347–363. Amsterdam: Rodopi.

Gavioli, L. 2005. *Exploring Corpora for ESP Learning* [Studies in Corpus Linguistics 21]. Amsterdam: John Benjamins.

Gavioli, L. & Zanettin, F. 2000. I corpora biiingui nell'apprendimento della traduzione.

In *I corpora nella didattica della traduzione: Corpus Use and Learning to Translate*, S. Bernardini & F. Zanettin (eds), 61–80. *Bologna: CLUEB.*

Gilquin, G. & Gries, St. Th. 2009. Corpora and experimental methods: A state-of-the-art review. *Corpus Linguistics and Linguistic Theory* 5(1): 1–26.

Grabe, W. 2002. Applied linguistics: An emerging discipline for the 21st century. In *The Oxford Handbook of Applied Linguistics,* R. B. Kaplan (ed.), 3–12. Oxford: OUP.

Granger, S., Lerot, J. & Petch-Tyson, S. (eds). 2003. *Corpus-Based Approaches to Contrastive Linguistics and Translation Studies.* Amsterdam: Rodopi.

Greaves, C. 2009. *ConcGram 1.0: A Phraseological Search Engine* [Studies in Corpus Linguistics Software 1]. Amsterdam: John Benjamins.

Greenbaum, S. 1991. The development of the International Corpus of English. In *English Corpus Linguistics. Studies in Honour of Jan Svartvik,* K. Aijmer & B. Altenberg (eds), 83–91. London: Longman.

Halliday, M. A. K. 1991. Corpus studies and probabilistic grammar. In *English Corpus Linguistics. Studies in Honour of Jan Svartvik,* K. Aijmer & B. Altenberg (eds). London: Longman.

Hatim, B. 2001. *Teaching and Researching Translation.* London: Pearson Education.

Hoey, M. 2005. *Lexical Priming: A New Theory of Words and Language.* London: Routledge.

Hunston, S. 2002. *Corpora in Applied Linguistics.* Cambridge: CUP.

Hunston, S. & Francis, G. 1999. *Pattern Grammar: A Corpus-Driven Approach to the Lexical Grammar of English* [Studies in Corpus Linguistics 4]. Amsterdam: John Benjamins.

Jääskeläinen, R. 2004. The fate of 'The Families of Medellín': Tampering with a potential translation universals in the translation classroom. In *Translation Universals: Do they Exist?* [Benjamins Translation Library 48], A. Mauranen & P. Kujamäki (eds), 205–214. Amsterdam: John Benjamins.

Jääskeläinen, R. & Mauranen, A. 2005. Translators at work: A case study of electronic tools used by translators in industry. In *Meaningful Texts: The Extraction of Semantic Information from Monolingual and Multilingual Corpora,* G. Barnbrook, P. Danielsson & M. Mahlberg (eds), 48–53. London: Continuum.

Johansson, S., Leech, G. N. & Goodluck, H. 1978. *Manual of Information to Accompany the Lancaster-Oslo/Bergen Corpus of British English, for Use with Digital Computers.* Oslo: Department of English, Oslo University. <http://khnt.hit.uib.no/icame/manuals/lob/index.htm> (20 May, 2009).

Johns, T. 1991. Should you persuaded: Two examples of data-driven learning. *ELR Journal* 4: 1–16.

Kelly, D. 2005. *A Handbook for Translator Trainers.* Manchester: St. Jerome.

Kennedy, G. 1998. *An Introduction to Corpus Linguistics*. London: Longman.

Kenny, D. 2001. *Lexis and Creativity*. Manchester: St. Jerome.

Kenny, D. 2005. Parallel corpora and translation studies: Old questions, new perspectives? Reporting *that* in GEPCOLT: A case study. In *Meaningful Texts: The Extraction of Semantic Information from Monolingual and Multilingual Corpora*, G. Barnbrook, P. Danielsson & M. Mahlberg (eds), 154–165. London: Continuum.

Kenny, D. 2009. Corpora. In *Routledge Encyclopedia of Translation Studies*, 2nd edn, M. Baker & G. Saldanha (eds), 59–62. London: Routledge.

Kiraly, D. C. 2003. From instruction to collaborative construction: A passing fad or the promise of a paradigm shift in translator education? In *Beyond the Ivory Tower: Rethinking Translation Pedagogy* [ATA Scholarly Monograph Series XII], B. J. Baer & G. S. Koby (eds), 3–27. Amsterdam: John Benjamins.

Kress, G. R. & van Leeuwen, T. 1996. *Reading Images: The Grammar of Visual Design*. London: Routledge.

Kress, G. R. & van Leeuwen, T. 2001. *Multimodal Discourse: The Modes and Media of Contemporary Communication*. London: Arnold.

Kruger, A. (ed.). 2004. *Corpus-Based Translation Studies: Research and Applications. Language Matters* 35(1). (Special issue).

Kujamäki, P. 2004. What happens to 'unique items' in learners' translations? 'Theories' and 'concepts' as a challenge for novices' views on 'good translation'. In *Translation Universals: Do they Exist?* [Benjamins Translation Library 48], A. Mauranen & P. Kujamäki (eds), 187–204. Amsterdam: John Benjamins.

Laviosa, S. 2006. Data-Driven learning for translating Anglicisms in business communication. *IEEE Transactions on Professional Communication* 49(3): 267–274.

Lederer, M. 2007. Can theory help interpreter and translator trainers and trainees? *The Interpreter and Translator Trainer* 1(1): 15–35.

Leech, G. N. 1991. The state of the art in Corpus Linguistics. In *English Corpus Linguistics. Studies in Honour of Jan Svartvik*, K. Aijmer & B. Altenberg (eds), 8–29. London: Longman.

Leech, G. N. 1992. Corpora and theories of linguistic performance. In *Directions in Corpus Linguistics. Proceedings of Nobel Symposium 82, Stockholm, 4–8 August 1991*, J. Svartvik (ed.), 105–122. Berlin: Mouton de Gruyter.

Leech, G. N. 2002. Corpora. In *The Linguistics Encyclopedia*, 2nd edn, K. Malmkjaer (ed.), 84–93. London: Routledge.

Leeson, L. 2009. Signed language interpreting. In *Routledge Encyclopedia of Translation Studies*, 2nd edn, M. Baker & G. Saldanha (eds.), 274–279. London: Routledge.

Malmkjaer, K. 2002. History of grammar. In *The Linguistics Encyclopedia*, 2nd edn, K. Malmkjaer (ed.), 247–263. London: Routledge.

Mauranen, A. & Kujamäki, P. (eds). 2004. *Translation Universals: Do they Exist?* [Benjamins Translation Library 48]. Amsterdam: John Benjamins.

McEnery, A. & Wilson, A. 1996. *Corpus Linguistics*. Edinburgh: EUP.

McEnery, A., Xiao, R. & Tono, Y. 2006. *Corpus-Based Language Studies. An Advanced Resource Book*. London: Routledge.

Mollin, S. 2009. Combining corpus linguistic and psychological data on word co-occurrences: Corpus collocates versus word associations. *Corpus Linguistics and Linguistic Theory* 5(2): 175–200.

Nuccorini, S. 2008. 'Phraseologies' and Italian-English dictionaries: Evidence for a proposal. In *Investigating English with Corpora. Studies in Honour of Maria Teresa Prat*, A. Martelli & V. Pulcini (eds), 171–187. Polimetrica: Monza.

O'Hagan, M. 2009. Computer-Aided translation (CAT). In *Routledge Encyclopedia of Translation Studies*, 2nd edn, M. Baker & G. Saldanha (eds), 48–51. London: Routledge.

Olohan, M. 2004. *Introducing Corpora in Translation Studies*. London: Routledge.

Olohan, M. 2007. Economic trends and developments in the translation industry. *The Interpreter and Translator Trainer* 1(1): 37–63.

Øveras, L. 1998. In search of the third code: An investigation of norms in literary translation. In *L'Approche Baseé sur le Corpus. The Corpus-Based Approach*, S. Laviosa (ed.), 571–588. *Meta* 43(4). Special issue). <http://www.erudit.org/revue/meta/> (20 May, 2009).

Ping, K. 2009. Machine translation. In *Routledge Encyclopedia of Translation Studies*, 2nd edn, M. Baker & G. Saldanha (eds), 162–169. London: Routledge.

Pulcini, V. 2008. Corpora and lexicography: The case of a dictionary of anglicisms. In *Investigating English with Corpora: Studies in Honour of Maria Teresa Prat*, A. Martelli & V. Pulcini (eds), 189–203. Milano: Polimetrica.

Quah, C. K. 2006. *Translation and Technology*. Houndmills: Palgrave Macmillan.

Robinson, D. 2003. Cyborg translation. In *Translation Translation*, S. Petrilli (ed.), 369–386. Amsterdam: Rodopi.

Scarpa, F. 2008. *La Traduzione Specializzata: Un Approccio Didattico Professionale*. Milano: Hoepli.

Shlesinger, M. 1998. Corpus-Based interpreting studies as an off-shoot of corpus-based translation studies. In *L'Approche Baseé sur le Corpus. The Corpus-Based Approach*, S. Laviosa (ed.), 486–493. *Meta* 43(4). (Special issue). <http://www.erudit.org/revue/meta/> (20 May, 2009).

Siemund, P. & Kintana, N. (eds). 2008. *Language Contact and Contact Languages* [Hamburg Studies in Multilingualism 7]. Amsterdam: John Benjamins.

Sinclair, J. M. 1987. *Looking Up*. London: Collins.

Sinclair, J. M. 1991. *Corpus Concordance Collocation*. Oxford: OUP.

Sinclair, J. M. 2003. *Reading Concordances*. London: Pearson Education.

Sinclair, J. M. 2005. Corpus and text – Basic principles. In *Developing Linguistic Corpora: A Guide to Good Practice,* M. Wynne (ed.), 1–16. Oxford: Oxbow Books. <http://ahds.ac.uk/linguistic-corpora/> (20 May, 2009).

Sinclair, J. M. 2008. Borrowed ideas. In *Language, People, Numbers: Corpus Linguistics and Society*, A. Gerbig & O. Mason (eds), 21–41. Amsterdam: Rodopi.

Sinclair, J. M. & Teubert, W. 2004. Interview with John Sinclair conducted by Wolfgang Teubert. In *English Collocation Studies: The OSTI Report. John M. Sinclair, Susan Jones and Robert Daley*, R. Krishnamurthy (ed.), xvii–xxix. London: Continuum.

Stewart, D. 2000. Conventionality, creativity, and translated text: The implications of electronic corpora in translation. In *Intercultural Faultlines. Research Models in Translation Studies 1: Textual and Cognitive Aspects*, M. Olohan (ed.), 73–91. Manchester: St. Jerome.

Stubbs, M. 1996. *Text and Corpus Analysis: Computer-Assisted Studies of Language and Culture*. Oxford: Blackwell.

Tognini-Bonelli, E. 2001. *Corpus Linguistics at Work* [Studies in Corpus Linguistics 6]. Amsterdam: John Benjamins.

Tognini-Bonelli, E. 2002. Functionally complete units of meaning across English and Italian. In *Lexis in Contrast: Corpus-Based Approaches*, B. Altenberg & S. Granger (eds), 73–95. Amsterdam: John Benjamins.

Tymoczko, M. 1998. Computerised corpora and the future of translation studies. In *L'Approche Baseé sur le Corpus. The Corpus-Based Approach*, S. Laviosa (ed.), 652–659. *Meta* 43(4). (Special issue). <http://www.erudit.org/revue/meta/> (20 May, 2009).

Ulrych, M. 2005. Training translators: Programmes, curricula, practices. In *Training for the New Millennium* [Benjamins Translation Library 60], M. Tennent (ed.), 3–33. Amsterdam: John Benjamins.

Vandeweghe, W., Vandepitte, S. & Van de Velde, M. (eds). 2007. *The Study of Language and Translation. Belgian Journal of Linguistics* (21). (Special issue).

Vintar, S. 2008. Corpora in translator training and practice: A Slovene perspective. In *Incorporating Corpora: The Linguist and the Translator*, G. Anderman & M. Rogers (eds), 153–167. Clevedon: Multilingual Matters.

Widdowson, H. 2000. The limitations of linguistics applied. *Applied Linguistics* 21(1): 3–25.

Zanettin, F. 2008. Parallel corpora in literary translation theory and practice. In *Literary Translation and Beyond/Traduzione letteraria e oltre: La traduzione come negoziazione dell'alterità,* R. Mallardi (ed.), 275–301. Bern: Peter Lang.

Zanettin, F., Bernardini, S. & Stewart, D. (eds). 2003. *Corpora in Translator Education*. Manchester: St. Jerome.

Principles and applications of Corpus Linguistics

Professor Emeritus of English Linguistics at Lancaster University (United Kingdom), Geoffrey Leech raises several points about Corpus Linguistics *per se* in a thought-provoking way. As far as the historical perspective is concerned, he indicates whom he considers the founding fathers of this field and justifies his choices. When writing about representativeness, he argues that the suffix '-ity' is better suited for this term when compared to '-ness'. This is because 'representativity' would allow for a continuum in which corpora could be classified as more (or less) representative of a (specific use of a) language. A corpus linguist at heart, Leech sees no drawbacks in this approach, but rather credits any shortcomings to the way it is put into practice. In terms of applications, Leech discusses his research experience in approaching both pragmatics and style by means of corpora.

1. Where do you place the roots of Corpus Linguistics? And to what do you attribute the growth of interest in the area?

I think for this purpose we can quickly pass over precursors from the pre-electronic era, people mentioned, for example, in early chapters of Kennedy's (1998) and McEnery and Wilson's (2001) introductions to Corpus Linguistics. I include here great people like Samuel Johnson and Otto Jespersen – who systematically collected the data of language in use in order to write dictionaries, grammars and the like. I would like to focus instead on two pioneers of modern Corpus Linguistics (although the term was not used at that time), Randolph Quirk and Nelson Francis, and the key dates are 1959 (when Quirk started his Survey of English Usage) and 1962 (when Francis, aided by Henry Kučera, started to collect the Brown Corpus). These two scholars both hit on the idea of collecting a large body of texts (and transcriptions) wide-ranging enough to represent, to a reasonable extent, the contemporary English language. In this, they must have been considerably influenced by the American structuralist school of the 1940s and 1950s, which placed fundamental emphasis on the need for a corpus of any language to be investigated. But such corpora as were collected during that era tended to be on a relatively small scale [for example, the corpus of spoken American English used by Charles C. Fries (1952)], and were not made available to the academic community at large. I suggest that there are two defining goals that made Quirk and Francis founding fathers of modern Corpus Linguistics:

a. That someone giving an account of a language should aim at what Quirk (1960: 49–54; Svartvik & Quirk 1980: 9) called 'total accountability': that is, all relevant data obtainable should be taken into account, not just the examples that the investigator finds useful or congenial.
b. That a corpus, compiled in the spirit of offering total accountability, should be made available as a resource for the world of scholarship at large.

Notice that I made no mention of computers. Francis did create the first computerised corpus of English, and it became increasingly clear through the seventies and eighties that the computer, with its power of storing, searching and processing linguistic data, was the essential empowering tool of Corpus Linguistics. But Quirk's Survey of English Usage (SEU) corpus was originally not computerised: it was stored on paper in cumbersome metal cabinets in a large room in University College London, where scholars were encouraged to come and consult and analyse the data manually – as many leading scholars of English did during the last four decades of the 20th century. Later it was converted to electronic form by Svartvik and Greenbaum; but those who wonder why Quirk avoided the computer – though he embraced the technology of the modern tape recorder – should recall that the main focus of his research in the 60s was on spoken English – for which the computer was so far of little use – whereas Francis, in those early days making pioneering use of primitive computing facilities, took the only practicable route, in compiling a computer corpus of *written* language.

I have emphasised these *resource-driven* beginnings of Corpus Linguistics: for both Quirk and Francis, the corpus building was the initial goal, and from that resource, which could be used by many, an enormous wealth of research projects, many not foreseen by its originators, would develop. A second origin of Corpus Linguistics can be described as *research-driven*. I believe this term fittingly applies to the beginning of Corpus Linguistics at Birmingham under John Sinclair, as documented in Sinclair et al. (2004). Here there was a prior research problem – how to investigate the lexical structure of collocation – which required the collection and quantitative analysis of a large amount of data of language use – and so the collection of data logically followed the problem it was designed to solve. Sinclair was reluctant to use the term 'corpus', referring to his first large-scale corpus-building programme as the 'Birmingham collection of English texts'. Later, when he collaborated with the publishers Collins on the COBUILD project in the 1980s, the corpus (by now vastly outstripping the early corpora in size) became a proprietary resource to be used – among other things – for creating usage-based dictionaries. The corpus was never distributed to the world of scholarship as the Brown and SEU corpora were. These two origins gave rise to distinct research traditions and cultures which are still distinguishable at the present day, although there is now much interchange between them.

The growth of interest in Corpus Linguistics was initially very slow, but has more recently grown exponentially. With the enormous increase in computational power, capacity has gone a vast expansion of corpus resources – not only corpora, but software and 'dataware' of various kinds – which have made it progressively more difficult to ignore what can be done with computers and corpora. Recognising the uses of corpora in linguistics has required the overturning of a powerful ideological orthodoxy: the Chomskyan paradigm which held (and still holds) that corpora, and the frequency data they provide, are virtually useless in linguistics. This has bit-by-bit been giving ground to the usage-based paradigm found, for example, in construction grammar, in cognitive linguistics and in phraseological studies. Frequencies and probabilities have become integrated with linguistic thinking again. A 'tipping point' in the acceptability of corpus-based research was probably reached in the early 1990s, when computational linguistics embraced corpora as the automated analysis of large quantities of text data started to make serious impact on the development of speech recognition, machine-aided translation, and other natural language processing tasks. Here again, *total accountability* was the key advantage of corpus-based methods. A machine-aided translation or speech recognition system needs to cope with any piece of text or discourse it meets, and this can only be achieved if the system has experience – through corpora – of the widest possible range of naturally occurring utterances.

2. Is Corpus Linguistics a science or a methodology? Where would you situate Corpus Linguistics in the scientific or methodological panorama?

'Corpus Linguistics' is a convenient umbrella term for linguistic research that depends on the use of corpora. But the coiner of the term 'Corpus Linguistics' in the early 1980s, Jan Aarts (see Johansson 2009: 34), was hesitant in using the term, and many others have been less than happy with it. Perhaps it misleadingly suggests a subdiscipline, comparable with sociolinguistics, psycholinguistics, forensic linguistics, clinical linguistics and the like, dealing with a particular interdisciplinary application of linguistics. It has often been noted, however, that Corpus Linguistics can combine with any such subfield: a corpus can be used as a source of data in syntax, lexis, pragmatics, sociolinguistics, psycholinguistics, and virtually every branch of language study. Moreover, the wide umbrella of 'Corpus Linguistics' can cover anything from the casual use of a corpus to obtain a suitable authentic illustration of some linguistic phenomenon to the development of general corpus-based or corpus-driven models of how language works.

Corpus Linguistics is not a methodology pure and simple, but is more like a methodology than a scientific domain. Using a corpus has led to the development of a growing collection of computer tools for searching, retrieving, annotating, and analysing electronic text data: concordancers, taggers, parsers and so forth. It is from these tools, as much as from the availability of abundant text data, that Corpus Linguistics has derived its special character and its unprecedented power to reveal the characteristics of real language use. From this point of view, then, Corpus Linguistics is a methodologically-oriented branch of linguistics.

That said, it should also be noted that Corpus Linguistics has implications for the theoretical conception of linguistics as a science. Tools and the technologies associated with them (like the Hubble telescope in physics and astronomy) can revolutionise science. It is arguable that the electronic corpus and its associated toolkit have been revolutionising linguistic science, by empowering us to do things with linguistic data that no one could have dreamed of fifty years ago, opening up the potential for a new empiricism in linguistics. Before the first electronic corpus was created, statistical models of language that made use of frequency of occurrence were unavoidably simplistic – even though conceived by brilliant minds (Zipf, Shannon).

After that, Chomsky's (1962) wholesale rejection of frequency marginalised statistical approaches to language for a generation, but since the 1980s, models of language (cognitive linguistics, construction grammar, usage-based theories) as well as theories of language learning and language change (in the study of grammaticalisation, for instance) have rediscovered a growing role for frequency. These developments have happened outside Corpus Linguistics (although increasingly involving the use of corpora), and meanwhile, within Corpus Linguistics, probabilistic language models building on frequency and co-frequency have become increasingly sophisticated. So a corpus-based approach, which began methodologically, is increasingly becoming central to much that is innovative in linguistic thinking, with far-reaching implications for how language works in the mind, as well as how it works in communicative use.

3. How representative can a corpus be?

Well, how long is a piece of string? A useful definition of *representativeness* is provided by Manning and Schütze (1999: 119): a sample is representative if what we find for the sample also holds for the general population. If we replace 'sample' by 'corpus' and 'population' by 'language', we see the difficulty of determining whether what is found to be true of a corpus can be extrapolated to the language as a whole. We cannot (in general) study the whole language in terms of use, so we are left with the problem of ensuring that the corpus is as representative a sample of the language (or language variety) as possible.

When I first started drafting this answer, I began by describing representativeness as the Achilles' heel of Corpus Linguistics. Afterwards, I changed 'Achilles' heel' to 'Holy Grail', to sound a rather more positive note – representativeness is something we are optimistically looking for, but may never exactly find. In this respect it is like truth. Very rarely can complete representativeness, like complete truth, be attained. What we can do, though, is work towards greater *representativity*. I prefer to use this term (Leech 2007: 140) to denote a scalar concept (one corpus being *more* representative or *less* representative than another), rather than 'representativeness', which tends to suggest an all-or-nothing quality.

If a corpus is a sample of language in use, then obviously the language (the 'population') of which it is a sample has also to be considered as consisting of language in use – language as performance, rather than competence. A general corpus of English in the year 2000 should be considered a sample of all utterances/texts that were produced in English at that time. But this is a mindbogglingly impractical population to measure a corpus against, and in practice the 'population' of which the corpus is a sample is defined not just as being in a particular language, but as being circumscribed by parameters of language variety. For example, the Brown Corpus was designed to be a sample of *written American* English published in the year *1961.*

It is probably uncontroversial that the bigger a corpus is and the greater the variety of text types (genres, registers) it contains, the greater its representativity. However, this is not sufficient. We have also to consider the *quantity* of particular varieties that must be contained in a corpus of a given size: how a corpus can become 'balanced' by including appropriate proportions of different text types. This is the issue of proportionality: the proportion of a text type in a corpus should ideally equate with the proportion of that text type in the population as a whole. The one-million-word Brown Corpus contains c. 88,000 words of newspaper reportage and c. 12,000 words of science fiction writing. We may feel satisfied that the news report genre is a bigger, more important category than science fiction, and that this proportion of 88,000 to 12,000 is intuitively reasonable. But how would we demonstrate this, and how can we determine the right quantities more precisely? The most likely answer to this would be to find a library with a classification of all the publications in the US in the year 1961, and replicate the proportions found there in the Brown Corpus.

Biber (1993) rejected proportionality as a means to achieving representativeness, because this would, he argued, lead to a highly skewed sample of the language. Since about 90 per cent of all linguistic usage is ordinary private conversation (an estimate less convincing now than it was), the corpus would consist largely of conversational data, and some important genres, such as the language of statutes, or of the inaugural addresses of American presidents, would have scarcely no existence in the corpus. However, my position is that we should rather concentrate on the *addressee*'s end of the message, rather than the *addresser*'s, in calculating the proportions of usage. The author of a message is normally an individual, whereas the number of receivers can vary from one individual to many million individuals (in the case of a popular newspaper or a TV broadcast). The number of receivers a message has provides a reasonable way of determining its importance. If this position is adopted, a radio news bulletin listened to by a million people deserves to be in a corpus sample a million times more than a conversation between two private individuals. The conclusion is that the design of a general corpus should ideally be built on extensive language reception research (see Čermák 1997 on the Czech National Corpus). This does not, however, solve our problem of representativeness – it is difficult to obtain precise information on the number of readers of a written text, or the number of listeners to a spoken discourse. But the receiver-centred view of representativity gives us a conceptually sound model for defining a 'balanced corpus', and where we have no precise figures (which is very often), we can do our best by relying on estimates. The Holy Grail of complete representativeness is still far away, but we can aim to achieve better coverage of genres and better approximations to proportionality. As a sample of written American English, the Brown Corpus may not be entirely representative, but it is better than a million words of the *Wall Street Journal*, for instance.

4. How far should an analyst rely on intuition?

The term 'intuition' applies to two kinds of knowledge available to the human analyst. One is something that used to be called 'native speaker's intuition', although – especially for an international language like English – I would say that a non-native speaker's intuition can be as reliable as, or sometimes better than, a native speaker's. This 'intuition' is our implicit, operational knowledge of what the language is like, which can be retrieved up to a point by introspection. A second kind of intuition is the explicit, analytic knowledge of a language that an analyst has, but which is often lacking in native speakers. Confronted with a corpus, the corpus linguist can use both kinds of knowledge to make sense of the data. This is how we do what is called 'qualitative analysis'. In Corpus Linguistics, there needs to be a partnership between both types of intuition, both focusing on the observational evidence of corpora.

The question of 'how far we should rely on intuition' comes to the fore particularly when we ask whether our intuition can overrule the data in the corpus. Where corpus and intuition conflict, I believe that there is a certain trade-off of plausibility. A single instance of an aberrant feature in a large corpus can be set aside as not part of the language: it might be a mistake, a typo, a slip of the tongue or the pen. On the other hand, a set of aberrant examples, especially if occurring systematically, even though in small numbers, may be sufficient to outweigh the analyst's intuition. This might attest, for example, a genuine dialect feature with which the analyst is not familiar. In general, a corpus linguist will have a strong predilection in favour of what is attested in a corpus. But users of the BNC or (even more) of the 'Web as Corpus', will be familiar with fair sprinklings of errors due to dysfluency, hasty or inexpert transcription, spontaneous unedited writing, and so on.

5. What kind of questions should an analyst think of?

Typical questions are:

a. Does the corpus data provide a suitable, adequate sample of what I want to investigate?

b. Can I extrapolate from this corpus to some general conclusions about this or that variety of some language(s)?

c. Concerning some linguistic phenomenon of interest X, what significant differences of frequency of X are observed in different subdivisions of corpus C? What contextual factors are associated with these differences?

d. In comparing parallel/comparable corpora or subcorpora C and D, what significant differences of frequency of X are observed, and what contextual factors are associated with them?

e. What functional or qualitative explanations can be offered for the frequency patterns observed in answering questions (c) or (d)?

The above questions follow a bottom-up methodology, starting with the data and working towards abstractions, generalisations and tentative explanations. The opposite top-down methodology may then be employed, following the cyclic inductive-deductive method, in trying to confirm or refine the findings resulting from questions (a) to (e). Or, in contrast, we can start with the top-down method, beginning with an abstract hypothesis, and work down to the data. I know of no way of determining in advance what questions people will want to ask at this abstract level. They may be questions prompted by a particular theoretical position. In Corpus Linguistics, the only requirement is that such questions should be capable of being answered by observing what is attested in corpus data. Obviously, for example, questions about the psycholinguistic processing of languages or their social or cultural interrelations cannot be directly resolved by corpus analysis, although corpus data may well contribute to their solution. The beauty of a corpus is that it places no prior constraints on the imagination or curiosity of the investigator. Any question within the domain of language use or performance may be asked: but we may not find it easy to get the answer, and – fortunately rather than unfortunately – we may not get the answer we are expecting.

6. What are the strengths and weaknesses of corpus analysis?

The main strength of corpus analysis is that the descriptive generalisations, hypotheses, or theories one makes about a language are based on, and answerable to, the empirical evidence of (appropriately sampled) language use. The strength of this position can best be shown by comparing it with the influential rejection of corpus data by Chomsky and the generativist linguists who followed him.

a. The opposition between the all-sufficient corpus of the American structuralists of the 1950s and the all-sufficient intuitions of the generative linguists who succeeded them from 1957 onwards is a false opposition, ignoring intermediate positions. The corpus linguist uses *both corpus data and intuition*. This is necessary if we are both to observe and to understand the nature of language.

b. The generativist's reliance on the native speaker's intuition begs a question about the analysis of language by non-native-speaking scholars. Such analysts often have knowledge and reliable intuitions about what is possible in a language, and, especially in the context of present-day worldwide use of English, it is artificial to restrict information about a language to that provided by native speakers. It is no coincidence that English Corpus Linguistics has flourished in countries where a tradition of English studies is very strong, but where English is not a native language – in Germany, Sweden and Japan, for instance. Once again, it must be emphasised that corpus analysis relies both on the concrete evidence of language use and the insight, intuition and understanding that the corpus analyst (not necessarily a native speaker) brings to the task.

c. The generativist's reliance on 'intuition' required the positing of an 'ideal native speaker/hearer' who speaks an invariant variety of the language in question (Chomsky 1965). But sociolinguistics and other usage-oriented branches of linguistics have highlighted the *variability* of the competences of different native speaker dialects or idiolects. As the non-uniformity of a language is widely accepted as self-evident, it is clear that the native speaker's knowledge of that language is bound to be incomplete, whether in terms of register, dialect or diachrony. Corpus Linguistics accepts this non-uniformity, and provides the tools to investigate it, compiling corpora and subcorpora representing different varieties of the language (e.g. the differences between spoken and written English have been brilliantly illuminated by corpus analysis).

d. The principle of *total accountability* is an important strength of corpus analysis. Studies of corpora bring to light phenomena that cannot be neatly accommodated by intuition-based generalisations or categories. These often occur systematically and cannot be rejected as performance errors. Rather, they invite analysis in terms of non-deterministic models of language, accepting that linguistic phenomena do not always have neat boundaries, but can be characterised by prototype effects, gradients, or fuzzy categories. From this point of view, reliance on the linguist's intuition unsupported by corpus evidence is suspect, as it is likely to discover only clear-cut, prototypical examples to back up a generalisation, or, in contrast, to find unrealistic counterexamples for which a corpus would provide no authentic support.

e. Corpora provide *frequency information*, which is typically difficult or impossible to obtain from other sources. This is a matter of growing importance to linguistic theory and to the study of linguistic processes such as acquisition and change.

The *weakness*es of Corpus Linguistics? I do not see any weaknesses in Corpus Linguistics *per se*, although there are certainly some in the ways it has been practised. Perhaps we should talk more of weaknesses in the *application* of Corpus Linguistics.

a. One source of misuse is in the tempting assumption that corpora provide the only kind of observable evidence linguists need in order to carry on their trade. Other kinds of evidence can be important – especially the evidence of intuition and the evidence of elicited data (for example in fieldwork or in psycholinguistic testing) which have their own spheres of validity, and can tap cognitive sources of information inaccessible to Corpus Linguistics.[1]

b. Another complaint about Corpus Linguistics is that it tends to be concerned with low-level descriptive facts about particular languages, whereas for many linguists, the high-level abstract universals of language are most significant. Again, I would argue that to some extent this impression is due

---

1 In brief, corpora yield performance data, while elicitation yields cognitive (competence) data. These are often mutually confirmatory, but, for example, the frequency phenomena provided by a corpus do not necessarily correspond closely with the prototype information to which elicitation experiments can give access. On this and related issues, see Gries et al. (2005) and Gilquin (2007).

to inadequate use of corpus methods: there has been a lack of ambition on the part of corpus linguists to engage with theory, but this is being overcome. One sign of this is the journal *Corpus Linguistics and Linguistic Theory*.

c. Most corpora furnish an impoverished picture of the speech events or written texts they contain. This arises from two sources. The first, which applies especially to corpora of spoken discourse, is poverty of contextual information. Audiovisual corpora, which provide a video record combined with an auditory record of the speech event, are beginning to overcome part of this problem, but are obviously more costly and problematic to create than purely textual renderings of discourse. Again, a prosodic transcription of discourse, with built-in pause, intonation and stress phenomena is an advantage in telling us not just *what* was said, but *how* it was said. However, it is all too common for spoken language corpora to be transcribed rather simplistically as an orthographic record, simply because of the difficulty of providing the alternative. An orthographic record, of speech as well as of writing, imposes its own limited perspective on the text, divided it into words through white-space word boundaries. Hence the typical window on to a corpus – a concordance based on plain orthographic text – is seriously limiting as a representation of a spoken discourse.

d. At the same time, there is a lack of the deeper analysis that can be provided by annotation. The most frequent form of annotation – POS-tagging – is the most simplistic, whereas parsing, semantic analysis, anaphoric annotation, etc. would provide much more.[2] The lack of these kinds of analytic information about the text in practice tends to restrict investigations to those kinds of phenomena that can be retrieved without them – lexical studies and simple word-based grammatical studies above all. Without doubt, these can be very revealing, but only give us a partial viewpoint on the multi-levelled nature of language.

---

2 Some parsed corpora do exist, and enable one to retrieve from the corpus more abstract syntactic phenomena such as topicalisation, zero relativisation, gapping and inversion. But these are in the minority. Examples are the Penn Treebank (Marcus et al. 1993) and the ICE-GB Corpus (Nelson et al. 2002).

7. What is the future of Corpus Linguistics?

Of course, this is speculation. But one can observe certain trends, and certain problems that have to be addressed.

a. One obvious point: there are many languages so far untouched by Corpus Linguistics. For most of the world's 6,000-odd languages there is no computer corpus. For others, there is much work to be done. In this scenario, there is little danger of corpus linguists running out of new material to study!

b. For languages that have already been studied in some depth using corpus methods, the availability of electronic textual data has mushroomed: there is no need, perhaps, for the painstaking assembly of textual data such as was undertaken in the early days of the Brown and LOB Corpora. But other areas of data collection are still far behind: spoken data and manuscript data still have to be collected in sufficient quantity, quality and variety. There is need to go beyond the simplistic transcription methods which have too often been employed – for economic reasons – on spoken corpora. Prosodic transcription has made surprisingly little progress recently, simply because it is a painstaking and highly-skilled activity which costs too much money and time. Perhaps there will be a breakthrough when automatic speech recognition is sufficiently advanced.

c. In other respects, too, we need more richly transcribed, marked-up and annotated corpora. Corpus parsing is a big log-jam that needs to be shifted. Multimedia and multimodal corpora are beginning to develop, and are likely to become a big area in the future. Other levels of annotation – semantic, pragmatic, discoursal – will probably develop much more than at present. The difficulty with all these plans for the analytic enrichment of corpora is that they mostly involve (at present) a great deal of tedious work with little reward (and little financial support). Until further breakthroughs are made in automated transcription and annotation, corpus linguists will tend to accept existing levels of resource, relying on the vast quantities of minimally-annotated machine-readable written text, which will mean ignoring many of the most challenging areas of investigation.

d. One scenario is that Corpus Linguistics, as a separate area of linguistics, will simply melt away, as a sub-branch of linguistics, because using corpora will be the most obvious natural way to do linguistics. Also the notion of a finite corpus like the BNC will fade away, as people become used to relying on the world-wide web as a virtually limitless corpus,[3] and full-text databases. The special technologies developed within Corpus Linguistics will spread more generally, and a linguist who does not use corpora will be like a psychologist who does not use statistics. But I still believe that the more interesting challenges of Corpus Linguistics lie in achieving more sophisticated methods of analysis, rather than in exploiting the copiousness of data.

8. In what ways can corpus analysis help pragmatic understanding of language use?

My interest in pragmatics and my interest in corpora developed independently of one another, and have only overlapped once. This was in 2000–2002 when, with Martin Weisser, I undertook dialogue-act (speech-act) annotation of corpora of service dialogues (e.g. the Trainline corpus of train ticketing dialogues between a call centre and customers). This was an interesting project, which showed how semi-automatic pragmatic annotation could be undertaken with considerable success, in cases where a spoken corpus represents 'well-behaved' task-oriented dialogue.

However, the annotation algorithm was heavily dependent on routinised or quasi-formulaic dialogue strategies, e.g. discourse markers such as *Yeah, Right, Thanks*, etc., and opening moves such as *Could I ... ? Would you mind if ... ?* For more complex and variable dialogue situations such as one meets in general conversation, such algorithms were found to be less successful.

For deeper probing of the communicative goals of interactants in real dialogue, corpora tend to be impoverished through lack of depth in contextual information. Yet a further drawback is that any inventory of dialogue acts misrepresents pragmatic reality by drawing clear-cut boundaries between speech act categories. Indeterminacy, in practice, is a fundamental part of pragmatic behaviour and interpretation.

While I cannot envisage a time when pragmatic analysis of corpora will provide all the answers, I believe that corpora will continue to be useful for investigating the meaning and frequency of particular pragmatic strategies.

---

3 The world-wide web can be regarded as a corpus of virtually limitless size and unprecedented ease of access. Unlike other corpora, however, it lacks 'quality control', and there appears to be no way of determining its contents and the filtering mechanisms of the search engines by which access is provided. The pros and cons of the Web as Corpus are explored at length in Hundt et al. (2007).

Other methods of data collection, such as DCTs, role-plays, and the like, although they have the advantage of eliciting precise responses to given stimuli, all suffer in large measure from lack of spontaneity and authenticity. These qualities are an important 'plus' for corpus pragmatics.

9. How can style be accounted for (semi-)automatically by means of corpus investigation?

As with pragmatics, so with stylistics: my interests in these fields developed totally independently of corpus-based research. In the last two or three years, however, I have begun to bring my corpus work and my stylistic interest together, and to help others (such as my Lancaster colleagues Mick Short and Elena Semino) to open up the new field of *corpus stylistics*.

I can report two methods of investigating style with corpora. One method studies the change of style over time. I have engaged in a study of style extending over the period 1931–1991, using the exactly comparable corpora of the Brown family. Nick Smith and I (in collaboration with Marianne Hundt and Christian Mair – see Leech et al. 2009) investigated a number of general stylistic trends in written English, including *colloquialisation* (the ongoing diachronic process by which written language tends to adopt the habits of speech – e.g. in the increasing use of contractions like *don't* and *it's*) and *densification* (the process of achieving more compact expression of meaning, for example by using noun + noun sequences instead of more wordy equivalents – e.g. *patient behaviour* instead of *the behaviour of the patient*). In this type of study, we find the same trends evidenced by significant increase or decrease of frequency across the whole range of text types in the Brown family corpora. These are, in other words, general stylistic trends, showing changing norms of style in written English.

Another method uses the stylistic norms provided by a reference corpus such as the Brown Corpus as a standard against which to measure the 'differentness' of a text from the norm. Paul Rayson's programme Wmatrix automatically identifies the *key words* which make a chosen text most different from the norm, and also carries out a similar comparison to determine POS-tags and semantic tags which are likewise '*key*' in being most strongly characteristic of the text. The text I chose for this purpose was Virginia Woolf's 'The Mark on the Wall' (see Leech 2008). Arguably these three levels of analysis can give a deeper appreciation of the characteristic stylistic features of a text than would be provided by the purely lexical 'keyword' model that is familiar in the work of Mike Scott and others (see Scott & Tribble 2006). But as elsewhere, the lack of sufficient automatic 'intelligent identification' of stylistic features (through parsing, for example) so far limits the usefulness of the technique. Nevertheless, I would argue that an important start has been made in the identification of significant features and changes of style by corpus linguistic methods.

10. What are the advantages and shortcomings of annotating a corpus from a linguistic perspective?

Annotation is a general term for the adding to a corpus of additional linguistic information – such as part-of-speech (POS) tags identifying the word class of each word token in the corpus. I will begin to answer this question with a disclaimer. We should always remember that the corpus and the annotation are logically separate, and it is a cardinal principle of annotation that it should always be possible to separate the corpus and the annotated material. Hence the argument that the annotation of the corpus somehow 'tampers with' or vitiates the corpus in its pure form is largely groundless – I say 'largely', because there are exceptions. When we undertook the tagging of the LOB Corpus in the early 1980s (one of the earliest annotation projects) we did alter the form of the corpus by making some minor changes to simplify the task of automatic tagging – e.g. changing sentence-initial capitals to lower case. This fault has since been corrected. Also, when some corpora are made available online, it is sometimes the case that the POS-tagged version is the default form of the corpus, so that it is easier to use the tagged corpus than not to. This is unfortunate: the annotation should be a completely optional addition.

I move on now to the major advantage of annotating: the reason why annotation is undertaken in the first place. Annotation can be thought of a kind of 'value added' to the raw form of the corpus. Each level of annotation (POS-tagging, parsing, semantic tagging, discourse annotation, etc.) adds additional information about the linguistic form and content of the text, and therefore enables us to retrieve from the corpus instances of the phenomena so represented. In this way, the searching of the corpus, or extraction of statistical data from the corpus, can be made more powerful and abstract. With POS-tagging we can extract, for instance, examples of *lives* as a verb, and distinguish them from *lives* as a noun. But with POS-tagging we cannot extract all relative clauses: for this, the additional level of syntactic annotation (or corpus parsing) is required. Here I would emphasise the *empowering* nature of annotation. If corpus use is restricted to the raw, unannotated corpus, we can only extract information that is available from the orthographic form of the text: largely just (combinations of) words and punctuation marks. If we are interested in investigating syntax or semantics, for instance, we can only do this if we can find what we want by searching individual word spellings and the like. A vast amount of manual sifting of the data may be necessary to identify even low-level morphosyntactic abstractions such as past or present participles.

Moving on now to disadvantages, the two main ones are (a) error, and (b) lack of consensus about annotation schemes. Error occurs because, with any extensive corpus annotation project, automated or semi-automated methods have to be used. Even a good POS-tagger will produce a wrong result in 2–4 per cent of tokens. Parsers or semantic taggers produce a bigger error rate than that. Ideally, errors should be manually corrected in a carefully controlled way, to avoid inconsistencies, before the release of the corpus. But this is an expensive and time-consuming process. So in practice it is common to use annotated corpora which contain a considerable number of errors. Although analysts can make allowance for errors, and can if necessary do their own error checking, this can be too onerous for the everyday user, so that inaccurate or even erroneous findings can result. The user has to beware of the consequences of error!

Perhaps a more fundamental disadvantage than this is that the annotation scheme may impose on the user a set of categories which is inappropriate for the user's purposes. Taking POS-tagging as our example, the annotator's position is similar to the position of the lexicographer: we label words according to well-established, *consensual* categories with which linguists, grammarians, and language teachers are likely to agree. In general, there is little dispute about whether a noun like *car* is a noun, and whether a verb like *find* is a verb. But even the basic parts of speech are subject to disagreement. One authoritative reference grammar of English considers *now* and *here* to be adverbs, whereas another one considers them to be prepositions. When we move on to higher levels of annotation, such as those of syntax and semantics, the amount of disagreement over categories and their application is bound to increase. To such objections the annotator replies: 'The annotations are optional, and are added to help those who find them helpful. If you don't, then please ignore them'.

I have said enough to indicate the strengths and weaknesses of annotation.

Many users find annotation helpful, and indeed indispensable for what they want to investigate. But not everyone wants to 'buy in' to the annotation provided for a particular corpus. *Caveat emptor*!

References

Biber, D. 1993. Representativeness in corpus design. *Literary and Linguistic Computing* 8(4): 243–257.

Čermák, F. 1997. Czech National Corpus: A case in many contexts. *International Journal of Corpus Linguistics* 2: 181–197.

Chomsky, N. 1962. Paper given at the University of Texas in 1958, *3rd Texas Conference on Problems of Linguistic Analysis in English.* Austin TX: University of Texas.

Chomsky, N. 1965. *Aspects of the Theory of Syntax.* Cambridge MA: The MIT Press.

Fries, C. C. 1952. *The Structure of English.* New York NY: Harcourt Brace.

Gilquin, G. 2007. To err is not all: What corpus and elicitation can reveal about the use of collocations by learners. *ZAA* 55(3): 273–291.

Gries, St. Th., Hampe, B. & Schönefeld, D. 2005. Converging evidence: Bringing together experimental and corpus data on the association of verbs and constructions. *Cognitive Linguistics* 16(4): 635–676.

Hundt, M., Nesselhauf, N. & Biewer, C. (eds). 2007. *Corpus Linguistics and the Web.* Amsterdam: Rodopi.

Johansson, S. 2009. Some aspects of the development of Corpus Linguistics in the 1970s and 1980s. In *Corpus Linguistics: An International Handbook,* A. Lüdeling & M. Kytö (eds), 33–54. New York NY: de Gruyter.

Kennedy, G. 1998. *An Introduction to Corpus Linguistics.* Harlow: Longman.

Leech, G. 2007. New resources, or just better old ones? In *Corpus Linguistics and the Web*, M. Hundt, N. Nesselhauf & C. Biewer (eds), 133–149. Amsterdam: Rodopi.

Leech, G. 2008. *Language in Literature: Style and Foregrounding.* Harlow: Longman.

Leech, G., Hundt, M., Mair, C. & Smith, N. 2009. *Change in Contemporary English: A Grammatical Study.* Cambridge: CUP.

Manning, C. D. & Schütze, H. 1999. *Foundations of Statistical Natural Language Processing.* Cambridge MA: The MIT Press.

Marcus, M., Santorini, B. & Marcinkiewicz, M. A. 1993. Building a large annotated corpus of English: The Penn Treebank. *Computational Linguistics* 19(2): 313–330.

McEnery, T. & Wilson, A. 2001. *Corpus Linguistics,* 2nd edn. Edinburgh: EUP.

Nelson, G., Wallis, S. & Aarts, B. 2002. *Exploring Natural Language: Working with the British Component of the International Corpus of English* [Varieties of English in the World G29]. Amsterdam: John Benjamins.

Quirk, R. 1960. Towards a description of English usage. *Transactions of the Philological Society 1960,* 59: 40–61.

Scott, M. & Tribble, C. 2006. *Textual Patterns: Key Words and Corpus Analysis in Language Education* [Studies in Corpus Linguistics 22]. Amsterdam: John Benjamins.

Sinclair, J., Jones, S. & Daley, R. 2004. *English Collocation Studies. The OSTI Report*, R. Krishnamurthy (ed.). London: Continuum.

Svartvik, J. & Quirk, R. (eds). 1980. *A Corpus of English Conversation*. Lund: CWK Gleerup.

Philosophical and literary concerns in Corpus Linguistics

Chair of the English Department at the University of Zimbabwe, Bill Louw contributes with an account of the philosophical aspects in Corpus Linguistics. He states that the popularity of corpora among language researchers in the recent years relates most directly to the search for truth. As regards literary research, Louw brings out the challenges corpora have posed to traditional (and long-held) notions in literature as well as the possibilities of (re)introducing the social aspect in corpus stylistics. In terms of the literature curriculum, he argues that students/ teachers should not be forced to use corpora. Instead, the potential of the corpus approach should be demonstrated as a way of inviting them to follow the empirical way.

1. Where do you place the roots of Corpus Linguistics? And to what do you attribute the growth of interest in this area?

I shall begin with the second part of your question, because the answer is simple. Interest in CL has grown because everyone is interested in *truth*. The fact that a fake institution such as the Truth and Reconciliation Commission (Louw 2003) is easily detected and falsified from its title alone, continues to fascinate and astonish the older generation. Who would have thought that language would become its own instrumentation and that linguistics would establish itself (through the work of John Sinclair) as a 'harder' science than mentalist linguists ever envisaged, and, for that matter, as a science that is at least as 'hard' as physics? The mentalists used the principles of reductionism to elevate psychologism to the level of 'science' in order to lend apparent respectability to the fact that *their* form of linguistics was, at best, little more than a gigantic thumb-suck. Corpora have proved them both dishonestly motivated and factually wrong, to the point that the apparent defeating of the science of language is now the only avenue left open to them. Stewart (2010) is a good example of this. John Sinclair (personal communication), commenting on lexical priming (Hoey 2005) remarked that mentalist studies are easily recognised because they all end in the same way: the *'truth remains elsewhere'*. The mentalist establishment doubtlessly continues to find this comforting.

The roots of Corpus Linguistics are to be found within the same peculiar trait of human intellectual curiosity: a desire to sample the world and the 'worlds' it purports to contain. In creating pre-computational samples of the world through language, philosophers and some linguists hoped to come to a fuller understanding of how factual truth (Wittgenstein 1922: 7), or the logic inherent in states of affairs, is represented within those worlds. There were no computers in 1921, but eventually the research conducted at that time by philosophers, mathematicians, ethnographers and linguists, became capable of automation through the use of electronic corpora. Scholars began to gain insights into how language cannot but 'gesture' both the logic and, therefore, the truth (Ayer 1971) of those states of affairs in which language forms an essential part of their nature as repeatable events (Russell 1948; Louw 2008d)[1]. This gesturing of truth is correctly referred to by Wittgenstein as 'picturing' in section three of the *Tractatus Logico-Philosophicus* (1922).

The main players in about 1921 were the empiricist, analytic philosophers, starting with Gottlob Frege, Bertrand Russell, Wittgenstein and Carnap. Other disciplines were also involved. Within ethnography, Bronislaw Malinowski published his *Corpus Inscriptionum Kiriwiniensium* in 1922 as he sampled the institutional worlds of the Kiriwinians in the Trobriand Islands. A good example from mathematics was Markoff's (1913) stochastic processes. His research very nearly found collocation 35 years ahead of its discovery by J. R. Firth. The *automata* that resulted from his work began to 'build' the 'corpus' probabilistically [from a single word, just like Sinclair's (2006) *Phrasebite*]. Chomsky (1957) deliberately downplays Markoff's (1913) work in the opening pages of *Syntactic Structures*. He dismisses corpora in a footnote in *Aspects of the Theory of Syntax* (Chomsky 1964).

We see that non-electronic corpora were in existence long before

---

1 Louw (2008d) was delivered as a paper at *Corpus09* in Liverpool on 22nd July 2009. This public address may have resulted in the release from prison of Simon Mann. The paper proved, using Russell's (1948) postulates, that the removal from Haiti of Jean Bertrand Aristide was the same event as the mercenary mission to Equatorial Guinea, only days later. No mention of Aristide appeared in the press reports of 4th November, 2009 concerning the release of Mann. We await further disclosures in that regard.

the arrival of computers. These early attempts fell into two categories: (a) research that attempted to build corpora logically from truthful propositions and (b) attempts to record authentic language as 'modes of action *in rebus*' (Malinowski 1946: 216). The latter provide what is arguably the best early example of what our modern corpora would look like: Malinowski's (1922) *Corpus Inscriptionum Kiriwiniensium*. The two best examples of the former were Wittgenstein's (1922) picture theory of language, in the first half of his *Tractatus Logico-Philosophicus* and Carnap's (1928) *Der Logische Aufbau der Welt*. Their intention was to build the corpus from logical propositions until it reflected 'all that is the case ... the totality of facts not of things ...' (Wittgenstein 1922: 7). The idea is, of course, Fregean. Frege noted that even though the 'Morning Star' and the 'Evening Star' refer to the same referent, the terms are uttered in totally different circumstances, often by different categories of people and with different intentions. In order to correct this, Frege took the unusual and highly original step within the quasi-mathematical discipline of logic, of introducing *contextual* detail in the form of *arguments* that would always accompany *functions* [Fa]. Firth and Malinowski may have been responsible for the introduction of contextual linguistics, but its true origins took place almost 60 years earlier in the work of Frege and we are all indebted to Russell for drawing our attention to that research.

None of these developments has received satisfactory recognition within the discipline of Corpus Linguistics. The reason for this is that most linguists are not really interested in dealing with them. Almost all linguists are incorrigibly oriented towards *structure* and *description* rather than provide direct empirical access to *meaning* through the co-selection of collocates. The biggest challenges that corpora have brought into linguistics have been to show (a) that direct access to situational meaning is possible through corpora (see also Louw & Chateau, forthcoming), and (b) that this involves a form of empiricism that has never been encountered before. It is a form of empiricism that totally revises notions and limitations that philosophers believed were well settled within their discipline (cf. McGinn 1982: 89).

One of these problems is *a priori* knowledge. Ayer (1987: 26) refers to an impasse regarding probability. Corpora easily overcome this difficulty. If a predicted, event-related linguistic phenomenon only occurs sometimes (or even if it occurs very frequently), the Vienna Circle and other empiricist philosophers took the view that the safe course was to reject it and regard the phenomenon as pure metaphysics and, therefore, non-sense. But corpora offer their own highly converting form of empiricism. They are capable of furnishing '*a priori*' knowledge, by proxy, of events that many people have never encountered previously. A good example has surfaced with the arrival of the current world 'credit crunch'. When times are normal, there is no need to mention an institution called *the lender of last resort*. And yet even a small concordance is capable of establishing the lenders' ontological status and only a small clutch of collocates is needed to sketch such lenders' roles in repeatable, if often widely spaced, events (Louw 2008d). This fact vindicates the belief of Russell (1945) that such sense-data need not be present on each and every occasion that the event in question takes place. They need occur only sufficiently often to trigger inductive reasoning. Russell (1945: 647) claimed that induction alone is an independent logical principle that is both inherent in science and makes science possible.

MicroConcord search SW: lender of last resort
80 characters per entry
Sort : 1R/SW shifted 1 characters.

1	alled the Bank of England the	lender of last resort, a description which, in the
2	nt of exchange rates and as a	lender of last resort, as well as towards co-opera
3	Bank of England, traditional	lender of last resort. Barings' directors are re
4	enever a central bank acts as	lender of last resort. By letting Barings fail,
5	England in 1946, the role of	lender of last resort has always involved the use
6	themselves without a reliable	lender of last resort if Britain were to join? 2
7	an unquantifiable risk as the	lender of last resort; if it had offered some ulti
8	he Bank's refusal to act as a	lender of last resort in this case has permanently
9	case for the Bank to act as a	lender of last resort. Unlike BCCI and other banks
10	office of the local Fed, his	lender of last resort. 'You seem to have a problem

(Data from *The Times* 1995)

If we have been enjoined to 'trust the text' (Sinclair 2004a), our examination of the origins of corpora must bear upon truth and logic (Ayer 1971). It must move through Popper's (1959) serial falsification of weak theories as we bear out Wittgenstein's (1922) (*Tractatus* section 4.003) assertions concerning 'the logic of our language' and claim the ineluctable scientific fact that language is now its own instrumentation (Louw 2000, 2003, 2007a, 2008c), for Firth

(1955: 91) maintained that scientific facts do not exist until they are claimed. What did the logic of our language imply for philosophy? Corpora alone have confirmed this: tautologies picture nothing. '*Business is business*' looks like a tautology, but it is a *fact* or state of affairs, in which the uttering of these words brings to an end a form of exploitation in which one player, through his/her favoured status, has been endangering the profitability of another player. We find exploitation to the left of the phrase and its cessation or resistance to the right of it.

2. Is Corpus Linguistics a science or a methodology? Where would you situate CL in the scientific or methodological panorama?

Let me say at once that a 'scientific or methodological panorama' is simply not a truthful possibility in scientific terms within CL. In an unscientific community, like the community of linguists, methodological eclecticism is made to sound both easy and desirable. However, the truth of the matter is that we are bound unwittingly by the Greek etymology of the word *method*: *meta + hodos* or an *after + path* (Louw 2008a: 243). In other words, methodology is shaped and dictated by developments inside science (Kuhn 1996; Kitcher 1993). New methods are born as a result of paradigm shifts and scientific revolutions. They are the *paths* that we adopt *after* they have been dictated by momentous discoveries in science.

A good example would be the fact that Firth's (1957: 196) formula for 'meaning by collocation' can be automated (Louw 2008a, 2008d) and converted into instrumentation for disclosing facts or states of affairs in a corpus of natural language (Wittgenstein 1922: 7). Sinclair's Scottish Schools project, Cain, uses software called Phrasebox© that invites primary school children to enter *two* expressions for a co-selected search. Co-selection is the preferred method for finding events. Eclecticism in methodology may be motivated by curiosity alone and such curiosity is often of a fairly trivial kind. An example might be Hunston and Thompson's (2006) desire to ascertain how much of Halliday's intuitively-derived theories can be recovered from corpus data. Note that Halliday, and not the corpus as instrument, has primacy in this enterprise. The volume is entitled *System and Corpus*, but even if the order of these terms were reversed, they would remain rather strange bedfellows: an intuitively derived postulate and a scientifically unrecognised instrument. All mentalist and NLP activity within CL falls into this category and inexplicably remains largely unquestioned. Quine (1961) and Davidson (1973–1974) were responsible for replacing the first dogma of empiricism with the scientifically weak third dogma. It enshrines the given and the 'interpretation of the given or the *conceptual scheme*'. However, CL reveals clearer evidence for the existence of analytic and synthetic truth.

So, the answer to the question is that CL, as it is mostly being used, is neither a science nor a methodology. But the corpus is undeniably an instrument of science in the right Sinclairean hands. What led Sinclair to take the view of trusting the text? What had he witnessed in the course of coming to it? As we try to answer these questions, it is almost inevitable that parts of our investigation will be unwelcome.

We must remember that Sinclair was the first person to witness the computational power of collocation. He discovered semantic prosodies, although he and I collaborated in naming them. He witnessed the apparent censorship of what he had found (personal communication): all copies of the OSTI report disappeared except for his own copy of it. The British Library apparently lost its only copy. Attempts to get it published bounced from publisher to publisher. Krishnamurthy (2004) finally rescued it from the growing pile of censored material, such as Sinclair's ill-starred proposed *Dictionary of Collocation*. The world was fobbed off instead with a collection of collocations on CD ROM (Sinclair 1995). Sinclair's indefatigable generator of paraphrase, Project Lucid, met a similar fate. By the time he wrote *Trust the Text* (Sinclair 2004a), he had also witnessed the falsification of the Truth and Reconciliation Commission, from its title alone (Louw 2003) and he had logged the spin-doctors' hidden positive semantic prosody inherent in and to the left of *and + reconciliation*. Small wonder then that Chapter 14 of *Reading Concordances* (Sinclair 2004b) – and devoted to dealing with semantic prosody – is subtitled 'hidden meaning'.

The community of linguists seems reluctant to allow the corpus rather than a human being to 'read' a target text. Yet humans are manifestly gullible enough, in large numbers (families of about 23,000 victims of *Apartheid* murders), not to see that 'truth and reconciliation' is 'truth and waiver'. Institutions and their often questionable ideologies feel a need to survive the process of analysis (Louw 2006: 183; 2007a: 391). This fact may make linguistic science unwelcome in institutional circles.

One serially censored aspect of the author's work is the deception of long standing inherent in the expression *natural justice* (see also the delayed Louw 2008b). Censorship allows a researcher to know when she/ he is on the right track within science and methodology. Indications often come quite unexpectedly and often pre-emptively. I became suspicious that homogenisation of the instrument, the corpus itself, had been taking place when the British National Corpus was released throughout the world, but with the signal exception of Africa. Correspondence with Lou Burnard offered little reassurance. I finally had access to the BNC in Granada in 2004 and found that its power to read *natural justice* (Louw 2003) as a 'mode of action *in rebus*' (Malinowski 1946: 296) had apparently been tampered with and thwarted: sampling of the form was mostly drawn from a legal textbook on the subject rather than from press accounts of authentic court cases, as was the case in the Bank of English. Was an eclectic method used to emasculate the instrument itself with a view to protecting judicial discretion for the settling of scores from the bench? The table which follows is available at the Brigham Young University website. It provides a picture of the sampling involved. We find that 245 instances of *natural justice* (four fifths more than from any other source) were sourced from academic books. Furthermore, the BNC contains a disproportionately high number of citations for *natural justice* by comparison with the Bank of English, which is five times larger than the BNC. Does that reduce the trustworthiness of the BNC as a text? If the sampling was made deliberately poor in order to save an ideology, what name would we give it? Is *homogenisation* the right label or should it be termed *event-fraud*?

REGISTER	SPOKEN	FICTION	NEWS	ACADEMIC	NONFIC MISC	OTHER MISC
TOKENS	7	12	8	245	19	11
SIZE (MW)	10.33	16.19	10.64	15.43	16.63	28.39
PER MIL	0.7	0.7	0.8	15.9	1.1	0.4

3. How representative can a corpus be?

The intention to sample has always been very broad. If the world exists in exactly the form that Wittgenstein states it, then his wide, almost lexicographic vision of sampling was brought about by one academic alone: John Sinclair, in 1987 with the first edition of the *Collins COBUILD English Language*

Dictionary, using a main corpus of 7.5 million words in conjunction with reserve corpora of up to 21 million words of running text.

However, a much more exciting enterprise involves asking the question: Can a corpus ever be too representative? This question forces us to ask whether there are any details within those institutions to be represented by the corpus that are, without comment, not for general public consumption. *Natural justice* is certainly one of these in the judiciary and the legal profession. There are others such as the remedy of judicial review, so named because it does not, in court, give rise to a remedy (*sic*), but is its own remedy! However, where any institution begins to be sampled so closely that its ideology shows, it is *there* that the sampling shoe pinches. Over-representation is usually to be found in fakes such as the Truth and Reconciliation Commission or in specialised corpora. Monitor corpora could potentially be set up in order to prevent too much flank from being shown, but this would be worryingly close in character to censorship.

The Sizewell Corpus is a corpus of 16 million words of spoken language that is made up entirely of the transcript of one of the longest enquiries in history: the enquiry into leaks of radiation at the Sizewell B Nuclear Power facility.[2] It exists today in a magnetic medium and has even been used in research leading to a data-assisted approach to negotiating skills (Louw 2006). From a judicial point of view, the Sizewell Corpus is arguably *too* representative, in the sense that it reveals too much ideological flank about what goes on inside the courtroom. Some fairly harmless, short concordances are offered below. Cover-up is easily detected to the left and right of *happy + to* and insincerity abounds as we find that it is an essential part of at least one official's duties at a nuclear enquiry to interrupt those giving evidence, by using the words *sorry + to + interrupt*. This occurs so often that in this case, frank remorse is simply not a logical, Gricean possibility (Grice 1975). Clients frequently ask insurance brokers this question: 'Of course, I can always cash this policy, can't I?' Do we ever hear the words in reply?: 'One third of the

---

2 The proceedings of an enquiry into a leak of radioactive material from the Sizewell B Nuclear Power Station in the United Kingdom took place before Sir Frank Layfield QC at the Maltings, Snape, Suffolk UK in late July 1982. It was initially recorded by shorthand writers. They produced it in the form of a typescript that was later captured in a magnetic form on computer tape. A number of universities were offered copies. The University of Birmingham opted for the magnetic format. The result is an untagged corpus of 16 million running words and arguably the longest record of a negotiation.

cash amount realised must always be reinvested in an insurance-based product … ' It spoils the fun somehow. It is easier and more profitable to say: 'Yes'.

49	blem in the US. Again, I would be very	happy to	make that available to the Boa
50	gain, this is something I would be very	happy to	make available to you on Ameri
52	y document, sir, but would be quite	happy to	obtain a copy of this for Rev.
53	e by giving those references – I am	happy to	omit them – the reason I do is
55	that is why I said initially we are	happy to	provide the factual informatio
56	o not have them to hand. I shall be	happy to	provide them. 478. Q. Than
57	Thank you, Mr. Baker. I would be quite	happy to	provide you with my calculatio
58	Table 11. A. Certainly, we will be	happy to	provide it. 66. Q. The oth
28	_____ 660. Q. Professor, I am	sorry to	interrupt you. Could you go with m
29	upply … 137. Q. Mr. Parker, I am	sorry to	interrupt you, but can we trace th
30	THE INSPECTOR: Mr. Fitzgerald, I am	sorry to	interrupt you, but we promised we w
31	… . 262. Q. THE INSPECTOR: I am	sorry to	interrupt you, but you keep on usi
32	ou not? A. That is correct. 605. Q.	Sorry to	interrupt you. A. To some extent, t
33	THE INSPECTOR: Mr. Fitzgerald, I am	sorry to	interrupt, but it has happened on a
34	CPRE/S/155. 39. THE INSPECTOR: I am	sorry to	interrupt, Mr. Taylor. What is this

(Source: The Sizewell Corpus)

4. How far should an analyst rely on intuition?

Any activity that is not science runs a fairly substantial risk of turning out to be trickery. One characteristic of the devil is that he offers his victims good things in order to deprive them of the best. So it is with many of the products of mentalism. Why would anyone choose to follow a school of thought whose only remaining trick in the age of corpora is flattery? All that it can provide is the unproven suggestion that we have good minds and that their judgement is unerring. And many believe this until they encounter the victims of deception: 23,000 families of the murdered victims of *Apartheid* waived their rights to ordinary justice in exchange for details of murders that would have come out anyway in *any* murder trial in *any* court of justice that was worth its salt! The Chief Justice of South Africa enforced this national waiver when the family of Steve Biko appealed to the Constitutional Court for the remedies of ordinary justice rather than remedies that an untried waiver commission might purport to provide (Louw 2003).

The philosopher C. S. Peirce gained recognition for introducing pragmatics into philosophy (Peirce 1905). What price are we to set upon 'theories' that specialise in telling you what you know already in the hope of keeping you away from the empiricism in which truth manifestly resides and is easily revealed? For example, cognitivists (Stockwell 2002; Gavins and Steen 2003) will tell you that you have a schema for *pubs* and that as a result you know that you can purchase food and drink in them. We accept this form of claptrap far too readily and the system behind it works because most of us will never see the *proof* of what only a corpus can show: that the most frequent collocates of *pub* are the terms *groups*, *chains* and *organisations*. Pubs organise our drinking habits and their own profitability, far more than anything else they do, and only a corpus will show you that (Louw 2007a: 348, 360). Philosophers like Wittgenstein tried to fill this appalling lacuna in our logic by building into their theories the mechanisms needed to find instances where $p = non-p$ and show them the door (Pears 1971). As a result, Wittgenstein's work was played down in America to the point that some collections of essential readings in philosophy (Martinich 1985) leave out the work of arguably the most important philosopher in the 20th century. Wittgenstein's only sin was to write three sections of the *Tractatus* before hitting the mentalist iceberg. We lose interest as he declares at the beginning of Section 4, that 'a thought is a proposition with a sense' (TLP 4).

However, even Wittgenstein was easily duped, in the absence of computers, into the belief that psychology had been accorded the status of science by means of the ruse of reductionism (the second dogma of empiricism). This resulted in the production by Wittgenstein (1980) of two and a half volumes on the philosophy of psychology. Today, collocation automates his picture theory of meaning as it is set out in the first few sections of the *Tractatus* and leaves the content of his later volumes looking like little more than a list of 'things'. Frege (1884) alone stands out against psychologism. He warns against the use of uncontextualised sentences (what else was Chomsky ever about?) and single words (because these relexicalise once their collocates are trimmed away) (Philip 2003). Frege declared that most of philosophy was ' ... infected through and through (*verseugt*) by psychology' (Beaney 1997: 201). Another ideology to preserve psychologism in these early years was the unfounded belief that analysis alters the text. Believe that and you will believe anything.

The community of linguists has neither fully understood the extent to which intuition is flawed nor come to terms with what is involved in 'trusting the text' over intuition whenever the opportunity arises. As a result, the colonisation of Corpus Linguistics by mentalists who care nothing for corpora is at present almost fully accomplished. The cash value of phlogiston, considering what it is, remains remarkably high in a market governed by bullish forms of irrational exuberance and the instruction from powerful insiders to: 'Buy!'

5. What kind of questions should an analyst think of?

Any question that an analyst asks of the corpus as a scientific instrument must be predicated upon methodology born of theory. For example, it has become apparent in Sinclairean Corpus Linguistics that different types of question are methodologically governed. These depend on the standpoint of the researcher. If we take collocation as an example, the type of question asked will depend upon the investigator's understanding of what exactly collocation is and how it functions. Hence, in relation to the Figure 1, Kjellmer (1984) would ask

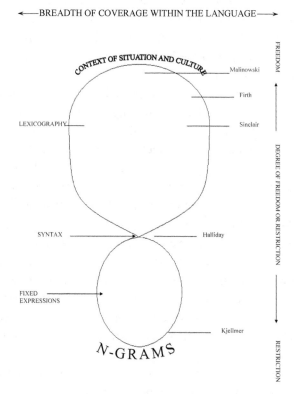

Figure 1. Different scholars' views of collocation

a question based upon his view that, like Halliday's (1966), is predicated upon the belief that collocation is a sentence-bound phenomenon. Kjellmer (1984) may see collocation as slightly less flexible in terms of word order than Halliday (1966), but there would be nothing much in any difference between them. Hence, their query to the corpus would look like either or both of these two query instructions: *fan* + *the* + *flames* or *fan@* + *2flames*. These two queries, a string search or a skip-search would be suitable in terms of the diagram for any search 'south' (Kjellmer 1984) of where the lines of the figure of 8 cross (Halliday 1966). They are based on syntactic structure.

However, anywhere *'north'* of this crossing point, would reflect a vision of collocation that is truly Firthian, that is to say, 'abstracted at the level of syntax' (Firth 1957: 191). This can mean that the questioner believes in a moving 9-word window of collocative power (Sinclair 1991). Such a window ought to be totally ungoverned by syntax. Thus, the question asked of the corpus must be a search for what Firth terms 'meaning by collocation' of the kind where, as Firth (1957: 191) says, 'one meaning of the word *night* is its collocability with *dark*'. The form of that question, therefore, must set the co-selected items free from the constraints of syntax, as we see in the concordances below.

MicroConcord search SW: truth CW: justice

80 characters per entry

Sort: 1R/SW shifted −4 characters.

1	ind of work being on the side of	truth	and justice, if you like and this involve
2	of social justice than empirical	truth.	For example, many alcoholics with pancre
3	grown Arthur might have put it:	"Truth,	justice and the American way." Or as AC
4	ng with rectitude, declares that	truth,	justice, humanity the Heavens themselves
5	expert witnesses who got to the	truth.	Lord Justice Swinton Thomas, sitting w

(Source: *The Times* 1995)

In the search line, SW is the *search word* and CW is the *context word*. Line 5 demonstrates that *judges* and *truth* are meant to inhabit the same Wittgensteinian fact or state of affairs. This is totally unaffected by the sentence boundary that separates them. Syntax 'chunks' bits of the sentence (Sinclair 1991: 132; Sinclair & Mauranen 2006), but collocation 'chunks' the world of the northern bulb of Figure 1 into contexts of culture and of situation. Co-occurrence is proof of Malinowski's determinism of events (Berofsky 1971). Malinowski called this science and Firth agreed with him.

However, syntax has not become completely surplus to requirements. Because philosophical propositions and mathematical equations are also syntactic, syntax may be used to confirm the detection of fraudulent or fake states of affairs that fly in the face of the law because they are demonstrably without that which the law purports to value: precedent. The only ontological link between *truth* and *reconciliation* is through the fake collocate *commission*. The spin-doctors threw them together in order to create a plausible *symbol* (Gk. *syn* + *ballein*: *together* + *to throw*) (Louw 2007b). Before the establishment of the Commission, Sinclair's reserve corpora of 21 million words offer the result 'no matches' for the same search query as the one we see today if we co-select the terms in the Bank of English. The collocation table below demonstrates the spin-doctors' 'success' and hence the necessity for collocation as instrumentation (Louw 2003). A table like this ought to warn the reader that although *truth* and *reconciliation* have been forced together, they represent no institutional depth of long standing.

log likelihood	Chi square
1. tell (12,011.8)	Urquhart (170,913)
2. truth (11,711.7)	Ruth (135,969)
3. is (8,490.32)	truth (83,659.3)
4. telling (8,482.61)	telling (54,560.6)
5. Ruth (8,422.57)	tell (52,199.1)
6. Urquhart (4,915.43)	***Reconciliation*** (30,272.9)
7. the (4,704.42)	DEAR (27,588)
8. that (4,012.31)	falsehood (12,281)
9. about (3,126.72)	is (11,997.5)
10. told (1,957.6)	Sojourner (8,937.53)
11. DEAR (1,668.93)	unpalatable (8,150.95)
12 know (1,630.64)	falsity (7,951.66)
13. The (1,619.81)	RUTH (7,302.71)
14. I (1,585.56)	www.eu.microsoft.com (7,205.68)
15. In (1,522.92)	unvarnished (6,513.04)
16. ***Reconciliation*** (1,344.99)	economical (5,682.15)
17. lies (1,182.89)	the (5,556.43)
18. whole (1,174.51)	that (5,138.48)
19. not (1,161.63)	about (4,727.06)
20. lie (1,072.85)	literal (4,506.04)

21. ." (979.812)	Truth (4,446.34)
22. matter (976.616)	TRC (4,329.31)
23. simple (901.219)	'death (4,128.57)
24. nothing (875.149)	lies (4,010.42)
25. you (850.123)	kiri (3,935.73)

(Source: The Corpus Hub at Birmingham [CHAB])

MicroConcord search SW: truth CW: reconciliation
80 characters per entry
Sort: 1R/SW unshifted.

```
1 wrangling delays the creation of the   Truth  and   Reconciliation Commission for whi
2 er misdemeanours before the nation's   Truth  and   Reconciliation Commission, recent
3 for clemency by revealing all to the    Truth  and   Reconciliation Commission when it
4 nt Mandela to head the controversial    Truth  and   Reconciliation Commission which i
5 d Tutu, who was put in charge of the    Truth  and   Reconciliation Commission, a body
```
(Source: *The Times* 1995)

It is in *Phrasebite*, as we shall see later that Sinclair asks more profound questions that go against Halliday's (1966) advice to us to ignore the grammar word collocates. An analyst should ask whether the institutions that appear in texts are institutions with a rich historical tradition that favours mankind or whether they are 'institutions of straw', that may, like natural justice, even be denied ontological status and written out of existence by their collocates. The analyst owes humanity a duty of care to ask all and only the right questions of the text. This takes Sinclairean 'trusting' of the text a stage further.

6. What are the strengths and weaknesses of corpus analysis?

For corpus analysis to be any good, the corpus itself needs to be beyond reproach. In the case of the *natural justice* example from the BNC, the entire sample is compromised, not just for reasons of *prima facie* dishonesty to thwart the analysis of an institution, but also, because the apparent dishonesty may be aimed at neutralising scholarship, as it develops, using Malinowski's (1946) theory. So it would trivialise the serious nature of what may have occurred in this case if we see it simply as a question of 'garbage in – garbage out'.

The abuses ought perhaps to be graded on a cline, with homogenisation at one extreme and naïve or unwitting practice at the other. However, not very far from homogenisation we would need to place something akin to a breach of natural justice in real life. *Mentioning* the corpus or saying that one has a home-made one allows bogus practitioners to be judges in their own cause and to reap the benefits of credibility by means of fake objectivity (see the so-called Bootcamp Debate on the Corpora List and in *The International Journal of Corpus Linguistics*, in press). For corpora to prosper as instrumentation they must be allowed to surprise the investigator and this means that they must be accorded primacy on the basis of their recognised heuristic power. Anything less would be indicative of the malady identified by Firth as 'fishing in one's own tank' (Palmer 1975). All mentalist approaches do this. The problem is particularly acute where the act of name-dropping the existence of a corpus is hastily got out of the way at an early stage and, thereafter, entirely intuitive analysis purports to proceed. Swales (1990) would have introduced a labelled 'move' for this manoeuvre. Readers are referred to Gries and Stefanowitsch (2007) where some, but not all, of the papers are guilty of this form of piggy-backing on the name of science, especially by ignoring collocation or treating it as 'off limits' for some inexplicable or all too explicable reason.

Further along this proposed cline we find *hybridisation* of theory and the imposition of it upon the corpus through the importation of labels derived from revered practitioners [what Kitcher (1993) calls 'science as myth'] who have deliberately eschewed corpora in favour of intuitively derived theory. Michael Halliday falls into this category, not so much because of his own choice (especially as he has only recently shown a little more interest in corpora than he did on visits to COBUILD in the 90s), but because his followers are determined, in support of Householder's *God's Truth* distinction, to place him inside the corpus, fighting to get out. O'Halloran (2007: 1), for example, coins the term 'register prosody' (*sic*). This hybridises the scientifically respectable term semantic prosody by mixing it with intuitive Hallidayan notions of markedness rather than Firthian meaning by collocation. Hoey (2005, 2006: 53) refers to 'priming prosody' in the full knowledge that what he calls 'priming' is a mentalist phenomenon that has no objective markedness to match relexicalisation brought about by collocation in a moving 9-word window of *relexicalising* collocative power and which demonstrably sustains the fact that all *devices* relexicalise (Louw 1991; Sinclair 2004a: 198). By the time we reach Stubbs's 'discourse prosody' (2001: 65), there is a sense of 'anything goes', but we need to remember that to Firth, discourse merely meant *conversation*. In the case of Stubbs, the label 'discourse' adds nothing. It may be an attempt to make his work look less derivative than it is from my own. Long and Doughty (2009: 333) struggle unsuccessfully to make a distinction between discourse prosody and semantic prosody. It may simply be a case of impoverished intellectual property in the first place. If you have a lot of work in the area of discourse, you stick that label onto other things in passing that you may wish had been yours. But it does science the disservice of hybridising it. The recoverable markedness of Sinclairean semantic prosody has no reason to rely upon intuition or questions of purported genre. With the publication of Stewart (2010), hybridisation has apparently abandoned all reliance on piecemeal instances of the use of intuition in favour of the creation a hybridising volume under the apparent guidance of a series editor with a conflict of interest (Hoey 2005: 24). Nobody spoke or wrote about semantic prosody in the pre-computational period simply because they could not recognise it intuitively. Furthermore, science as *themes* rather than *proofs* is not science (Stewart 2010: 6).

The acid test is that Firth's meaning by *collocation* has been automated by *that* very phenomenon, *collocation* itself in a digital form (Louw 2008a). If meaning by collocation is automated by collocation, then language *is* its own instrumentation (Louw 2007a). Hallidayan hybrids would not pass this test. The empiricism to support their extraction from corpora is available, but *they* do not all exist very prominently. They exist intuitively and, some of them exist for the convenience of what Firth, in the case of Wegener, calls 'trinities of association'. Halliday's entire theory is perched upon such trinities. Firth either did not notice them, or they may have appeared in documents released by Halliday after his death. If anyone doubts this, set your students an assignment to automate 'mode of discourse' using the Bank of English. The request will result in reactive psychotic depression throughout the class! Meaning by collocation, by comparison, brings with it such abundant empiricism that, in a large corpus, it has the power of a fire-hose for delivering language examples. The sad aspect is that the unwary may be taken in and all of our advances in scholarship on our careful journey through Malinowski, Wittgenstein, Firth, Sinclair and the history of science may be rubbished in the process by 'interested' outsiders. Malinowski points out that there are 999 ostriches with their heads in the sand among every 1000 academics.

Having examined crippled corpora, we need to appreciate what corpora are capable of at their best. A crucial article on Contextual Prosodic Theory has been 'out of print' almost since the day it appeared and has, at last, been re-published with the assistance of Carmela Chateau and Professor Francois

Rastier (www.revue-texto.net/index.php?id=124) and now receives, I am informed, an agreeably large number of 'hits'.

The serious use of corpora in truth studies tends to frighten the geese in a world whose moral axioms are at least as dodgy as Plato's in mathematics were found to be by the crestfallen Russell and Whitehead between the years 1910 to 1913. A corpus that can falsify the Truth and Reconciliation Commission from its title alone (Louw 2003) is a difficult beast to tame, even for spin-doctors and trained spoilers.

7. What is the future of Corpus Linguistics?

The future of CL looks bleak in general but bright within the particular, small, neglected area of science and instrumentation for language. My fear is that insultingly mundane, pedestrian, hybridising and dishonest approaches to CL will continue to prosper and be peddled to an entirely unsuspecting world in the guise of truth. These approaches will attempt to defeat the vision of meaning by collocation and that without the use of concepts that we see in Firth, Malinowski and Sinclair. In philosophy, the restoration into empiricism of the *conceptual* marked the re-entry of *phlogiston*.

The community of linguists is powerless to assist in bringing corpora back to their heyday in COBUILD on the first and second floors of Westmere. It was the empiricist philosophers and sadly not the linguists who were trained to recognise science, aim for science and hand matters in their discipline over to science as soon as they achieved the status of settled knowledge (Russell 1960: 12). Corpus linguists believe (wrongly in my respectful view) that somehow they *are* scientists. The corpus linguists continue working within their own narrow fields on largely traditional, structural language research as though corpora are simply an add-on, just a carriage rather than the locomotive of CL. Most of them recognise that a paradigm shift or a scientific revolution subsists within their discipline, but they appear almost to have been suborned out of referring to it. Collocation is as 'off limits' today as it was when Sinclair penned the OSTI Report. Some of those linguists are imposing mentalism on the corpus in the guise of intuitive markedness (Hoey 2005; Stewart 2010).

The attack on semantic prosody continues to gain vitriolic momentum among linguists even as its markedness on the delexical/relexical cline (Sinclair 2004a: 198; Louw 2008a) is daily borne out with ever greater clarity. It is time for us to consolidate semantic prosody and collocation studies by concentrating on their *applications*, such as humour, spin, negotiating theory and stylistics.

8. In what ways has Corpus Linguistics challenged traditional literary concepts?

CL's challenge to literary concepts has taken twenty years to develop. I would date the commencement of that process around 1987, the year in which the COBUILD corpus reached 21 million words, combining main and reserve corpora and the production of the first edition of the *Collins COBUILD English Language Dictionary*. Your question identifies a reason that goes beyond mere disc-space: literary critical studies form part of a very traditional and fiercely independent discipline. Literary criticism may well become the last bastion for the intuitive study of language. A striking example of this conservatism is to be found in the fact that scientific proof continues to be resisted by literary critics, even where their own theories have been demanding it for years. A good example surrounds the stylistic theory that sees style as literary deviance or deviation from a norm. For as long as providing access to the norm seemed an utterly impossible dream, literary critics continued to demand it. However, once the COBUILD project made it available, the clamour ceased instantly and the matter was never mentioned again, either in scholarship or in polite company!

A further weakness in the literary tradition is that its concepts are almost entirely taken for granted to the point that they form a backdrop to the discipline, in much the same way that linguists never question whether their practices are scientific or even misguided. It was Auberon Waugh who wrote that 'if ever the Prime Minister wants an excuse to close down a university, she has only to look at its department of linguistics' (Waugh 1993: vii). This means that errors can lurk within concept-based scholarship and remain undetected for centuries. Concepts carry with them an inherent flaw that is inimical to science: they are used to explain data rather than allow data to speak for themselves (Palmer 1975). Phlogiston is the best example of this in the history of science (Kitcher 1993: 98). Its adherents set back the discovery of oxygen for almost a year by persuading the scientists that they were working with 'phlogistonated air' instead of oxygen.

Firth's (1957) view of meaning by collocation makes demands that literary scholars may be unwilling to abandon. Concepts would need to be disposed of, for example. That would be the death-knell, not before time, of the cognitive. Sinclair's Scottish Schools Project, Cain, before it was apparently halted, came close to destroying the root-room of *concepts* in the primary school.

And yet, the shedding of concepts is what Firth demands: 'Meaning by collocation is an abstraction at the syntagmatic level and *is not directly concerned with the conceptual or idea approach* to the meaning of words' (my emphasis) (Firth 1957: 196). The task is accomplished effortlessly by the mutually defining nature of co-selection within a 9-word window of collocative power. Co-selection is at least as powerful in computational terms as Frege's F(a) is powerful within logic.

The fact of the matter is that if traditional literary concepts are to be made scientific, they will need to be given definitions that are corpus-attested and these will need to be strenuously protected from the hybridisers (Louw 2008a). This means that almost every entry in a dictionary of literary terms will need to be recast along the lines of Louw's article on the implications for literary criticism of the advent of CL (Louw 1997). What these published works all have in common was stated long ago (Louw 1991): all literary devices relexicalise. *That* is what gives them their markedness (Enkvist 1993). All of Lakoff and Johnson's (1980, 2003) 'metaphors we live by' are delexical. They are 'dead'. That is how they remain. We do not live with or by them, but are stuck with them because, between them, they make up a vast amount of the detritus of the English language and many of them are gathered up in fixed expressions in English. Moon and Knowles (2006: 30) take a contrary view.

A further huge problem subsists within and around the notion of *subtext*. It was Roman Jakobson (Culler 1975: 6) who declared that what is *not* said in a literary text is just as important, and sometimes more important than what actually appears in the text. It is the grammar words in text that provide it with the *subtext of its logic.* The term *logical* semantic prosody would be an appropriate label because logic cannot hybridise the approach: it can only enhance it (Louw 2010a, 2010b). Again, this looked like another impossible dream. It was speculated about endlessly, but the moment a corpus threatened to provide subtexts, with a corpus stylistician saying that if an underlying collocate sketches a literary work's entire world, then it is an undeniable part of that text, even in a state of *absence* (Macherey 1966; Louw 2008a: 256), everyone looked the other way. Critics will simply not surrender their right to eschew empiricism, but they are wrong to do so, because subtexts, although they are recovered externally are not exophoric but deeply and provably endophoric. They are our only hope for getting rid of connotation from the scientific study of language.

9. In what ways should corpus analysis be integrated into the literature curriculum?

The corpus should never be imposed upon students and colleagues. The best method is simply to operate by means of demonstration and invitation. I issued an invitation to students on a recent visit to a university in Northern Ireland. One student came and announced that she was a doctoral student in creative writing and a 'total corpus sceptic'. During our conversation it emerged that she was going through a worrying period of writer's block. I asked her to read to me from her notes about incidents she was incorporating into her novel. I co-selected two words that I thought may chunk a particular type of event within its context of situation and of culture. It does not take much to conjure up an event: in the world of cinema, KNIFE co-selected from the corpus with SHOWER would take us directly to the Hitchcock movie *Psycho*. Eleven instances in 44 million words of a newspaper corpus appeared on the screen. I announced that what she was working with comes up as an event every 4 million words in real life, showed her how to open each context and then made a point of leaving the room to get coffee and not reading them with her. On my return she had undergone a conversion, claiming that the results were 'incredible'. I said that I had not read any of the citations. I offered her copies of the corpus and concordancer on her flash drive. The writer's block was cured and the corpus is now in use, with subscriptions to the Bank of English seen as the next step. We not only need to trust the text, but also the text as instrument.

The best way of integrating the corpus is to appoint a sensitive, tactful, Firthian corpus stylistician (there are so many!) to the staff on a short contract. We need to be aware that service personnel are usually on the staff of English departments anyway. In reacting to this question, I examined the establishment of a medium-sized university in the South Midlands that I thought might be typical of many universities. In addition to literary theorists, literature period specialists and traditional English language specialists, I was delighted to find the following areas of special interest, in no particular order: the philosophy of Russell, scriptwriting, creative writing, poets in residence, film and documentary producers, editing (in the person of a distinguished visitor), feminist and gender critics, theatre and drama producers, etc. The mix is perfect for introducing the use of corpora in ways that are not face-threatening.

Imagine simply leaving the following pamphlet entitled *Phrasebite* by

John Sinclair (2006) with the same university's feminist critics. John (personal communication) told the author that women in his class always knew unerringly that linguistics was a 'male trick'. *Phrasebite* provides some proof that takes their argument further. Note how the worlds of this huge worldwide semantic prosody act in ways that Wittgenstein would call 'family resemblances'.

"When she was – *Phrasebite*© John Sinclair, 2006.

1. The first grammatical collocate of *when* is *she*
2. The first grammatical collocate of *when she* is *was*
3. The vocabulary collocates of *when she was* are hair-raising. On the first page: *diagnosed, pregnant, divorced, raped, assaulted, attacked*
   The diagnoses are not good, the pregnancies are all problematic.
4. Select one that looks neutral: **approached**
5. Look at the concordance, first page.
6. Nos 1, 4, 5, 8, 10 are **of unpleasant physical attacks**
7. Nos 2, 3, 6, 7, 9 are **of excellent opportunities**
8. How can you tell the difference?
9. the **nasties** are all of people out and about, while the nice ones are of people working somewhere.
10. Get wider context and look at verb tenses in front of citation.
11. In all the nasties the verb is past progressive, setting a foreground for the approach.
12. In the nice ones, the verb is non-progressive, either simple past or past-in-past ...

Data for para 4 above.

(1) walking in Burnfield Road, Mansewood, **when she was approached** by a man who grabbed her bag
(2) teamed up with her mother in business **when she was approached** by Neiman Marcus, the department store
(3) resolved itself after a few months, **when she was approached** by Breege Keenan, a nun who
(4) Bridge Road close to the Causeway Hospital **when she was approached** by three men who attacked her
(5) Drive, off Saughton Mains Street, **when she was approached** by a man. He began talking the original
(6) film of The Stepford Wives **when she was approached** by producer

Scott Rudin to star as

(7) bony.' 'Kidd was just 15 **when she was approached** to be a model. Posing on

(8) near her home with an 11-year-old friend **when she was approached** by the fiend. The man

(9) finished a storming set of jazz standards **when she was approached** by SIR SEAN CONNERY. And she

(10) on Douglas Street in Cork city centre **when she was approached** by the pervert. The man persuaded

(from: *Phrasebite,* John Sinclair 2006)

10. How can a corpus-based analysis of literature be combined with its social functions?

If we get the science right and follow our 'after-path' or method, the corpus and the social functions of literature ought to merge spontaneously as science: collocation as instrumentation for language. What we see in *Phrasebite* (Sinclair 2006) is proof of what Malinowski referred to as scientific determinism. Why should our gender predictably cause us to have a rough or a smooth 'deal' throughout our lives?

Once we have read *Phrasebite* (Sinclair 2006), on the matter of *when + she + was*, we are scientifically bound to test out *when + he + was* (see table below). When we find that life is altogether more distinguished and comfortable universally for men, we need to allow *that* finding to percolate through to writers of feminist texts and in this way influence their literary theory. After all, the first article in corpus stylistics proper (with access to large corpora) only appeared in Louw (1989). The gender problem and its solution need to become co-extensive and co-continuous. The International Convention on Economic, Social and Cultural Rights entitles all of us to the benefits of science. We must let the corpus write us and our predicaments (Louw 1993, 2000).

N	Word	With	Rela-tion	Total	Total left	Total right	L5	L4	L3	L2	L1	Cen-tre	R1	R2	R3	R4	R5
1	TO	When he was	0	267	113	154	23	30	26	33	1	0	0	75	24	30	25
2	IN	When he was	0	458	222	236	23	46	39	114	0	0	55	71	39	35	36
3	BY	when he was	0	153	31	122	7	4	14	6	0	0	1	69	18	20	14

(continued)

(continued)

N	Word	With	Rela-tion	Total	Total left	Total right	L5	L4	L3	L2	L1	Cen-tre	R1	R2	R3	R4	R5
4	THE	when he was	0	550	254	296	62	49	68	75	0	0	18	54	96	68	60
5	AND	when he was	0	188	72	116	15	16	17	14	10	0	0	49	26	22	19
6	A	when he was	0	367	137	230	33	23	48	33	0	0	81	42	42	34	31
7	OF	when he was	0	275	124	151	34	33	35	22	0	0	0	41	35	38	37
8	HIS	when he was	0	233	127	106	23	30	38	36	0	0	0	40	16	28	22
9	HE	when he was	0	173	80	93	15	16	19	30	0	0	0	34	24	19	16
10	AS	when he was	0	91	40	51	10	16	12	1	1	0	1	31	7	5	7
11	FOR	when he was	0	107	47	60	8	14	20	5	0	0	1	24	11	11	13
12	MINISTER	when he was	0	37	5	32	1	0	2	1	1	0	1	18	7	5	1
13	ON	when he was	0	78	31	47	5	10	10	6	0	0	11	18	6	6	6
14	FROM	when he was	0	81	35	46	4	10	8	11	2	0	0	15	6	10	15
15	YEARS	when he was	0	56	33	23	4	3	2	16	8	0	0	14	4	4	1
16	UP	when he was	0	27	11	16	4	5	2	0	0	0	0	13	0	1	2
17	WITH	when he was	0	73	32	41	4	10	7	7	4	0	2	12	10	10	7
18	YOUNG	when he was	0	29	2	27	0	2	0	0	0	0	11	12	2	2	0
19	OFF	when he was	0	15	2	13	0	1	1	0	0	0	0	9	2	1	1
20	DIRECTOR	when he was	0	12	1	11	0	1	0	0	0	0	3	7	0	1	0
21	LAST	when he was	0	59	42	17	1	2	2	37	0	0	2	7	4	3	1
22	STUDENT	when he was	0	11	2	9	1	0	0	1	0	0	0	7	1	0	1
23	ABOUT	when he was	0	28	11	17	1	2	5	3	0	0	6	6	2	3	0
24	BOY	when he was	0	13	2	11	0	0	0	0	2	0	0	6	3	2	0
25	CHILD	when he was	0	13	2	11	0	1	0	0	1	0	1	6	4	0	0
26	ELECTED	when he was	0	22	0	22	0	0	0	0	0	0	16	6	0	0	0
27	OUT	when he was	0	20	8	12	0	1	3	1	3	0	3	6	0	0	3
28	AFTER	when he was	0	33	15	18	3	2	4	6	0	0	0	5	3	4	6
29	AT	when he was	0	92	38	54	8	9	19	2	0	0	19	5	9	13	8
30	AWAY	when he was	0	6	0	6	0	0	0	0	0	0	1	5	0	0	0

(continued)

(continued)

N	Word	With	Rela-tion	Total	Total left	Total right	L5	L4	L3	L2	L1	Cen-tre	R1	R2	R3	R4	R5
31	HIGH	when he was	0	11	4	7	1	1	1	1	0	0	0	5	0	2	0
32	LEADER	when he was	0	10	1	9	0	0	0	0	1	0	2	5	2	0	0
33	OPPOSITION	when he was	0	9	0	9	0	0	0	0	0	0	0	5	1	3	0
34	OVER	when he was	0	12	3	9	0	1	1	0	1	0	1	5	1	2	0
35	SECRETARY	when he was	0	11	0	11	0	0	0	0	0	0	1	5	2	3	0
36	10	when he was	0	11	0	11	0	0	0	0	0	0	7	4	0	0	0

Figure 2. Fragment of the collocation table for *when + he + was* from the British National Corpus

The collocates in this table settle the point that Sinclair makes in *Phrasebite* (above). They do this in *two* ways. Firstly, we notice that the collocates to the right of the phrase (*minister, director, leader*, etc.) settle the fact that men's career paths are unjustifiably more distinguished and comfortable than those of women in corpora of natural language. However, the second way in which they are empirically different is to be found in the *grammar-word collocates* that Halliday (1966) urges us to ignore. These are *to, in* and *by*, and must *not* be seen as prepositions. We have left grammar and syntax behind in order to utilise collocation as instrumentation. We are allowed logic. These words act as *truth-functional logical constants* (Carnap 1928; Russell 1948) to disclose the states of affairs or *facts*, in which men perform their privileged roles as part of our lived realities. A short extract from the concordance for *when + he + was + in* from a newspaper corpus follows. If we exclude *to, in* and *by* as 'stop words' (*sic*), we simultaneously discard their critical *argumentative* power as truth constant logical operators.

MicroConcord search SW: when he was in
80 characters per entry
Sort: 1R/SW unshifted

1	d by the Ministry of Defence and	when he was in	a position to influence the pla
2	nager, will be wary of Rothwell.	When he was in	charge of the Bridlington Town s
3	uir are well drilled and shrewd.	When he was in	charge of Meadowbank Thistle, o
4	law as the city's deputy mayor,	when he was in	charge of finances and economic
5	e on both Cambridge and Leander,	when he was in	charge in 1951 and 1952. His con

6	ve been little more than routine	when he was in	his heyday. His share of four
7	f reality, as it sometimes did	when he was in	office. I have heard people des
8	r Lafontaine's criticisms of him	when he was in	power. </Group> </Story>
9	rous role in combating the Mafia	when he was in	power. 'After two years of inve
10	known. "He was prescribed them	when he was in	public life to help him get thr
11	er P5. Campbell bought his car	when he was in	talks with Rolls-Royce to provid
12	Sittard. I played against Gullit	when he was in	that role for PSV Eindhoven and
13	dramatic shift in his view from	when he was in	the cabinet,' Tebbit said, poin
14	on as a sort of Cuban James Bond	when he was in	the Interior Ministry's elite sp

We also need to settle the issue that the Malinowskian determinism we witnessed in *Phrasebite* is borne out in corpora of *literary* texts and the phenomenon is *not* the product of *primed* (*sic*) individual minds (Hoey 2005). Such proof will be welcomed by Toolan (2009: 194), who finds difficulty in dealing with purportedly primed individual minds as a source of empiricism. This will form the subject matter of research during the early period of integration to which your question alludes. The evidence that this is so, exists and must be made available on an interdisciplinary level and as part of the new agenda for comparative literature and translation studies.

It must surely be more than coincidence that the string *she* + *was* occurs in *all* of the poetry of Philip Larkin only *twice*. *Both* instances occur in the same poem, 'Sunny Prestatyn'.

Sunny Prestatyn
Come to Sunny Prestatyn
Laughed the girl on the poster,
Kneeling up on the sand
In tautened white satin.
Behind her, a hunk of coast, a
Hotel with palms
Seemed to expand from her thighs and
Spread breast-lifting arms.

She was slapped up one day in March.
A couple of weeks, and her face
Was snaggle-toothed and boss-eyed;
Huge tits and a fissured crotch

Were scored well in, and the space
Between her legs held scrawls
That set her fairly astride
A tuberous cock and balls

Autographed Titch Thomas, while
Someone had used a knife
Or something to stab right through
The moustached lips of her smile.
She was too good for this life.
Very soon, a great transverse tear
Left only a hand and some blue.
Now Fight Cancer is there.

A poem of this kind is just the beginning for the type of work your question demands. For example, the entire notion of subtext is available for detailed explication (see Louw 2011 on subtext and especially Milojković 2011a for an illustration of how the grammatical string 'but when did' affects our understanding of Larkin's line and contributes to research on inspiration). The approach has established conclusively that the notion of text must now be extended. Material that *might* have appeared in it can no longer be disregarded or treated as an undecided absence. The universality of the approach and its transferability to other languages has now been confirmed (Milojković 2011b). As this paper goes to press, Aristide is back in Haiti and Mann is free and has renounced mercenary activity. Both parties have lost their day jobs.

References

Ayer, A. J. 1971. *Language, Truth and Logic.* Harmondsworth: Penguin.
Ayer, A. J. 1987. The a priori. In *A Priori Knowledge*, P. K. Moser (ed.). Oxford: OUP.
Beaney, M. (ed.). 1997. *The Frege Reader*. Blackwell: Oxford.
Berofsky, B. 1971. *Determinism.* Princeton NJ: PUP.
Carnap, R. 1928. *Der Logische Aufbau der Welt.* Berlin: Weltkreis Verlag.
Chomsky, N. 1957. *Syntactic Structures.* The Hague: Mouton.
Chomsky, N. 1964. *Aspects of the Theory of Syntax.* Cambridge MA: The MIT Press.
Culler, J. 1975. *Structuralist Poetics.* London: RKP.
Davidson, D. 1973–1974. On the very idea of a conceptual scheme. In *Proceedings*

and Addresses of the American Philosophical Association, 1973–1974, J. Rajchman & C. West (eds). New York NY: Wiley.

Firth, J. R. 1955. Structural linguistics. *Transactions of the Philological Society* 54(1): 83–103.

Firth, J. R. 1957. *Papers in Linguistics 1934–1951.* Oxford: OUP.

Frege, G. 1884. *The Foundations of Arithmetic: A Logico-Mathematical Enquiry into the Concept of Number,* translation (1974) by J. L. Austin. Oxford: Blackwell.

Gavins, J. & Steen, G. 2003. *Cognitive Poetics in Practice.* London: Routledge.

Grice, H. P. 1975. Logic and conversation. In *Syntax and Semantics* III: *Speech Acts,* P. Coles & J. L. Morgan (eds), 41–58. New York NY: Academic Press.

Gries, St. Th. & Stefanowitsch, A. (eds). 2007. *Corpus-Based Approaches to Metaphor.* Berlin: Mouton de Gruyter.

Halliday, M. A. K. 1966. Lexis as a linguistic level. In *In Memory of J. R. Firth,* C. E. Bazell, J. C. Catford, M. A. K. Halliday & R. H. Robins (eds). London: Longman.

Hoey, M. H. 2005. *Lexical Priming: A New Theory of Words and Language.* London: Routledge.

Hoey, M. H. 2006. Language as choice: What is chosen. In *System and Corpus: Exploring Connections,* S. Hunston & G. Thompson (eds). London: Equinox.

Hunston, S. & Thompson, G. (eds). 2006. *System and Corpus: Exploring Connections.* London: Equinox.

Kitcher, P. 1993. *The Advancement of Science.* Oxford: OUP.

Kjellmer, G. 1984. Some thoughts on collocational distinctiveness. In *Corpus Linguistics,* J. Aarts & W. Meijs (eds). Amsterdam: Rodopi.

Krishnamurthy, R. 2004. *English Collocation Studies: The OSTI Report.* London: Continuum.

Kuhn, T. 1996. *The Structure of Scientific Revolutions,* 3rd edn. Chicago IL: University of Chicago Press.

Lakoff, G. & Johnson, M. 1980[2003]. *Metaphors We Live By.* Chicago IL: University of Chicago Press.

Long, M. H. & Doughty, C. H. (eds). 2009. *The Handbook of Language Teaching.* Malden MA: Wiley.

Louw, W. E. 1989. Sub-Routines in the integration of language and literature. In *Literature and the Learner: Methodological Approaches* [British Council ELT Documents 130], 47–54. London: MEP.

Louw, W. E. 1991. Classroom concordancing of delexical forms and the case for integrating language and literature. *ELR Journal 4:* 151–178. [Special issue *Classroom Concordancing,* T. Johns & P. King (eds)].

Louw, W. E. 1993. Irony in the text or insincerity in the writer? The diagnostic potential of semantic prosodies. In *Text and Technology: In Honour of John Sinclair*, M. Baker, G. Francis & E. Tognini-Bonelli (eds). Amsterdam: John Benjamins.

Louw, W. E. 1997. The role of corpora in critical literary appreciation. In *Teaching and Language Corpora*. A. Wichmann, S. Fligelstone, T. McEnery & G. Knowles (eds). Harlow: Longman.

Louw, W. E. 2000. Contextual prosodic theory: Bringing semantic prosodies to life. In *Words in Context. In Honour of John Sinclair*, C. Heffer & H. Sauntson (eds). Birmingham: ELR. <www.revue-texto.net/index.php?id=124>

Louw, W. E. 2003. Dressing up waiver: A stochastic-collocational reading of the Truth and Reconciliation Commission (TRC). Harare: mimeo, also available in the *Occasional Papers dei Quaderni del CeSLIC* <http://www.lingue.unibo.it/ceslic/e_occ_papers.htm>

Louw, W. E. 2006. Data-Assisted negotiating: Will it produce a new class of negotiator or destroy the ideology of negotiating? *Language Matters* 37(2): 183–205.

Louw, W. E. 2007a. Truth, literary worlds and devices as collocation. Closing Keynote presentation at TaLC6 on 7th July 2004. In *Proceedings of the Sixth Conference on Teaching and Language Corpora*, E. Hidalgo, L. Quereda & J. Santana (eds). Amsterdam: Rodopi.

Louw, W. E. 2007b. Are literary texts and their worlds 'thrown together' as collocation? Keynote presentation to ACORN Symposium, in Honour of John Sinclair, on 4th May 2007. <http://www.aston.ac.uk/symposium.htm>

Louw, W. E. 2008a. Consolidating empirical method in data-assisted stylistics: Towards a corpus-attested glossary of literary terms. In *Directions in Empirical Literary Studies. In Honour of Willie van Peer,* [Linguistic Approaches to Literature 5], S. Zyngier, M. Bortolussi, A. Chesnokova & J. Auracher (eds). Amsterdam: John Benjamins.

Louw, W. E. 2008b. Two chapters. In *Approaches to Corpus Stylistics. The Corpus, the Computer and the Study of Literature* [Routledge Advances in Corpus Linguistics], D. Hoover, J. Culpeper & B. Louw (eds). London: Routledge.

Louw, W. E. 2008c. Is it time to change your linguistic or stylistic theory? Paper presented at PALA, Sheffield.

Louw, W. E. 2008d. Establishing a historiography for corpus-events from their frequency: A celebration of Bertrand Russell's (1948) five postulates. Harare: mimeo.

Louw, W. E. 2010a. Collocation as instrumentation for meaning: A scientific fact. In *Literary Education and Digital Learning: Methods and Technologies for Humanities Studies*, W. van Peer, E. Asimakopoulou & N. Bessis (eds). Hershey PA: IGI Global.

Louw, W. E. 2010b. Automating the extraction of literary worlds and their subtexts from the poetry of William Butler Yeats. In *Para por y Sobre Luis Quereda,* M. Falces Sierra (coord.). Granada: Granada University Press.

Louw, W. E. 2011. Relabelling subtext as logical form. In *Proceedings of the Sixth International Conference on Corpus Linguistics.*

Louw, W. E. & Chateau, C. Forthcoming. The smoothing of semantic prosody in science: A contextual prosodic approach. Rome: JADT Proceedings.

Macherey, P. 1966. *Pour une theorie de la production litteraire.* Paris: Maspero.

Malinowski, B. 1922. *Argonauts of the Western Pacific. An Account of Native Enterprise and Adventure in the Archipelagoes of Melanesian New Guinea* [Studies in Economics 65]. London: George Routledge & Sons.

Malinowski, B. 1946. The problem of meaning in primitive languages, Supplement 1. In *The Meaning of Meaning,* C. K. Ogden & I. A. Richards (eds). London: Kegan Paul.

Markoff, A. A. 1913. Essai d'une recherché statistique sur le texte du roman Eugene Trench and Trubner. Onegin. *Bull. Acad. Imper. Sci. St Petersbourg* VII.

Martinich. 1985. *The Philosophy of Language.* Oxford: OUP.

McGinn, M. 1982. The third dogma of empiricism. In *Proceedings of the Aristotelian Society,* Vol. *LXXXII.* London: Aristotelian Society.

Milojković, M. 2011a. Time and transitions in Larkin's poetry. In *Online Proceedings of the 2011 PALA conference.*

Milojković M. 2011b. Semantic prosody and subtext as universal, collocation-based instrumentation for meaning and literary worlds. In *Труды международной конференции «Корпусная лингвистика – 2011,* Zakharov V. P. (et al.). St Petersburg: St Petersburg State University, Faculty of Philology. 47–52.

O'Halloran, K. 2007. Critical discourse analysis and the corpus informed interpretation of metaphor at the register level. *Applied Linguistics* 28(1): 1–24.

Palmer, F. R. 1975. *Semantics: A New Outline.* Cambridge: CUP.

Pears, D. 1971. *Wittgenstein.* London: Fontana Collins.

Peirce, C. S. 1905. What pragmatism is. *Monist* 15(2): 161–181.

Philip, G. S. 2003. Collocation and Connotation: A Corpus-Based Investigation of Colour Words in English and Italian. PhD dissertation, School of English, University of Birmingham.

Popper, K. R. 1959. *The Logic of Scientific Discovery.* London: RKP.

Quine, W. van O. 1961. Two dogmas of empiricism. In *From a Logical Point of View,* 20–46. Cambridge: Harvard University Press.

Russell, B. 1945. *The History of Western Philosophy.* London: Routledge.

Russell, B. 1948. *Human Knowledge: Its Scope and Limits.* London: Routledge.

Russell, B. 1960. *Bertrand Russell Speaks His Mind.* London: Arthur Baker.

Sinclair, J. M. et al. 1987[1993]. *Collins COBUILD English Language Dictionary*. London: HarperCollins.

Sinclair, J. M. 1991. *Corpus, Concordance, Collocation*. Oxford: OUP.

Sinclair, J. M. 1995. *Collocation on CD-ROM*. Glasgow: HarperCollins.

Sinclair, J. M. 2004a. *Trust the Text*. London: Routledge.

Sinclair, J. M. 2004b. *Reading Concordances*. London: Longman.

Sinclair, J. M. 2006. *Phrasebite*. Pescia: TWC.

Sinclair, J. M. & Mauranen, A. 2006. *Linear Unit Grammar: Integrating Speech and Writing* [Studies in Corpus Linguistics 25]. Amsterdam: John Benjamins.

Stewart, D. 2010. *Semantic Prosody: A Critical Evaluation*. London: Routledge.

Stockwell, P. 2002. *Cognitive Poetics*. London: Routledge.

Stubbs, M. 2001. *Words and Phrases: Corpus Studies of Lexical Semantics*. Oxford: Blackwell.

Swales, J. 1990. *Genre Analysis in Academic and Research Settings*. Cambridge: CUP.

Toolan, M. 2009. *Narrative Progression in the Short Story: A Corpus Stylistic Approach* [Linguistic Approaches to Literature 6]. Amsterdam: John Benjamins.

Waugh, A. 1993. *The Linguistics Wars*. Oxford: OUP.

Wittgenstein, L. 1922. *Tractatus Logico-Philosophicus*. Trans. D. F. Pears & D. F. McGuiness, 1960. London: Routledge and Kegan Paul.

Wittgenstein, L. 1980. *Remarks on the Philosophy of Psychology,* 2 Vols. Oxford: Blackwell.

A two-way exchange between
syntax and corpora

In his contribution, Geoffrey Sampson, Professor Emeritus at the University of Sussex (United Kingdom) and currently Research Fellow at the University of South Africa, highlights the relationship between Corpus Linguistics and Syntax. He shows how this bond has a two-way nature. In his view, the use of corpora in language research allows one to better understand syntactic issues and the development of language complexity. However, the relationship also runs in the other direction in Sampson's view since he believes the focus on syntax is one of the major factors contributing to the growth of interest in Corpus Linguistics. From a more general perspective, Sampson argues in favour of linguistics remaining a creative activity which develops in unexpected ways. As for the prospects of Corpus Linguistics, he predicts its death – not of this approach itself, but of the term. He believes the label 'Corpus Linguistics' will disappear when corpora become just another resource available to linguists.

1. Where do you place the roots of Corpus Linguistics? And to what do you attribute the growth of interest in the area?

2. Is Corpus Linguistics a science or a methodology? Where would you situate Corpus Linguistics in the scientific or methodological panorama?

I must take these questions together, because answering either one involves discussing the other.

The first thing that needs to be said about these and the rest of this series of questions (I shall be surprised if I am the only contributor who makes essentially the same point) is that it is misleading to think of 'Corpus Linguistics' as a branch of linguistics, alongside sociolinguistics or historical linguistics. Corpus linguists are just people who study language and languages in an empirical, scientific manner, using whatever sources of empirical data are available; at the present time it happens that, for many aspects of language, the most useful data sources are often electronic corpora. I work a lot with corpora, but I think of myself as a linguist, not a 'corpus linguist'. If some aspect of language is better studied using other tools, I will use those.

The reasons why corpora have become more significant in linguistics than they used to be include: (i) the availability of computers; (ii) change of emphasis from phonology to syntax; and (iii) the bankruptcy of intuition-based techniques. I discuss these points in turn:

Availability of computers

It is hard to do much with a corpus unless it is in electronic form and you have access to a computer to process and search it. The Brown Corpus, the first electronic corpus, was published in 1964, which as it happens was close to the time when I began learning to work with computers – but that was very unusual then for someone with a humanities background. Everyone had heard of computers, but most academics knew little about them and had certainly never seen one. I remember the air of imperfectly-concealed condescension with which engineers and mathematicians greeted the idea that some of us arts types wanted to play with their machines. When we managed to do so, the low-level programming languages of those days and the batch-processing approach of 1960s computing environments meant that, although one could use computers to find out things about language which would be hard to discover any other way, the process was horribly slow and cumbersome relative to what is possible and easy now.

It was not until some time in the 1980s that computers began to become routinely available to linguists. Even that is quite a while ago now; but when a complex new technology does become convenient and widely available, it inevitably takes time for a profession to adjust to its possibilities. Corpus-based techniques have taken decades to catch on in linguistics, but I am not sure that one could have expected the process to occur faster.

Change of emphasis within the discipline

Until some point in the 1960s, the intellectual 'centre of gravity' of linguistics lay in phonology, which deals mainly with finite systems of a few dozen phonemes that combine in a limited number of ways. Corpora do not offer much to the phonologist. One can survey the possibilities adequately using traditional techniques. Only with the rise of generative linguistics did the 'weight' of the discipline shift to syntax, which deals with large numbers of elements combining in effectively infinitely many ways. That meant that one needed to study very large samples to have a chance of encountering a representative range of possibilities, so corpus compilation became the way forward.

Bankruptcy of intuition-based techniques

Ironically, while the generative movement shifted linguists' attention to an aspect of language – syntax – which is difficult to study empirically without the use of corpora, the unempirical style of research advocated by the generativists led very many linguists to ignore the virtues of corpora for a long time after they started becoming available. No one in the modern world would suggest that, say, meteorologists or marine biologists should decide what their basic data were without looking at evidence: it is too obvious that the weather, and marine organisms, are things independent of us and that we can find out about them only by looking. Language is not in the same sense independent of human cognition, so it may at first have been reasonable for the Chomskyans to believe that a linguist can decide what is in and what is not in his language by introspection, without external observation. And, as well as arguing that grammar-writing *can* be based on introspection, they cited the 'absence of negative evidence' (that is, we don't hear starred sentences) in order to argue that grammar-writing *cannot* successfully be based on observation.

For a short while these ideas may have been reasonable, but it soon turned out that eliminating the dependence of science on observation is just as bad an idea in linguistics as in physical sciences. This was clear at least from the time when William Labov (1975) demonstrated that speakers simply do not know how they speak, and that generative linguists ascribe an authority to their own judgements which they manifestly do not possess. The argument from absence of negative evidence represented a misunderstanding of how empirical science works (Sampson 1975); if it were a good argument, no physical science would be possible (Sampson 2005: 89–91).

By now there are many cases where core elements of non-empirical linguists' theories rest on intuitive beliefs that are wildly at variance with reality. One of Noam Chomsky's leading arguments for innate knowledge of language (see e.g. Chomsky 1980: 40) is the claim that, without innate knowledge, children could not succeed in mastering the English rule for forming questions, because structures that are allegedly crucial for determining the correct rule are so rare that one can live one's life without ever hearing an example. Chomsky seems to have based that statement on guesswork (or 'intuition', if one wants to use the more dignified term). Although I do not believe that one needs to hear these particular structures to get the question rule right, I used the demographically-sampled speech section of the British National Corpus to check how rare the structures are in real life. It turned out that one can expect to hear thousands of relevant examples in a lifetime's exposure to casual chat (Sampson 2005: 81). This is not an isolated case of mismatch between generative linguists' intuitions and empirical reality (though it is perhaps the most egregious case, in view of the frequency with which the generative literature has relied on this baseless assertion – cf. Pullum & Scholz 2002: 39–40).

Even in face of absurdities like this, quite a few linguists do continue to cling to the idea that grammatical research can progress independently of empirical evidence. But by now they are starting to resemble upper-middle-class Edwardian ladies who cannot conceive of cooking or cleaning with their own hands. Fiddling about with scripts for searching text files or with tape recordings of spontaneous speech looks like servants' work to some of the more precious inhabitants of linguistics departments. But the reality of many areas of present-day linguistics is that, if one wants to make progress rather than just go through the motions, that is the kind of work that has to be done; and I think this is now obvious to many younger linguists. So it is no surprise that corpus work has been coming to the fore.

The remaining point in Questions 1 and 2 concerns the 'roots' of Corpus Linguistics. Diana McCarthy and I surveyed the historical origins of corpus work briefly in our *Corpus Linguistics* anthology (Sampson & McCarthy 2004: 1–4). One might argue that Dr Johnson's dictionary was based in part on a 'corpus' of literary quotations, and the work of Wilhelm Käding (1898) seems to have been a clear early case of Corpus Linguistics in the modern sense. But these are matters of fact and of definition (what counts as a 'corpus'?), rather than of intellectual controversy; there is little to be gained from contributors repeatedly rehearsing the history at length.

3. How representative can a corpus be?

Representativeness seems to have become something of a bugbear for corpus researchers, but I am not quite sure why it is felt to be a worry. Any corpus is a sample of language use, and naturally one wants it to be an unbiased 'fair sample'. Statisticians who discuss sampling talk in terms of drawing a sample from a 'population' – the (perhaps infinitely) numerous set of entities for which the finite sample is intended to stand proxy. If there is a worry about corpus representativeness, perhaps the problem is less about sampling techniques than about deciding what 'population' is to be sampled. Thus, for written language ought we to think in terms of acts of writing, or acts of reading (some pieces of written language are read very many times, others only once)? Or perhaps the problem arises because of tensions between groups who want to use language corpora for different purposes and have not fully recognised that the same kind of sample will not suit all purposes equally. The written-language section of the British National Corpus includes quite a lot of literary writing, sometimes decades old. For a sociolinguist interested in what written usage the average Briton encounters, this might be inappropriate; for the dictionary publishers who were among the leading sponsors of the BNC project, it may be very desirable to give extra weight to writing that is recognised as more authoritative than, say, hastily-composed office memos. This would be a case of conflicting interests; I wonder whether 'representativeness' is invoked in order to suggest that such conflicts have scientifically correct solutions.

To me it is hard to get worked up about this issue, because (at least with respect to English grammar, the aspect of language that I have chiefly been involved with) such evidence as I have examined suggests to me that any differences between genres of English are trivial relative to what they have in common (Sampson 2001: Chapter 3). There is one English language, not a set of Englishes. Clearly we should avoid obvious bias in the way we sample the language, when we can easily do so, but I am sceptical about whether our findings will be much affected by how far we go to achieve perfect representativeness.

4. How far should an analyst rely on intuition?

I have discussed intuition to some extent in an earlier answer. The standard line, according to the hypothetico-deductive scientific method, is that the scientist uses intuition to generate plausible hypotheses – hypotheses will not emerge mechanically from any amount of accumulated data – and then uses empirical evidence to corroborate or refute the hypotheses. This is as applicable to linguistics, I believe, as to other fields, and in linguistics the empirical evidence often comes from corpora.

5. What kind of questions should an analyst think of?

This one really is unanswerable! Linguistics is a science, and science is a creative affair – a scientist who hopes to be told what kind of questions to ask (what hypotheses to formulate, in the jargon) is unlikely to produce much of value.

Admittedly that might not be true of present-day 'Big Science': 21st-century genetics, for instance, seems to involve armies of researchers uncovering and assembling numerous small pieces of new knowledge in response to strategic research guidelines which perhaps can be laid down successfully well in advance. Whoever formulated the guidelines needed to be creative, but the individual researchers possibly do not. However, linguistics, realistically, will never be like that (and probably should not be like that even if it could be). Linguistics will always be 'craft science' rather than production line science, organisationally more like 17th-century physics than 21st-century Big Science. That means that it is heavily dependent on individuals with original minds spotting novel questions whose answers might move our understanding forward. One cannot lay down long-term research strategies, because tomorrow's questions grow in an unpredictable fashion out of today's answers.

Now that the management of universities is increasingly shifting out of the hands of practising academics into those of professional managers, these points are beginning to be lost sight of. In my experience the managerial types in suits would like university research to move into predictable, production line mode, and they have little understanding of (or patience with) the idea that for many subjects it just cannot be like that. Younger academics, whose memory does not stretch back to a time when university governance was in a healthier state, are sometimes browbeaten into accepting that the managerial perspective must be correct. But, for linguistics, the 'production line' research model could only be a system for raising and spending funds in an orderly manner and providing researchers with a career structure. If it generated any significant advances in our understanding of language and languages, these would surely emerge more or less accidentally, out of the tea-breaks or things done after the end of the shift, as it were, rather than rolling systematically off the end of the production line.

Whether as a consequence of managerialism or for other reasons, linguists who work with corpora do often seem to misunderstand the essentially creative aspect of the discipline. One symptom of this is the way that groups who publish new corpus resources are routinely expected nowadays to complement the data files with software for manipulating them. When I began to work with the British National Corpus and subscribed to its online forum, I was surprised (and quite disappointed) to find that it was full of messages about how to implement the software accompanying the BNC (called Sara, if I remember correctly), while there was hardly anything about people using the BNC to explore the nature of the English language in novel ways. I have even had people complain to me that the corpus resources I have made available to the public are only half-finished, because I provide no software to go with them – though I do provide documentation which defines their file structures very precisely.

Personally, when I get hold of new corpus resources, I use the data files and discard or ignore any software that comes with them. However good the software might be, it will be designed to allow users to answer some fixed range of questions which the designer anticipates that people will want to ask. The chances that this range will cover the questions I find myself wanting to put to the data are not good enough to make it worth learning to use the software. Clearly that cannot be an absolute rule: when the recordings underlying the spoken section of the BNC are digitised by the 'Mining a Year of Speech' project which John Coleman is leading at Oxford, I shall have to use that project's software to explore the material – it would be folly to try to analyse acoustic signals independently. But most electronic corpora, from Brown and LOB to the existing BNC, comprise straightforward text files, so that it is easy to write one's own scripts to analyse them in whatever way one wants. If a linguist is not willing to learn enough Perl to write simple analytic routines, then I'm sorry, but he or she is in the wrong job.

Now that corpus development has become a widespread activity within the discipline, one is hearing complaints by sceptics that for all the effort going into corpus-building, there does not seem to be a commensurate volume of new knowledge and insights emerging from corpora. I have sympathy with this complaint. At the present juncture I have a sense that there are a number of linguists around the world who like the idea of getting funding to develop a corpus of their language or their favourite genre of language use, but who do not really look beyond the busy-work of getting the corpus compiled; they perhaps hope vaguely that when their corpus exists, valuable knowledge will emerge from it almost automatically. That won't happen. A corpus is only a tool, and there is little point in equipping oneself with an expensive tool unless one has plans for using it.

6. What are the strengths and weaknesses of corpus analysis?

A 'corpus' just means a collection of samples of language usage recorded in some manner or other. If one is tempted to say that language corpora are unsuitable for certain kinds of linguistic research, one must be careful that the appearance of unsuitability does not merely reflect unduly narrow assumptions about the nature of corpora. For instance, traditional corpora of transcribed speech might not be adequate for studying child language development, even if the speech is that of children, because one cannot see what the child is doing or what is going on around him as he speaks. But a collection which videotaped the scenes as well as recording the sound would still be a 'corpus', though one very different from the classic language corpora.

Nevertheless, it is true that corpora are more useful for some areas of linguistic research than others. When we are dealing with small finite systems (the phoneme systems already mentioned being the obvious example), corpora tend not to be needed; we can often get on fine without them (though there are aspects of phonology, notably intonation systems, where corpus work will often be valuable or essential). At the other 'end' of linguistics, it seems to me that corpora have limited relevance (though some relevance) to the study of semantics. But that is not because the semantics of a language is studied using other sources of empirical evidence which do not fit the definition of 'corpus'. It is because to a large extent the study of semantics is not an empirical scientific discipline at all, but something more like a branch of philosophy (cf. Sampson 2001: Chapter 11). Subjects which can be studied scientifically ought to be studied that way, but we must recognise that science has limits.

7. What is the future of Corpus Linguistics?

As suggested in my previous answer, for the immediate future the priority needs to be (and I hope will be) a shift of emphasis, away from creating yet more corpora, towards extracting worthwhile knowledge from those we already have. By now we have lots. Of course I understand that if you are from a country whose national language has no corpus at all yet, building its Brown/LOB equivalent will be a high priority. But searching out and seeking to fill increasingly narrow 'gaps in the market' strikes me as a questionable use of linguists' time. The world does not truly need, say, a corpus of informal conversation between legal professionals (an example which I hope is hypothetical – no offence to anyone is intended). If the legal profession needs such a resource, let them take the initiative towards compiling it; they presumably will know how they want to use it. At present, the existing array of corpora are underexploited, so our profession ought to be putting effort into formulating novel questions to put to them.

Looking a little further ahead, in a sense I believe that Corpus Linguistics as such has not got a future. I began by saying that 'Corpus Linguistics' is not a special branch of linguistics. I would hope that its future is simply to fade away as a concept, because all concerned will take corpora for granted as one important set of tools in any linguist's toolbox. Some linguists will work with corpora most of the time, others more sporadically, and no doubt some will specialise in areas where corpora have little or no relevance. But it seems to me that it will be quite a failure if in forty years' time the phrase 'Corpus Linguistics' continues to be an established collocation.

8. What issues does one have to face when developing treebanks?

If we want to use a corpus to find out about aspects of a language other than vocabulary, we will probably need it to be equipped with annotation making explicit the grammatical structures into which the words are organised. Almost from the beginning of electronic corpus compilation it was usual to add part-of-speech tags to the words, and for a long time now many corpus developers have been adding information about phrase and clause structure – turning raw corpora into 'treebanks'.

The biggest problem here lies in taxonomy. What range of syntactic structures does a language possess, and where are the boundaries to be drawn between different categories of constituent? Linguists who became used to the aprioristic syntactic theorising of the 1960s and 1970s learned a few standard categories – noun phrase, adjective phrase, complement clause, relative clause, and so on; but, as soon as one encounters real-life language samples (even if these are drawn from edited, published writing, let alone from casual speech), one is rapidly at a loss to know how to apply the familiar categories, or to decide what further categories should be postulated. What labelled bracketing should we assign to a postal address? In the sequence *we kept adding to our ritual without daring to abandon any part of it*, is *without* functioning as a preposition introducing a separate constituent headed by *daring*, or is *without* a subordinating conjunction acting as the first word of a non-finite clause, parallel to, say, *while seeking to* … ? In my experience, one begins treebank compilation imagining that after a few debatable issues like these are cleared out of the way, the rest of the work will be fairly plain sailing – but it does not take long to discover that the debatable issues are almost more numerous than the straightforward cases, and new debatable issues never stop cropping up.

The point was demonstrated experimentally at a workshop at the 1991 ACL annual conference. Computational linguists from nine institutions were given a set of English sentences and asked to indicate what bracket-structure their respective groups would assign to them; and the analyses were compared. They were not asked to label the brackets; it is easy to imagine that different groups might use different nomenclature for grammatical categories even if they meant essentially the same thing. But one might have expected that at least the placing of brackets would agree fairly well. Yet, although the sentences were not notably 'messy', agreement was strikingly poor. In the following sentence (from a *New York Times* article included in the Brown Corpus):

One of those capital-gains ventures, in fact, has saddled him with Gore Court.

the *only* constituents identified as such by all nine participants were the name *Gore Court*, and the prepositional phrase *with Gore Court*.

In this situation it seems inescapable that if we want to get anywhere with building meaningful treebanks and generating findings that can meaningfully be shared between research groups, a high priority must be to define analytic schemes that will not just specify a comprehensive range of categories but will offer detailed, rigorous guidelines specifying how they are to be applied to as many debatable cases as possible. Our situation is akin to that confronting Carl Linnaeus when he developed the first standard system for naming biological species. Without it, there was just no way for botanists in different places to know whether or not they were discussing the same plant.

When, with colleagues at Lancaster University, I began developing what I believe may have been the first-ever treebank in the early 1980s, rigour and comprehensiveness in the analytic scheme seemed to me a more important goal than size of the treebank. Although scheme and treebank grew in parallel, I think the wordage of the scheme definition was always substantially in excess of the wordage of the analysed samples comprising the treebank. But, as treebank development has become an international industry, others involved in it do not always seem to have seen things the same way. My impression is that commonly it is seen as much more important to produce the largest-possible treebank than to adopt rigorous definitions of the analytic categories.

Academics are at the mercy of research sponsors, of course, and in dealing with funding agencies it is undoubtedly easier to 'sell' an enormous treebank than a tightly-defined treebank. Yet, without tight definition, the larger the treebank the more likely it is that its annotations will not reliably be counting apples with apples and oranges with oranges. Research sponsors may not initially appreciate this problem, but it is our role to educate them. There is of course a long history of downplaying the importance of taxonomy in linguistics. Generative linguists have in the past expressed hostility to taxonomy. Consider for instance Jerrold Katz's comments (1971: 31ff.) on linguistics as 'library science', as he put it, or the negative connotations of Chomsky's use (1964: 11) of the term 'taxonomic model'. And now that the generativists have moved on from NP and VP to 'Spec C', 'TP', and their other latter-day syntactic symbols, they seem to have shifted, if anything, even further away from the nitty-gritty issues of 'Where exactly does this unusual-looking constituent begin and end, and how do we classify it?', which constantly face anyone who tries to turn a real-life corpus into a treebank.

No corpus linguists, I think, are actually hostile to the taxonomic enterprise. The point I am trying to make in this section was made with more eloquence than I can muster by Jane Edwards at the Corpus-Linguistics Nobel Symposium (Edwards 1992: 139):

> The single most important property of any data base for purposes of computer-assisted research is that *similar instances be encoded in predictably similar ways.*

But this is a principle which I feel the community of corpus analysts in general has not yet taken fully to heart. Defining detailed, comprehensive analytic guidelines is an unglamourous, indeed downright tedious activity, but it merits a larger share of corpus linguists' efforts than it has been receiving.

9. In what way(s) can Corpus Linguistics enhance our understanding of syntax? And how is it reflected in grammar books?

As already suggested, syntax is to my mind the aspect of language where corpus-based research is supremely useful. It can answer questions that could scarcely be addressed any other way, ranging from highly specific queries such as whether some individual construction remains current, or what features in the environment favour or disfavour its use, to very general issues about the nature of human language behaviour.

One of these general issues which corpus work has led me to see with new eyes concerns the concept of 'ungrammaticality'.

For half a century now, most theoretical linguists have understood the grammar of a natural language on the model of the artificial 'languages' of mathematical logic, such as the propositional calculus, where the concept *well-formed formula* is central to the system. Rules generate a(n) (infinitely numerous) class of symbol-sequences that count as meaningful formulae of the calculus; other sequences of the same symbols are meaningless jumbles. Linguists, similarly, have identified a language such as English with a(n) (infinitely numerous) class of grammatical English sentences. They have seen the task of grammar-writing as being in large part to devise rules to distinguish between the grammatical sentences and the 'starred strings' or 'word-salad'.

Linguists have always recognised that the rules of grammaticality for a natural language must be massively more complex than those of artificial formal languages. And they have nuanced the picture in further ways. Some linguists suggest, for instance, that rules of natural-language grammar should be supplemented with probabilities, or with information about social variables, so that rather than merely defining a two-way grammatical/ungrammatical classification of strings of words, the grammar might characterise a sentence as 'grammatical but unusual', or 'used by men more than women'. But the idea that below this detail there is a fundamental distinction between grammatical and ungrammatical, whatever type of rules may be needed to formalise that distinction, has scarcely been challenged. For many years I took it for granted myself.

There were always linguists who questioned the orthodoxy. Fred Householder (1973: 371) pointed out that it is remarkably difficult to construct a sequence of English words for which one cannot imagine any use whatever. Studying the statistical distribution of constructions in English-language corpora eventually convinced me that the concept of 'ungrammaticality' is fundamentally mistaken. I no longer believe that any two-way classification of that sort can be imposed on word-sequences; the analogy with logical calculi is severely misleading.

Clearly, any language has some grammatical constructions which are very familiar and heavily used, and others which are less standard but will be used on occasion – but the evidence I have seen suggests that this is a cline with no particular termination. In a 'target article' in the 'Grammar without grammaticality' special issue of the journal *Corpus Linguistics and Linguistic*

Theory (Sampson 2007), I discussed this evidence, and likened the situation as I now see it to the pattern of tracks in open savannah country inhabited by a population which has not developed formal systems of land law, rights of way, and so forth. There will be some wide, heavily-used roadways, other lesser tracks, and so on down to scarcely-visible marks in the grass where one or two pairs of feet have passed. But it will not make sense to ask 'Is there a track from point X to point Y?' – in the imaginary scenario I postulated, if X to Y does not coincide with a heavily-used route the answer would have to be something like 'I don't remember seeing anyone walking just that way, but if you want to, go ahead'.

Similarly in the case of language, it makes sense to ask 'Can one say *The farmer killed the duckling* in English?', and the answer will be 'Yes, subject–verb–object is one of the central sentence-patterns of the language', but it does not really make sense to ask 'Is XYZ ungrammatical?' – if XYZ is a peculiar string of words, the only reasonable answer would be something like 'Well, what do you mean by it? – of course if that is how you want to use it, nothing stands in the way'. The situation is quite different from the case of the propositional calculus, where permuting the symbols of a well-formed formula gives a sequence that is just meaningless and useless, full stop.

Many commentators on my target article disagreed with me; but much of the disagreement read more as if the commentators could not believe that I was serious about holding such an unorthodox position, than as if they understood what I was saying and believed it was mistaken for identifiable reasons. The ungrammaticality concept appears to have such a hold over present-day linguistics that people find it difficult to entertain the possibility that it is a mistake.

Yet it is a fairly recent concept. The asterisk notation for ungrammaticality was never used, so far as I know, before the rise of generative linguistics. (I believe it was adapted from historical linguists' use of the asterisk to indicate that a reconstructed form is not actually attested – a quite different concept.) The 'pedagogical' or 'descriptive' grammar books that have been published down the centuries, before theoretical linguistics existed, listed constructions that do occur in a language but it seems to me that they did not express (or imply) any complementary concept of impossible constructions or word-sequences. If they mentioned that some form of wording was to be avoided, that was because people *do* often use it but it is socially deprecated.

In this respect it seems to me that descriptive grammars of languages, which theoretical linguists have sometimes seen as anecdotal or intellectually lightweight relative to their own attempts to formalise grammar rules, are more faithful to the reality of human language than a formal grammar can be. Someone who made a map of tracks in the savannah would include the broadest paths and some of the lesser ones, but would have to choose an arbitrary cut-off point below which paths were too narrow and temporary to mark on the map. Descriptive grammar-books do something very like that for natural languages: they list the heavily-used constructions and some of the less heavily-used ones, and it is an arbitrary decision where to stop and treat more unusual forms of wording as too occasional or specialised to mention.

Without corpus experience, I personally would probably never have come to see language this way. Perhaps it is no coincidence that Geoffrey Leech, one of the co-authors of the best-established descriptive grammar of English (Quirk et al. 1985), was also the pioneer of Corpus Linguistics on our side of the Atlantic. My current 'take' on the ungrammaticality concept may itself be misguided, of course – but I cannot imagine what category of evidence other than corpus evidence could be used to construct a serious argument against it.

10. What do corpus-based studies tell us about the development of language complexity? And how have/should they impact(ed) language teaching?

If one believes, as Noam Chomsky and Steven Pinker do, that the overall architecture of human language is laid down in our genes, then development of language complexity is scarcely an issue. One would expect all human languages to be similar in structure and hence similar in complexity, and an individual's idiolect would not be expected to develop much in complexity after he or she has passed the 'critical period' when the innate Language Acquisition Device is biologically programmed to switch off. But we know more about genetics now than we did when Chomsky was developing his ideas about innate knowledge of language, or even than we did when Pinker wrote *The Language Instinct* (Pinker 1994), and it has become harder to see how their picture of language acquisition could possibly be correct. (Chater et al. 2009 have produced a formal argument that it cannot be correct, though some have rejected that argument.)

Whether language structure *could* be genetically encoded or not, I find Chomsky's and Pinker's arguments that it *is* so quite empty (Sampson 2005); and others (notably Evans & Levinson 2009) are independently drawing attention to the fact that patterns of diversity among languages seem incompatible with the Chomsky/Pinker picture. The reasonable conclusion at this point is surely that languages are cultural constructs, constrained only in minor respects by biology. In that case, one would expect to find differences in complexity among languages, growth in complexity over time, and so forth, as one finds in other areas of human culture.

One way in which I have brought corpus data into relationship with this idea was by looking at correlations between syntactic complexity and speakers' demographic characteristics in a subset of the BNC demographically-sampled speech section. Measuring 'complexity' in the schoolroom sense of the incidence of subordinate clauses embedded within higher clauses, I found (to my considerable surprise) that there appears to be a statistically-significant correlation with speakers' age, in the sense that (not just through childhood but on beyond the 'critical period' into the thirties, forties, fifties, and sixties) people's speech grows more complex as they get older (Sampson 2001: Chapter 5). If this effect is genuine, it is surely not just fascinating but potentially has implications for social policy and the like.

The proviso 'if it is genuine' is important: creating a treebank of casual speech is a time-consuming, expensive business, so the sample available to me was small and the statistical test I applied achieved only a modest level of significance. (Currently I am developing a larger sample, which may in due course establish the finding more robustly – or may show it to have been a meaningless blip.)

If the finding is indeed genuine, because the BNC gives us a snapshot of British speech at one point in history (the early 1990s), it can be interpreted in alternative ways. It might mean that individuals' speech patterns regularly grow syntactically more complex as the individuals' age; they always have and they always will. Or it might mean that changes in British society over the 20th century, perhaps the spread of television and internet use, have led adults born in the 1960s and 1970s to adopt grammatically simpler styles of speech than those which people born in the 1930s adopted at the same age: the younger generation will never come to speak in the way that was natural for their parents.

Syntactic structure is so intimately related to human thought processes that we should surely want to know which of these interpretations is correct. Without corpora, questions like this could never emerge.

I cannot comment to any extent on language teaching, since this is not a topic I know much about. But if it really were the case that the speech of younger Britons is not spontaneously developing the levels of structural complexity found in the speech of previous generations, then one might feel that it should be a priority for primary and secondary education to do what it can to remedy this. Complex speech is not desirable for its own sake; when something can be put simply, that is the best way to put it. But many topics are inherently complicated, and citizens who are capable of engaging with complication in their thinking and speaking will, I would suppose, be better and more fulfilled citizens than those who are forced to oversimplify.

Let me repeat that at present it is far from clear that the correlation of complexity with age is a real phenomenon, let alone which explanation for it is the correct one, if it is real. But a style of linguistics which even potentially leads to consideration of issues like these is surely more worth pursuing than aprioristic theorising about artificially neat invented examples of language.

References

Chater, N., Reali, F. & Christiansen, M. H. 2009. Restrictions on biological adaptation in language evolution. *Proceedings of the National Academy of Sciences* 106(4): 1015–1020.

Chomsky, N. 1964. *Current Issues in Linguistic Theory*. The Hague: Mouton.

Chomsky, N. 1980. On cognitive structures and their development: A reply to Piaget. In *Language and Learning*, M. Piattelli-Palmarini (ed.), 35–52. London: Routledge & Kegan Paul.

Edwards, J. 1992. Design principles in the transcription of spoken discourse. In *Directions in Corpus Linguistics*, J. Svartvik (ed.), 129–144. Berlin: Mouton de Gruyter.

Evans, N. & Levinson, S. C. 2009. The myth of language universals: Language diversity and its importance for cognitive science. *Behavioural and Brain Sciences* 32: 429–492.

Householder, F. W. 1973. On arguments from asterisks. *Foundations of Language* 10: 365–376.

Käding, F. W. 1898. *Häufigkeitswörterbuch der deutschen Sprache*. Steglitz: Privately printed.

Katz, J. J. 1971. *The Underlying Reality of Language and Its Philosophical Import*. London: Harper & Row.

Labov, W. 1975. Empirical foundations of linguistic theory. In *The Scope of American Linguistics*, R. Austerlitz (ed.), 77–133. Lisse: Peter de Ridder Press. (Also published separately as *What is a Linguistic Fact?* Lisse: Peter de Ridder

Press, 1975.)

Pinker, S. 1994. *The Language Instinct*. New York NY: William Morrow.

Pullum, G. K. & Scholz, B. C. 2002. Empirical assessment of stimulus poverty arguments. *The Linguistic Review* 19: 9–50.

Quirk, R., Greenbaum, S., Leech, G. N. & Svartvik, J. 1985. *A Comprehensive Grammar of the English Language*. London: Longman.

Sampson, G. R. 1975. Chapter 4 of *The Form of Language*. London: Weidenfeld & Nicolson (Reprinted as Chapter 8 of Sampson, 2001).

Sampson, G. R. 2001. *Empirical Linguistics*. London: Continuum.

Sampson, G. R. 2005. *The 'Language Instinct' Debate,* rev. edn. London: Continuum.

Sampson, G. R. 2007. Grammar without grammaticality. *Corpus Linguistics and Linguistic Theory* 3: 1–32 & 111–129.

Sampson, G. R. & McCarthy, D. (eds). 2004. *Corpus Linguistics*. London: Continuum.

The technological aspect of Corpus Linguistics

Reader in Corpus Linguistics at Aston University (United Kingdom), Mike Scott is perhaps mostly associated with WordSmith Tools, the computer programme he has designed and has been working on since 1996 (currently in its sixth version). The author's technological concern is clear from the onset of his interview when he comments on the role played by the availability of personal computers in the development of Corpus Linguistics. In line with this practical concern, Scott writes about one of the major problems in compiling corpora: the issue of copyright. What lies ahead in the future, according to the researcher, is the creation of a newer generation of corpora, which will allow users to have audio and visual materials (in the first stage) together with the transcribed text. This specific technological concern, however, does not stop Scott from claiming that the questions to be asked by practising corpus linguists should always be socially relevant in the first place.

1. Where do you place the roots of Corpus Linguistics? And to what do you attribute the growth of interest in the area?

CL arose out of the traditional interest of linguists in having a corpus of text to study to exemplify usage. In the 1960s and 1970s, linguists typically used their own intuitions in deciding whether a given structure was or was not attested/ plausible/grammatical. But if they could show that the structure was actually found in text, then that was a much better way of proving their point. For that, it had to be quoted. In the same way the Oxford English Dictionary would provide a couple of quotations from eminent authors to show where a word was first used in a specific sense and that was a highly respectable method in lexicography. Deciding whether a given structure was attested or not was a major part of trying to pin down the edges of acceptability of a grammar and arguably represents a fore-taste of modern corpus study; many linguists saw understanding grammar (the system underlying the language) as their true goal. However, often this was done by discussing what was imagined to be attested, appealing, *faute de mieux*, to a notion of common intuitions.

When computer resources became available and especially when personal computers became affordable in the 1980s, CL was really ready to take off. There had been attempts by some enthusiasts much earlier to build corpora and to compute word-lists (Kučera & Francis 1967), but it was in the 1990s that many more linguists began to perceive the possibility that they might themselves actually owe or easily access a corpus of texts and find things out about what is and is not actually present in those texts.

The growth of interest in CL came because of two things. First, many linguists wanted themselves to know what is said and what isn't, to be able to be knowledgeable about how words are used. Some wanted this in the wish to be better language teachers, others as discourse analysts, text linguists, grammarians, etc. It was not too difficult to get access to a small corpus and a concordancer, to play with the new technology and incidentally to appear more up-to-date than one's colleagues. Second, it soon became apparent that what had always been said to be the 'true' structures of the language, e.g. the various patternings of tense in indirect speech or in the relations of conditional clauses to main clauses, did not correspond well to what was found in corpora. Performance began to raise its head and overtly challenge the rule of competence. For example, the neat sequences of tenses often propose for indirect speech, where tenses match in adjacent clauses, are very often not found in text, and the three classical conditionals with their matching tenses are often replaced by mixed forms such as those found in the BNC's KS6 text: ' ... and I might be doing something, so by the time I've picked it up to make that connection, suppose 3414 is then making another outgoing call, do I have to camp on yet again to 3414? Yes if it was erm, if it was ringing through, alright, and it's a two seconds ring that you get, okay, you can either get it because the party is engaged, still, alright, in which case it's not successful. So if it was, you wouldn't know that of course if you'd picked up the phone'.

2. Is Corpus Linguistics a science or a methodology? Where would you situate Corpus Linguistics in the scientific or methodological panorama?

It is not a separate science but is instead a tool, a resource. Simply put, computer resources have been created to enable researchers and students to find things out that they could not have found out otherwise, and examine patternings in ways that would have been prohibitively expensive if carried out by hand. In other words, CL is a resource, a new potential way of working. It is closer to a 'methodology'. As such, however, it is worth pointing out that the sheer power of the tools and the corpora have brought about not a simple quantitative change but a qualitative one too. With the possibility of checking a hypothesis or testing an idea quickly and easily, so many more tests end up being made that language theory itself changes. With a chance to produce word lists easily, it becomes possible and practical to consider comparing not just the texts where these lists were computed from but the very lists themselves, and thereby to reach the notion of a 'keyword', one whose frequency in one text or one set of texts is significantly unusual by comparison with a norm of some kind. The invention of the dictionary centuries earlier is similar: without it language work is still possible but much poorer. I think it does not make sense to think of CL as something a totally different field of human interest but as a powerful, transforming development akin to the dictionary or to Grimm's Law or the tape-recorder for studying speech sounds.

3. How representative can a corpus be?

Not very. Copyright does not allow one to gather a representative corpus. It may be worth commenting that copyright is something that is easy to worry too much about. In the last analysis, one does need permission to quote any largish extract taken from text, but the idea that a few words on either side of a node word or phrase, as in the case of a typical KWIC concordance, needs permission seems to me kowtow unnecessarily to copyright owners. I do not believe it is necessary to ask permission for simply collecting large amounts of publicly available text, either. But it is not OK to copy that and pass it on for commercial reasons without obtaining prior permission.

In any case, the very notion of representing human language is quite problematic. How can language be separated from its context, from the environment, the mood of the times and the culture which it sprang from? A corpus is typically opportunistic in the sense that the texts which it contains may well be incomplete (this applies to most of the BNC texts) and gathered attempting to satisfy (a) the overall design of some previous corpus such as Brown, and (b) copyright permission and the practical strains of gaining permission. The problem with the former is that there is no really suitable way of estimating what typical language users actually both encounter and produce each month or each year. The nearest attempt to a representative corpus that I know is the Czech National Corpus which had far fewer copyright difficulties and a better way of attempting to determine what users read than was the case with corpora of English – which itself is a much more internationally varied language. The Czech corpus builders had the advantage that copyright holders perceived the endeavour as leading to a valuable national resource, of interest chiefly within a clearly defined national context, and their methodology required them to study the differing uses of Czech before they started collecting text. The Czech National Corpus like the others has far fewer spoken resources than written ones, but in Czech as in English it is likely that most ordinary users encounter much more and more varied language in speech each day than in writing.

4. How far should an analyst rely on intuition?

Intuition should be relied on a very great deal. It is a mistake to think we can let our corpus methods or tools find the answers which we seek. By intuition I mean the human ability to think and understand, not simply an ability to think up an example of a language construction, or to match up a suggested example with one's own idiolectal usages. Intuition is judgement too, determining whether a string is coherent or incoherent in a given context, in connection with other words and phrases. It would only be possible to do away with intuition if one could also do away with the researcher and somehow leave it all to a drone. I would not want to be working in such an environment. CL is a support and a help, but our intuition is what makes us human.

5. What kind of questions should an analyst think of?

The questions an analyst should think of are the ones which might eventually identify answers to socially useful problems such as how to write clearly so that readers do not mistake our meaning, or how to persuade effectively as in the case of health or environmental education. But in order to do that, we also need answers to 'basic science' questions such as 'how are we to think about this or that construction in language'? In other words, there is a lot of ground work we have to perform before we can hope always to find answers to linguistic problems involved in schooling, industrial relations, better communications in business, language learning, etc. The ground work involves, thus, solving problems to do with ambiguity, with multi-word units, with collocation and colligation, with textual patternings, keywords, etc. We cannot in principle know in advance which of these concepts, once developed and refined, will pay big dividends in the practical linguistic problems mentioned above, though it is likely that they all will. In my own field, I would very much wish to understand how keywords relate to titles and sub-titles, and how key words are patterned in their dispersion through the text from its beginning to the end. Maybe having answers would end up being useful as well as interesting: it is all part of understanding how text 'ticks', so to speak.

6. What are the strengths and weaknesses of corpus analysis?

The major strength of corpus analysis is the possibility of ploughing quickly and tirelessly through enormous amounts of data, resorting and refiltering the data in almost endless ways, enabling the researcher to locate patterns, rather like the patterns we see in stars at night. An example is the pattern of the short head of extremely high frequency words followed by an enormous long tail of very low frequency items with hapax legomena taking up about half of the word forms. The weaknesses are (a) that the view from above is an overview, missing out often on the very fine contextual details which ordinary human reading might be able to spot, and (b) that the corpora we search through are flawed, as explained above. It is important to recognise that both blind corpus power and narrow human insight are limited but that working together more can be achieved.

7. What is the future of Corpus Linguistics?

The future entails corpora involving images and sounds (plus potentially smells, textures and tastes at a later date). If corpora do not reflect the whole of the ways in which the world impinges upon us, they will continue to be limited and the findings derived from them will be partial. The current generation of tools will need radical overhaul if they are to be adapted to handle sounds, images, smells, tastes and textures! I envisage a future where applications move towards what Computational Linguistics is good at; it has developed far further than Corpus Linguistics has been able to and produced socially useful tools like Google, automated purchase systems and so on. The problem is that by and large (this is a very coarse-grained generalisation) Computational Linguistics has not challenged the language problems but has concentrated on the algorithms and the technologies, making assumptions about language which the corpus linguist finds breathtaking, such as the supposition that a 'key word' must necessarily comprise or involve a noun phrase. My own work suggests that keyness can and often does reside in simple high frequency items such as *it* or *does* so that assuming that this cannot happen is risky.

8. How can an analyst cope with the speed of technological development?

The speed of technological development is an advantage, on the whole, not something we have to worry about. As Moore's Law shows, the computers we work with get faster and cheaper with time; this means that the technological resources get richer, on the whole. At the same time, people who develop them must remember (and do not always succeed in this) that human learning is not as fast and that it can be insulting to force the learner or researcher to struggle to relearn a system differently just because the software developers think they have found a more logical way of working. The MS Office 2007 programmes were, it seems, perceived by many as insulting and confusing in this regard, by those who had already painfully learned the MS Office 1997 or 2003 ways of working. For newcomers, it may be that the 2007 programmes are better, but the question has to do with an analyst coping with change, not starting from scratch. Change is inevitable, and software is no exception. This arises not just because of bug-fixes but also from user suggestions and from possibilities perceived by the software developers themselves. Some are aesthetic, as in new icons or skins, some have to do with accessing frequently used commands easily like Microsoft's ribbon layout, and others are directly related to the goal of the software itself as in concgrams built into WordSmith 5.0. The analysts cannot hope to prevent change and their *tried-and-tested* methods eventually need to be replaced by new ones as change occurs. That also means that findings of five years ago will begin to seem inadequate, however insightful and correct they seemed when new. By analogy, photographs of a few years ago look grainy. We are now entering an age of 3D movies. Corpora of the near future will incorporate sound and vision.

9. How much should a discourse analyst know before he or she engages in corpus work?

I don't agree with the presupposition. No discourse analyst needs to know anything about Corpus Linguistics before starting doing discourse analysis or before doing Corpus Linguistics. What they need (for either) is an open mind, a willingness to learn, to take risks, to make mistakes, and to ask for help or find it for themselves. There is not just one way of slicing bread, and the CL ways of slicing it are not necessarily superior to non-CL ways.

10. How may Corpus Linguistics help ESP research and teaching?

One fairly minor aspect of ESP is the nature of the language that the student will eventually engage with. The features of specific language were more or less equated with ESP forty years ago and since then we have all come to realise that the problem for the learner only concerns the special nature of grammar or phraseology in some target language variety to a rather minor extent. To that extent, it is possible that corpus methods may help learners themselves. (The greater problem usually has to do with the learning, the organisation of teaching so as to enable learning, as opposed to pinning down the language characteristics.) Corpus methods may be much more helpful, though, in assisting those who have to organise their learning schedules and procedures – the teachers and materials writers. By identifying patterns which do exist in the target language, or in the intermediate kinds of language to be studied in ESP classes, as opposed to ones which are merely assumed or supposed to, CL has a real part to play. Frequency, for example, is a guiding (if not over-riding) principle and CL helps us identify what is frequent. A glance at any issue of *English for Specific Purposes* reveals articles using corpus methods to identify language patterns – as in general language teaching, this has enabled teachers and materials writers to go beyond what is supposed to be usual English in a specific context, to the identification of what actually are the attested English patterns and forms. Finally, and Tim Johns' Kibbitzers illustrate this, Corpus Linguistics may enable what he called data-driven learning: in DDL, thinking comes from examining data, and it is driven by the data because it is the authority, showing what is attested, what is said and what is written.

Reference

Kučera, H. & Francis, W. N. 1967. *Computational Analysis of Present-Day American English.* Providence RI: Brown University Press.

A critical view on the use
of corpora

Professor Emeritus at the University of Michigan (United States), John Swales initially warns his readers that he is not an insider when it comes to the foundations of Corpus Linguistics. Perhaps this detachment allows him to report on how he changed his understanding of the corpus approach from a science to a methodology. Although he worked with both the Michigan Corpus of Academic Spoken English (MICASE) and the Michigan Corpus of Upper-Level Student Papers (MICUSP), Swales argues against the idea that the corpus approach should be the only one available to researchers. In fact, he holds that they need to be free to choose what better suits their research objectives. In his specific questions, Swales also comments on the role of corpora in the study of genres, academic literacy and pedagogy, and contrastive rhetoric.

1. Where do you place the roots of Corpus Linguistics? And to what do you attribute the growth of interest in the area?

I am in no way an expert in the origins of Corpus Linguistics, but my impressions are the following. The origins clearly lie in the early collections of texts prior to the availability of electronic databases. There were, for example, many print concordances, one of the better known being Bartlett's (1922) *A New and Complete Concordance or Verbal Index to Words, Phrases and Passages in the Dramatic Works of Shakespeare*. In addition, I would point to Michael West's (1957) *A General Service List of English Words* and Charles Fries' (1952) *The Structure of English*. Both of these works were valuable in their attempts to sort out prescription and folkloristic beliefs, on the one hand, and authentic attestation of what people were actually doing linguistically, on the other. In the former, for instance, the *General Service List*'s survey of the word *post* produced 450 tokens, of which 49% were to its use on the 'mail' sense, 26% in its 'job' sense, but only 9% to its use as a vertical pole. However, for many, I would guess that the 'lamp-post' meaning is the one that comes first to mind. As for the latter, Fries' grammar was based on a spoken corpus of 50 hours of telephone conversations subreptiously recorded at his house!

2. Is Corpus Linguistics a science or a methodology? Where would you situate Corpus Linguistics in the scientific or methodological panorama?

When I first started getting involved in Corpus Linguistics around 1997, I thought it was a science, a new empirical sub-branch of the language sciences relying heavily on quantitative methods – a view definitely underscored by packages such as Wordsmith Tools (Scott 1996). Like many other neophytes to CL, I suspect I was entranced by the sheer ease of manipulation that the packages provided; for instance, the quasi-magical way the user could now select, sort and delete strings of words, not to speak of features like plot and log likelihood. The contrast with the 'old ways' was roughly that of literal cutting and pasting with old manual typescripts and cutting and pasting on a keyboard. Somewhat later, and doubtlessly influenced by all those panel discussions at Corpus Linguistic conferences, I came around to the view that CL was a methodology, by which I mean a way of looking at large bodies of language data for a wide variety of purposes (historical, critical, pedagogic, etc.) rather than as a new branch of linguistics with its concern with a circumscribed area of content. Like all methodologies, CL has its own attendant strengths and weaknesses. One strength is its capacity for making generalisations about language use, but it is much weaker in its capacity to explain the forces that might give shape to those generalisations. The very act of electronic corpus compilation leads, on the one hand, to the rapid achievement of considerable data, but, on the other, it also leads to a necessary detachment from the situation of its origin; as Henry Widdowson (2002) has memorably said, in CL 'the text travels but the context does not travel with it.' Such decontextualisations are of course not necessarily fatal, nor indeed always unwelcome, as when constructing a corpus-based grammar. But today, as I see myself falling further and further behind colleagues who can manipulate complex and large bodies of linguistic data with increasingly sophisticated tools (such as K-grams), I have come to think of corpora as basically *resources*. For instance, one of my current projects is to investigate (along with Laura Aull and two undergraduate assistants from the University of Michigan) the use in student academic writing of that rhetorical device typically known as 'scare quotes'. For this, we are using the publicly-available Michigan Corpus of Upper-Level Student Papers, or MICUSP. Our original plan was to do this via an automatic search of the papers, following the tagging of this feature by interns from the School of Information Science. However, coding problems arose, and in the end we decided to use the raw texts, and identify and categorise scare quotes by hand. While the resulting process is labourious, the very act of eyeballing the texts produces various kinds of insights not so easily available via a few quick clicks of a mouse. For this project, MICUSP is a resource – a repository of texts to be consulted.

3. How representative can a corpus be?

This is an interesting question, but one to which I have no general answer. I certainly do not subscribe to the view that, *ceteris paribus*, the bigger a corpus the more representative it will be. Throwing everything you can get into the pot, as I believe was largely the case with the Bank of English, is not inevitably the most appropriate way to proceed. I remember years ago Michael McCarthy observing that in compiling a corpus it is important to strive hard to get the difficult material, otherwise you will over-represent the easy stuff. For example, in putting together a spoken business English corpus, it is presumably not too difficult to get exemplars of the discourse of job application interviews. Equally presumably, it is much harder to get examples of job termination interviews, but, especially these days, the latter are equally significant.

I can also approach this question by considering the corpus I know best – The Michigan Corpus of Academic Spoken English (MICASE). This is small (under 2 million words), but representative of the genres students are involved in at one major Midwestern university around the turn of the 20th century. These are clear and correct contextual constraints, and any extrapolations are for others to make. Further, this is a closed corpus so that the statistical data associated with it (i.e. 54% of the speech is uttered by women) are stable, and do not need to be continually updated as would be the case if further accessions to the database were permitted. Finally, there are two aspects of representativity that I think have been under-appreciated in the profession; the first is that a closed corpus is a time-capsule, and represents a language sample of a time that has passed or is passing. MICASE, for one example, is interesting in that all the lectures were recorded just before the emergence of PowerPoint as an increasingly popular lecturing device. Contemporary implications and applications of this phenomenon are obvious enough. The second is that however robust the design of a corpus, contingency and adventitiousness will still often play a part. Although MICASE generally covers the University of Michigan well, there are in fact no lectures from the Law School. But what might seem a design fault actually is a result of the fact that all the law instructors refused (to a man!) to let us record their lectures. And this example is but one of several MICASE instances of this kind that are known to me (and to a couple of others), but have never been discussed in print.

4. How far should an analyst rely on intuition?

Very far. The more negative aspects of my response to the Question 6 are essentially bound up with an avoidance of relying on intuition. Perhaps I can offer an example from one of my current projects. For many years now, I have been working on and teaching English written academic discourse – and writing textbooks thereto. About a year ago, when reading some of the texts being collected for MICUSP, I suddenly realised that the whole issue of when and when not to use 'scare quotes' and why they were used had been almost totally neglected in the literature. It turns out that only philosophers have taken up the topic of the use and misuse of scare quotes! An intuition has set me, albeit somewhat slowly, down the road of finding more about this topic, its disciplinary preferences, and whether certain groups of novice writers underuse or overuse them. Intuition then has shaped a project, and one that in terms of itself might be prone to the kind of 'incidentalism' in corpus studies that I have on occasion criticised. Of course, it couldn't have been done without access to the MICUSP database since 'scare quotes' are typically not that common – some 4–5 per 10,000 words. However, there is a further hermeneutical aspect to all this: once the research group began to get the hang of what was going on in this aspect of student writing, it became clearer to us that we *also* needed more socio-cognitive input than the texts themselves could provide. We did not even know whether the students had a term or phrase for the phenomenon under investigation; we are now collecting questionnaire data about student perceptions. Geertz (1980) talks about the need for a 'dialectical tacking' back and forth between small and large elements of a culture; so perhaps we need a 'dialectical tacking' back and forth between intuitions/perceptions and the data in order to complete the hermeneutical circle.

5. What kind of questions should an analyst think of?

A quasi-tautological but not unhelpful answer to this would be to say that the questions that the corpus analyst comes up with should be questions that a corpus can answer. These would obviously be, for example, questions about the patterning of texts or discourses, about broader lexico-syntactic regularities and about interesting exceptions. They would less obviously be questions about pragmatics, because of the well-attested difficulties in pragmatic tagging. Our efforts to tag pragmatically parts of MICASE ended in disarray because of poor inter-rater reliability; what was for one person a 'suggestion', was for another a 'request', and for a third a 'demand'. Similarly, investigations into the production and reception histories of the texts themselves will likely make only light use of corpora, relying more on ethnography, interview and citation analysis, or, in the case of literary texts, the established techniques and insights of the literary scholar. In the end, we will always do well to remember something that John Sinclair (1991) once said somewhere: 'When you look at a lot of language, it starts to look different'. It is that difference we should focus on.

6. What are the strengths and weaknesses of corpus analysis?

The achievements of corpus analytic work have been substantial, none more so than the splendid and comprehensive *Longman Grammar of Spoken and Written English* (Biber et al. 1999). Another is the increasing recognition of the key role of phraseology, in the sense that much of human verbal communication is acquired, stored and produced in the form of chunks rather than in the form of discrete words or morphemes. A third example would be the discovery of semantic prosodies that certain verbs, for example, have strong tendencies to be used in either positive or negative contexts. The verb *cause* illustrates this phenomenon nicely, since the complements of *cause* tend to be unfortunate, being, in the main, accidents, injuries, and the like.

On the other hand, there has been a trend that the well-known Chicago phonologist, John Goldsmith, called in a recent invited lecture, 'data fetishism', by which he meant an unswerving commitment to quantitative empirical data. Some of these assays have, in my opinion, proved rather unrewarding at least in terms of producing insights into the language *per se*, or usefully pointing the way to pedagogical improvements, especially some of those appearing in edited collections of papers from the smaller European academic publishing houses. Many years ago, the great cultural anthropologist, Clifford Geertz (1973: 16) expressed something similar when he observed, 'It is not worth it, as Thoreau said, to go round the world to count the cats in Zanzibar'. So, overall, corpus-based analyses have produced some important work, and quite a lot of relatively unimportant work. And I know this to my cost. Most of my numerous forays into the MICASE database have proved unenlightening or unrewarding, and have either been discarded, or have emerged in truncated 'kibitzer' format on the English Language Institute's MICASE website. Rather a long tail, then.

7. What is the future of Corpus Linguistics?

I have two quick reactions to this. One is that the future is very bright for this area; the other is a worry that the future might even be too bright. Recently, a colleague who works in Sweden told me that today it is almost impossible to do a PhD in linguistics in Scandinavia without using a corpus. Obviously, any such crowding out of alternative methods of linguistic enquiry may in the end lead to a new kind of scholasticism. I might illustrate this by returning to the 'reception history of texts' that was alluded to in Question 5 above. When I look at the increasingly large literature out there on academic texts, what I do not see enough of are studies that attempt to explain why one particular 1980 article has been hugely successful (i.e. Canale & Swain's paper on communicative competence in Applied Linguistics), while other comparable articles have fallen into the black hole of never having been cited. After all, without tracing the causes of citational success, we will never really know whether the way in which an article is written actually makes any real kind of difference. And this is a question that teachers of academic writing should be seriously interested in. For such a study, we certainly need electronic resources such as Science Direct or Google Scholar, but perhaps not so much a corpus.

8. In what ways can Corpus Linguistic techniques help one understand genres?

The work of Ken Hyland and others have obviously been able to tell us much about the surface features of genres, and this has led, among other things, to improved genre-based materials. On the one hand, it does not help us much to understand the social practices that revolve around the production and reception of specific genres. So, they are valuable, but only part of the story; ethnography and its variants are still essential. My own *Other Floors, Other*

Voices volume (Swales 1998) offered itself as a 'textographic' alternative to the straight textual analysis that I had been doing for many years. On the other hand, no sooner was that highly particularistic study completed, than I was using MICASE to try and make sense of little studied genres such as *research group meetings* and *dissertation defences* (Swales 2004). As the saying goes, 'different horses for different courses'.

9. How has corpus-based research contributed to the area of academic literacy and how have these results found their way into pedagogy?

This field is currently rather polarised: those associated with the 'academic literacy' movement *per se* (as led by Brian Street at London) have stressed the sociocultural individualities of apprentice academic writers, and so have little time for broad generalisations about exemplar texts; those in the English for Academic Purposes field (as best represented by Ken Hyland at Hong Kong) have, as applied discourse analysts, adopted corpus analytic techniques with considerable enthusiasm. It remains to be seen how, when and where a suitable rapprochement can be reached. That rapprochement, however, comes into much clearer focus when we consider the construction of EAP pedagogical materials. A suitable corpus provides the scientific basis for the work (along with relevant previous literature) as well as providing a wonderful resource for suitably-edited linguistic examples. The further fashioning of the basic material into a coherent sequence of texts and tasks then requires instructor experience, classroom testing and a certain imaginative flair. So corpus-based research provides the science, educational experience the craft, and creativity the art.

10. Does the corpus dimension add to contrastive rhetoric? Why/ Why not?

My sense of this is that much of the most useful work here has indeed used corpora, but has largely relied on intuition and on manual analysis. I would instance here, for example, the work of people such as Ulla Connor (e.g. 1996) and Anna Mauranen (e.g. 1993). The difficulty, however, with all comparative work of this kind is in establishing a suitable similarity between the two corpora; particularly problematic have been the all-too-many studies that have compared English-language research papers in high-impact journals with local low-impact journals in the other language. Indeed, I have been regularly arguing of late that an 'Angloother' contrastive rhetoric study of research articles will only achieve reasonable levels of comparability if the English-language papers selected are equally local and low impact. However, some recent studies I have been involved in with colleagues, comparing English research article abstracts with those in Arabic, French and Spanish (e.g. Van Bonn & Swales 2007), have used traditional, i.e. non-electronic, techniques brought to bear on carefully-constructed paper corpora. In effect, a corpus dimension remains essential, but it does not necessarily have to be electronic and have to depend on concordancing.

References

Bartlett, J. 1922. *A New and Complete Concordance or Verbal Index to Words, Phrases and Passages in the Dramatic Works of Shakespeare.* London: Macmillan.

Biber, D., Johansson, S., Leech, G., Conrad, S. & Finegan, E. 1999. *Longman Grammar of Spoken and Written English.* Harlow: Pearson Education.

Connor, U. 1996. *Contrastive Rhetoric.* Cambridge: CUP.

Fries, C. C. 1952. *The Structure of English.* New York NY: Harcourt Brace.

Geertz, C. 1973. *The Interpretation of Cultures.* New York NY: Basic Books.

Geertz, C. 1980. *Negara: The Theatre State in 19th-Century Bali.* Princeton NJ: Princeton University Press.

Mauranen, A. 1993. *Cultural Differences in Academic Rhetoric: A Textlinguistic Study.* Frankfurt: Peter Lang.

Scott, M. 1996. *WordSmith Tools.* Oxford: OUP.

Sinclair, J. 1991. *Corpus, Concordance, Collocation.* Oxford: OUP.

Swales, J. M. 1998. *Other Floors, Other Voices: A Textography of a Small University Building.* Mahwah NJ: Lawrence Erlbaum Associates.

Swales, J. M. 2004. *Research Genres: Explorations and Applications.* Cambridge: CUP.

Van Bonn, S. & Swales, J. M. 2007. English and French journal abstracts in the language sciences: Three exploratory studies. *Journal of English for Academic Purposes* 6: 93–108.

West, M. 1957. *A General Service List of English Words.* Harlow: Longman.

Widdowson, H. G. 2002. Corpora and language teaching tomorrow. Keynote lecture delivered at the Fifth Teaching and Language Corpora Conference, Bertinoro, Italy, 29 July.

The politics of Corpus Linguistics

Vander Viana

Queen's University Belfast[1]

1. Introduction

In a volume like *Perspectives on Corpus Linguistics*, readers assume special relevance as they are called in to infer the connections and controversies that bring together the interviewees' perspectives on the past, present and future of Corpus Linguistics. In this sense, this final chapter focuses specifically on one potential interpretation of what links all the fourteen contributions. If these texts are to share one feature, I would hold that it is 'politics' which prominently features as a common denominator.

Not different from what is proposed in dictionaries, the term 'politics' is here understood as '[t]he assumptions or principles relating to or underlying any activity, theory, or attitude, esp. when concerned with questions of power and status in a society' (Simpson & Weiner 1989). Corpus Linguistics may then be characterised by means of its political activities. The fourteen interviews grouped in this volume indicate at least five strands in 'the politics of Corpus Linguistics': scientific, research, educational, market and personal concerns. These are detailed and exemplified in the following sections.

2. Science

Perhaps the most common strand in the politics of Corpus Linguistics deals with the macro-aspects of the scientific scenario. In this sphere, the status of Corpus Linguistics is often put to question. Over the years, there has been a debate about the usefulness of investing time, effort and resources in empirical approaches to language studies. This discussion lies at the heart of Chomsky's

---

1 I am most grateful to Sonia Zyngier and John Kirk for their generosity in commenting on earlier versions of this chapter.

position as regards the corpus approach, a point that is again made clear in an interview he gave to József Andor and published in *Intercultural Pragmatics*:

> My judgement, if you like, is that we learn more about language by following the standard method of the sciences. The standard method of the sciences is not to accumulate huge masses of unanalysed data and to try to draw some generalisation from them. The modern sciences, at least since Galileo, have been strikingly different. What they have sought to do was to construct refined experiments which ask, which try to answer specific questions that arise within a theoretical context as an approach to understanding the world. (Andor 2004: 97)

In this excerpt, Chomsky indirectly describes the corpus way as 'non-standard', one which is not necessarily conceived as 'scientific'. It is noticeable that his criticism is targeted at the practice itself, that is, at *how* the investigation is done. A diverging perspective is seen in another fragment of the same interview where he states that

> People who work seriously in this particular area do not rely on Corpus Linguistics. They may begin by looking at facts about frequency and shifts in frequency and so on, but if they want to move on to some understanding of what's happening they will very quickly, and in fact do, shift to the experimental framework. (Andor 2004: 99)

Here, Chomsky's criticism goes well beyond positioning himself in relation to an objective topic. In fact, he questions the actual competence of researchers based on the type of study they carry out. The focus of negative evaluation is then moved from an objective to a subjective construct. This kind of positioning could, in a critical reading, imply that researchers' intellectual ability would be compromised if they developed corpus work.

The standing of Corpus Linguistics is indeed a major topic in the scientific strand. If it were by nature 'frivolous' as claimed by Chomsky, it would be pointless to carry it out. As a consequence, because all the strands are interconnected, they would be affected by this understanding of corpus work. This means that it would not be seen as an integral part of the research world. Neither would it have any impact on the educational context and job/ publishing market nor would we bother about the personal aspects involved in it.

Despite the recent publication of Chomsky's interview, there seems to be no need to justify corpus work any longer.[2] Corpora and their probing tools are actually considered a helpful way of gathering information about how language is used.[3] However, it is important to emphasise that corpora merely stand for one well-grounded method of approaching language, which might not suit each and every research project. For evolution to take place in science, researchers in general need to be aware that the more democratic and comprehensive their attitude to the study of language is, the more the field of linguistics will benefit from different approaches.

Once we assume Corpus Linguistics as a scientifically valid practice, the next step is how to characterise it. Would it be better described as a 'scholarly enterprise' (Kennedy 1998: 1), a 'pre-application methodology' (Tognini-Bonelli 2001: 1), an 'approach to language' (Teubert 2007: 50), 'a methodology' (McEnery & Wilson 1996: 2; McEnery et al. 2006: 6; Lindquist 2009: 1), 'an approach or a methodology for studying language use' (Bowker & Pearson 2002: 9), etc.? In a word, the status of the area is open to debate. In the fourteen responses to the second question of the interview, the notion that it is a method(ology) was the most prevalent,[4] but this position was not unanimous. Some contributors pointed out that there are elements which might characterise Corpus Linguistics as both a science and a methodology. In this sense, they stressed that its classification should be done according to the way it is applied, and that its identity should not be restricted.

Indeed, defining Corpus Linguistics as a discipline, a sub-discipline, a methodology, a method, among other possibilities, is primarily related to the politics of science. It must be made clear, however, that this classification also affects the other strands. Once an area achieves scientific status, it begins to enjoy a more advantageous position both in academic recognition and within the research community. This has a direct and explicit impact on market issues, which might be seen in the availability of funding, for instance.

---

2 Several publications on Corpus Linguistics cover the debate created between generativists and corpus researchers (e.g. McEnery & Wilson 1996; Hockey 2000; Meyer 2002; Teubert 2007; Lindquist 2009). This, however, seems to be done mostly as a way of keeping a record of how the discipline has evolved rather than to fight for the recognition of corpus research.

3 The advantages of corpus analysis have been discussed in each of the fourteen interviews (cf. Question 6) as well as elsewhere (e.g. Svartvik 1992).

4 The label 'methodology' might work as a superordinate term in those cases where interviewees have opted for 'tool', 'resource' or 'approach', to cite three examples.

As conceptualised in the present chapter, the politics of science is mostly related to that of research. While the former is more concerned with a general characterisation of Corpus Linguistics, the latter considers those aspects which are more specifically related to doing corpus analyses. These considerations are discussed below.

3. Research

In the strand of research, one of the early issues that corpus analysts have to tackle corresponds to the linguistic material to be used. The question of what a representative corpus involves has been quite recurrent. As a matter of fact, this topic was severely criticised in our pre-computational past when corpora were still inherently small and could not be said to represent much (see McEnery & Wilson 1996).[5] It is clear that the more specialised a corpus is, the easier it is to gather a relevant sample of the language to be studied – a point which has been made in several of the interviews in this volume as well as elsewhere (e.g. McEnery et al. 2006). However, the problem arises when general and wide-encompassing corpora are considered. In his interview, Gries proposes that further methodological investigations should be developed as a way of providing better guidelines for future studies. This is especially relevant in relation to corpora being representative of, for instance, a language.

The need for methodological investigation turns out to be more pertinent if we consider it from an educational perspective, which is a recurrent theme in this volume (see also Section 4). Once clearer guidelines are proposed, new generations of corpus linguists will face little difficulty in understanding, on safer (and more objective) grounds, what an 'adequate' corpus (i.e. one from which they might derive useful and accurate findings) needs to comprise. If these guiding principles are not provided, the future might hold one of the following scenarios: (a) researchers may be overtly criticised for carrying out work on corpora that are not representative of the language they are investigating, or, more worryingly, (b) the community may adopt an all-can-go attitude which would be a major drawback to the field. It is precisely because the weaknesses of Corpus Linguistics lie in its application, as suggested by Leech in his interview, that we should bring such a topic to our research

---

5 It could well be stated that this point lies on the borderline between the politics of science and of research, thus stressing once more the fluidity of the categories, as has been pointed out earlier.

agenda. This would possibly prevent researchers from interrogating a corpus from which there is not much to be gained.

A methodological research agenda would also be beneficial in other ways. The results of these investigations could let us know, for instance, which statistical tests would best suit specific goals, and which computer programmes would yield better precision and recall rates for each of the most recurrent corpus techniques. In the absence of these objective methodological findings, there should not be any dispute over methodological choices. In other words, provided the choices are well explained and adequate to the researcher's needs, they should not be criticised.

Once the internal questions are resolved, community members may productively work towards expanding research horizons. It is true that '[n]o longer the preserve of the computer "boffin", corpus-based research is increasingly influential in many areas of language study', as has been argued by Thomas and Short (1996: ix). What is perhaps needed now is to showcase how colleagues from other fields may best take advantage of what we do. Collaborative practice may develop in areas which have a wider reach of audience as is the case of journalism. For instance, broadsheet papers have recently published analyses which are – in a way or another – based on corpora. Some of them rely on the visual technique of designing word clouds to present the information in a more engaging way to readers (CBC 2010; Stoddard 2010). Others go beyond this visual level and count the number of certain words in several speeches of a given politician, plotting the results in graphs (BBC 2009). In both cases, the unanswered question is whether corpus linguists have been involved, at any level, in these analyses. Had collaborative work been carried out, corpus researchers could help refine these (sometimes simplistic) language conclusions. At the same time, they could also profit from journalists in the sense of disclosing corpus findings to a larger readership (mostly lay in this field).

Interdisciplinary practice may also be seen from a strictly academic angle. This would entail two (or more) researchers from different backgrounds who agree to pursue a common goal from which both would benefit. This kind of symbiotic enterprise might be exemplified by Goldschmidt and Szmrecsanyi's (2007) study. Here, an economist and a linguist examine texts that are circulated in economic journals. The results of this joint venture have been published in the *American Journal of Economics and Sociology*. The fact that this is not a linguistic journal *per se* draws our attention to the need of

254

overcoming research barriers and of making corpus analyses available to other communities of academic practice.

We do not need to go too far to notice that there is room for interdisciplinarity even in our own departments. A case in point would be what is now described as Corpus Stylistics, if we consider the activities within 'Schools of English'. It is true that Stylistics is already in itself an interdisciplinary venture (cf. Simpson 1996), but the corpus approach has added a new dimension to it. By looking more closely at the language used in literary texts, it is possible, for example, to open up new vistas to how literature might be characterised in more specific language terms (cf. Semino & Short 2004; Toolan 2009; Opas-Hänninen 2010) and to how it differs both within its canon and beyond it (Louwerse, Benesh & Zhang 2008; Viana et al. 2008).

From a quantitative perspective, Corpus Stylistics has been gaining momentum. A closer look at the 2010 Conference of the Poetics and Linguistics Association (PALA), the major forum for stylisticians, reveals that about 15% of the papers are corpus-informed. This might read as a low figure, but not when seen in the context of the thirteen different areas of interest of the Association.[6] Were these areas to be equally represented, then corpus studies would be expected to add up half of what it actually totaled.

In the politics of research, it is also important to take into account the geographical location of corpus linguistic centres. Not surprisingly, there are more centres in Europe (especially in the United Kingdom) than in North America (prominently in the United States).[7] This has a historical explanation as corpus researchers enjoyed less academic restrictions in the European continent.

Broadening the horizon could be easily justified on the grounds of a more democratic attitude to research. Any given community should aim at allowing other researchers to develop their own corpus projects, and at fostering

---

6 The full list includes narratology, literariness, literary linguistics, stylistics and pedagogy, critical discourse analysis, gender and writing, literary translation studies, linguistics and philosophy, metaphor, cognition, pragmatics, text linguistics and corpus stylistics.

7 The interviewees in this volume also show that the pendulum swings more towards Europe, where half of them work. At the same time, the list of contributors reveals the editors' concern in bringing together voices from continents other than Europe and North America. Therefore, in order to provide readers with a worldwide view of Corpus Linguistics, African, Asian and South American perspectives have also been included in this book.

high standards of academic practice. In addition, as more researchers from different national backgrounds experiment with Corpus Linguistics, the area might evolve into unforeseen directions (see, for instance, Berber Sardinha's interview on the possibilities of corpus practice in Brazil).

In expanding the reach of corpus tools and techniques among European countries, the role of the Common Language Resources and Technology Infrastructure (CLARIN) must be acknowledged. In 2009, for instance, the CLARIN Project issued a call for collaborative projects within the Humanities and Social Sciences by means of which European-based research groups could be aided in terms of the technology they needed to address specific research goals. It is hoped that more calls such as this one will take place in the future. It is also expected that the scope of these calls will include other continents and/or countries, especially those in which there is the will but not the means to develop corpus research.

When considering the prospects within the strand of research, the directions which the area might be taking should not be overlooked. Despite the unpredictability of this task, the fourteen interviewees agreed to voice their opinions on this matter. Here, I would like to add another direction: we may work towards uncovering the means by which corpus analyses are carried out. For instance, eye-tracking techniques may be used to check what it is that people look at first when they are presented with concordance lines. If coupled with verbal protocols, we could understand more clearly how practitioners make sense out of corpora output, which processes they employ in making generalisations, and so on. This type of 'meta-research' could be invaluable to the education of new generations of corpus linguists, which is the focus of the next section.

4. Education

In the politics of education, one of the initial concerns relates to the content which is to be invited to and discussed in the classroom. Rather than focusing on what is to be taught (see, for instance, Fligelstone's [1993] proposal[8]), I

---

8 The author proposes a three-tier model: 'teaching about', 'teaching to exploit' and 'exploiting to teach' (Fligelstone 1993: 98). While the first is more theoretically driven, the second has an applied nature in which students are introduced to ways of investigating corpora. Finally, the third category refers to the use of corpora to inform the teaching of, for instance, a language.

would like to stress the way of doing it. Different from long-established forms of education, the pedagogical application of corpus work requires a more autonomous setting in which (virtually) everybody can learn something from the exploitation of corpora. This means that we should avoid the principles of 'banking education', one 'in which the students are the depositories and the teacher is the depositor' (Freire 1996 [1970]: 53). Instead, the pedagogical application of Corpus Linguistics should pursue a more dialogical type of education:

> Through dialogue, the teacher-of-the-student and the students-of-the-teacher cease to exist and a new term emerges: teacher-student with students-teachers. The teacher is no longer merely the one who teaches, but one who is himself taught in dialogue with the students, who in turn while being taught also teach. They become jointly responsible for a process in which all grow. In this process, arguments based on 'authority' are no longer valid; [...] (Freire 1996 [1970]: 61)

This description does suit corpus practice even though Freire (1996 [1970]) had had a completely different setting when writing *Pedagogy of the Oppressed*. Should the 'arguments' refer to linguistic aspects, the 'authority' would correspond to our own intuitions of how language is used. As pointed out by several interviewees, there is nothing wrong with intuition (in whatever sense we may understand this word). The matter actually lies in how and for which purposes we use it. In the current corpus landscape, a question about language use must not be answered by stating rather concisely (and unconvincingly) that this is simply the way it should (or should not) be done. With plenty of data available in several languages, any claim about usage would need to be supported with empirical data.

Despite the gap of roughly 20 years between Freire's manifesto (1996 [1970]) and Johns's (1991) concept of 'data-driven learning', their similarity is easily noticeable. In the same sense the former writes about empowering students-teachers, Johns (1991: 1) suggests that 'the task of the learner is to "discover" the foreign language, and that the task of the language teacher is to provide a context in which the learner can develop strategies for discovery – strategies through which he or she can "learn how to learn"'. The main difference might lie in Johns's (1991) specific concern for the foreign language classroom; nevertheless, most of what he advocates for this learning setting abides by Freire's (1996 [1970]) proposal for the type of interaction that should take place between teachers and students.

The role played by teachers is extremely relevant in fostering learners' autonomy (see Benson 2001), one of the key aspects in bringing corpora to the classroom. If teachers believe they have to pass on the knowledge they have to their students, it is unlikely they will develop any sense of autonomy in the learners. By the same token, teachers who are reluctant to admit their intellectual fallibility will find it difficult to set up an educational atmosphere in which everybody feels free to contribute. While promoting learners' autonomy is not easy for those who were raised in traditional teacher-centred education, we must overcome this power barrier and share responsibilities in a class.

Another controversial topic in the educational context is integrating Corpus Linguistics into the university curriculum. In this volume, for instance, Louw argues against its insertion in the literature syllabus. Instead, he believes students (as well as staff members) should be introduced to the corpus approach in a more informal and relaxed way – one in which they are invited to come to demonstrations of what the approach is capable of achieving. It is perhaps more appealing to have people see and decide for themselves whether corpus methods are suitable to their own research needs. However, considering that the current model of education worldwide is based on courses (or modules) and that the curriculum is decided beforehand (with different degrees of freedom being assigned to students as regards their choices), the question to be asked is why not integrate Corpus Linguistics into the core component of education in languages and/or linguistics. After all, even if students come to realise that corpora are not particularly useful to their future academic/ professional careers, they would still be knowledgeable about it (as is the case with other disciplines).

In the education panorama, some consideration must also be given to the timing of introducing Corpus Linguistics to students who want to pursue language studies. In her interview, Conrad states that those who are introduced to corpus techniques earlier are those who might make the most of it. The question then is how early is 'early'. It seems that Corpus Linguistics entered the pedagogical setting by means of postgraduate education (both MA and PhD courses), where staff members generally enjoy more freedom in designing the curriculum and deciding which disciplines to teach.[9] For the sake of illustration, there has been a specific MPhil in Corpus Linguistics at the University of Birmingham since the academic year 2001–2002. This is not

9 See Renouf (1997) for a report on her experience of teaching Corpus Linguistics to postgraduate students of Applied Linguistics at the University of Birmingham.

to say, however, that corpora cannot be introduced at earlier university stages. In the United Kingdom, BA modules in Corpus Linguistics are, for instance, currently offered at Lancaster University, Swansea University and Queen's University Belfast.[10] The integration of such modules into the bachelor course, however, is not widespread. In describing the situation in Germany, Mukherjee (2004: 244) warns that 'it is still perfectly possible for each and every student of English language and literature in virtually all English departments in Germany to take a university degree without ever having delved into Corpus Linguistics.' We still seem to have a long way to go before the corpus approach is fully integrated into the university setting in different parts of the world.

The adequate timing for introducing Corpus Linguistics must actually be linked to its relevance to students. A case might be made for introducing corpora even earlier than the university level. Examples abound in the literature on teaching English as a foreign language (Tribble & Jones 1990; Johns 1991; also see Section 5) where learners might not yet have reached tertiary level. Other contexts of application, although not explicitly mentioned here, may also benefit from corpus analysis.

Adding to timing, we should always have in mind the audience to which Corpus Linguistics is introduced. By identifying who the interlocutors are, we will be in a position to adapt our discourse to their level of knowledge. This is indeed a major point in teaching Corpus Linguistics (or any other subject): clarity of expression must be a principle to be followed. Working with languages, corpus researchers are well aware of how the linguistic wording of ideas might play a role in putting off prospective learners. This is especially true when fostering interdisciplinary practice, a topic which shows the connection between the strands of education and research (see also Section 3).

Should there be more interdisciplinary projects in the future, they need to be promoted earlier in academia. In this sense, we need to go beyond academic departments and address audiences that might not necessarily consist of language and/or linguistics (under)graduates. A great deal of corpus techniques may be useful to those carrying out work in, for example, literature, education, history, social policy, and psychology. In several cases, these students are not equipped with the tools and knowledge that regular language students already have. We therefore need to overcome such barriers and clearly show the former how much they can profit from corpus approaches.

---

10 As regards the latter, for example, readers are referred to Kirk (1994, 2002), where they may find a more detailed description of two previous versions of this third-year module.

Finally, I would like to address yet another area at the intersection between education and research: the argument that corpus tools, techniques and resources add to the current language pedagogy. In this line, Tognini-Bonelli (2001: 14) suggests that

> In the context of the classroom, the methodology of Corpus Linguistics is congenial for students of all levels because it is a 'bottom-up' study of the language requiring very little learned expertise to start with. Even the students that come to linguistic enquiry without a theoretical apparatus learn very quickly to advance their hypotheses on the basis of their observations rather than received knowledge, and test them against the evidence provided by the corpus.

It is easy to find in the literature excerpts that focus on the advantages of the corpus approach. These are sometimes supported by impressionistic evaluations: 'The teacher reported that the students enjoyed the activity and that several students were using the KWIC function to check their paper for other classes' (Reppen 2010: 69). While we cannot dismiss the importance of teachers' impressions of student learning on their pedagogical practice, there are few empirical studies in this area.

From a general perspective, researchers have studied what students do with language (e.g. Granger 1998; Granger et al. 2002; Aston et al. 2004; Sinclair 2004; Nesselhauf 2005; among others), and also how corpora may be invited into the classroom (as discussed above). What is needed now is to check whether students who have been introduced to corpora actually do better than those who are unaware of their potential. So, the question is whether or not Corpus Linguistics adds to the learning experience. For the sake of illustration, we may ask two questions, indirectly referring to the terms 'precision' and 'recall', which are generally used in evaluating software:

a. Are students able to use the lexicon of a given language in a more clear-cut way to get their opinions across or do they continue to resort to longer paraphrases to express ideas which they do not know how to convey?
b. Given a specific context, are students able to select only those choices which are adequate to it, without bringing up any linguistic features which would be considered inappropriate?

These are two research questions which might be explored in the future. Their answers have implications to the market, which is discussed next.

5. Market

As is the case with the other strands, the relationship between Corpus Linguistics and the politics of the market is a two-way road: at one hand the area is influenced by the market, but at the other hand it helps shape market decisions.

In relation to how economical factors influence the practice in our field, one of the most noticeable effects has to do with the amount of financial resources which are made available to researchers. The more investment an area gets, the more chances it has to grow and establish itself. Therefore, a financially-privileged position allows researchers to better develop their investigations on a continuous basis. For instance, it will help them buy the hardware/software they need, carry out field work for data collection, and/ or hire other fellow researchers, thus expanding the human resources in the area.

The economy also plays a role in the availability (or otherwise) of corpora to the research community (see also Mark Davies's interview). Those who have been involved in the compilation of corpora know how much it costs (either directly or indirectly) to do so. It is true that charging for the use of corpora might be a way of obtaining some financial compensation, but their availability might then be restricted in some parts of the world. If we consider, for instance, the current state of affairs in the so-called developing countries where researchers have to deal with lack of financial support (cf. Tony Berber Sardinha's description), researchers/students might not be able to afford the licensing fees.

In any case, withholding corpora is a practice which ends up forcing users to start from scratch rather than investing effort in perfecting what has already been done. We would need to spend time and money (when it is available) to undertake a task which has already been accomplished by another researcher. Additionally, the unavailability of corpora also has a bearing on the strand of research: if our findings are based on corpora which are restricted, it then becomes impossible to replicate the study and check the accuracy of the claims that have been made. As a consequence, it holds the community back.

Unfortunately, the decision of making corpora available to the wider community is not always on the researchers' hands. There are several practical considerations which need to be taken into account before these compilations are released. The most pressing ones correspond to copyright restrictions, as indicated by Paul Baker, Mark Davies, Stig Johansson and

Mike Scott in this volume. It is indeed important to follow certain legal precautions before corpora are released since there is legal liability for copyrighted material.

A similar point may be made as regards the relationship between the accessibility of corpus software and the economy. In this case, financial resources are needed not only to buy a computer programme, but also to update it. As expected, whenever a major release is made available, users are required to upgrade it if they want to make use of the most recent built-in features.[11]

When considering the way in which the field has directed the market, we realise that Corpus Linguistics has notably had a bearing on the publishing world. The joint venture between the University of Birmingham and Collins, coordinated by John Sinclair, had a pioneering role in the production of dictionaries, grammars and other reference materials based on corpora. Nowadays these corpus-informed materials do not account for a trend in the publishing world, but rather correspond to a well-established reality.

An additional illustration of the corpus influence on the publishing market is the production of textbooks based on corpora. One clear example is *Touchstone* (McCarthy et al. 2005), a four-level series by the Cambridge University Press. This is an innovative publication which may be better placed on the crossroads between the market and education. On the one hand, it has been developed as a regular set of coursebooks for adoption in language learning centres, thus changing the way English is taught worldwide. On the other hand, it is because Corpus Linguistics has proved itself to be useful for education that these materials have been developed.

Some publications also aim at bridging the gap between teacher education and pedagogical practice. In this sense, they attempt to show language professionals how Corpus Linguistics can be used in the classroom (e.g. O'Keeffe et al. 2007; Viana & Zyngier 2008; Reppen 2010; Viana 2010).

Other publications cater for the needs of our own community of corpus linguists. In addition to some book series, one of which this volume belongs to, there are two main journals. One of them is the *International Journal of*

---

11 It should be pointed out, however, that some free computer programmes have functions which are similar to those available in commercial packages. In addition, researchers who know how to programme might wish to perfect open-source tools, or to develop their own script and/or software, as discussed by Stefan Th. Gries.

Corpus Linguistics, which dates back to 1996. Mentioned in Paul Baker's interview, the other one is *Corpora*, which was launched in 2006.

The politics of the market, however, is not restricted to publishing activities. It may involve job offers as well if we see this strand in a more wide-encompassing social perspective. In his interview, Tony Berber Sardinha expresses his desire to see more job opportunities being offered to corpus researchers in the future. This prospective view needs to be interpreted in terms of the other strands discussed here. Professionals in this field will only have more work opportunities if (a) Corpus Linguistics is recognised as a valid way of doing research (cf. Section 2), (b) interdisciplinary nets are sewn (cf. Section 3) and (c) corpora are shown to be a key aspect in education (cf. Section 4). In addition, corpus research will be more valued if it gives better return to the society from which it captures its data, a topic which is discussed in the following section.

6. Community

While the previous sections dealt mostly with objective topics, this last one is characterised by a more subjective nature. When examining the politics at the core of Corpus Linguistics, the personal aspect cannot be overlooked, as, ultimately, it is the community of practitioners that help shape the area. Put differently, it is both what the community members do with corpora and how they do it that contribute to the identity and recognition of the field. This strand of the community is then intrinsically tied to all the other ones.

It is commonly agreed that Corpus Linguistics opens up possibilities for challenging perspectives on language use. In this sense, Teubert (2005: 8) states that:

> Corpus linguists have to submit their findings to their discourse community and argue for their acceptance. The discourse community is, in principle, a democratic community. Every member has the right to contribute to the discourse, and to discuss, modify or reject what other members say.

Our academic conduct should therefore reflect this 'democratic' concern. Adopting such an open outlook does not only influence the way the community is perceived, but it also strengthens it.

By being willing to listen to others and assuming that their views are not (always or necessarily) the most appropriate ones, corpus linguists are more likely to develop collaborative projects.[12] If the two most important journals in this field are examined in terms of single- and co-authored papers, the figures are encouraging to some extent. There seems to be a balance between these types of papers in the nine published issues of *Corpora* (from May 2006 to May 2010): 55% of the papers were produced by a single author vs. 45% written by a team. As regards the *International Journal of Corpus Linguistics*, the number of co-authored contributions decreases to 33% as compared to 67% of single-authored papers.

Whenever a community is scrutinised, power relations among its members surge. In the case of corpus linguists, the question arises as to how open the field is to novices. This is especially relevant if we consider Condon et al.'s (2006: V) words about technological advances: '[...] students are more likely than teachers to be familiar with the latest incarnations. No teacher should ever be ashamed of learning from his or her students. Real learning involves everyone in the room living with a sense of wonder and anticipation.' Although the authors were referring to K-12 education in the United States, this description applies to universities as well. The technological aspect involved in Corpus Linguistics reinforces the need for a more democratic teaching/research practice, one in which power is more equally shared between community members.

The politics of the community, however, reaches beyond the university walls. In a sense, we are only able to carry out corpus studies because there are language users who allow us to work with their spoken and/or written production. And in what way do they benefit from our research results?[13] The answer to this ethical consideration of what to give back to society is of utmost relevance. As a matter of fact, this should be brought to the centre of our discussions. The more relevant corpus research proves to be in social terms, the more the society will value it. Showing the social relevance of corpus studies will provide us with more possibilities of investment. This will in turn help us develop stronger research clusters and make the research activity healthier.

---

12 See Section 3 for a discussion on the bonds that might be formed between researchers from different fields. In the present section, no distinctions are intentionally drawn between collaborators. The focus here lies on the cooperation *per se* of two or more researchers.

13 In detailing researchers' responsibilities, the British Association of Applied Linguistics, for instance, proposes that '[w]herever possible, final project reports should be made available in an accessible form to informants, and informants should have the right to comment on them' (BAAL 2006 [1994]: 5).

7. Final words

This chapter has focused on five strands – science, research, education, market and the community – which may be identified in the field of Corpus Linguistics. Because they have been discussed in separate sections, this might have conveyed the impression that they are discrete units. However, they should not been seen independently from one another. Figure 1 illustrates the mutual interaction between the five strands by means of dotted arrows. In addition, it shows how both the strands on their own and their interactions impact the field, visually rendered by solid arrows.

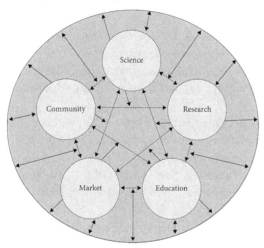

Figure 1. Strands in the politics of Corpus Linguistics

As can be seen in Figure 1, there are several interrelations within the politics of Corpus Linguistics. At the most basic level, any of the five strands on their own may affect the academic practice in our area. However, as they are part of a complex model, they may also interact with one another, and any of these relations may also impact our field of research. As the term 'strand' itself shows, all of them are woven together to form a more complex whole. Because of the central position politics enjoys in our lives, more attention should be given to the politics of Corpus Linguistics in the years to come.

References

Andor, J. 2004. The master and his performance: An interview with Noam Chomsky. *Intercultural Pragmatics* 1(1): 93–111.

Aston, G., Bernardini, S. & Stewart, D. (eds). 2004. *Corpora and Language Learners* [Studies in Corpus Linguistics 17]. Amsterdam: John Benjamins.

BAAL. 2006 [1994]. Recommendations on good practice in applied linguistics. <http://www.baal.org.uk/about_goodpractice_full.pdf>

BBC. 2009, January 9. Words that sum up Bush's America. *BBC News.* <http://news.bbc.co.uk/1/hi/world/americas/7813432.stm>

Benson, P. 2001. *Teaching and Researching Autonomy in Language Learning.* Harlow: Longman.

Bowker, L. & Pearson, J. 2002. *Working with Specialised Language: A Practical Guide to Using Corpora.* London: Routledge.

CBC. 2010, March 3. A graphic look at what the Governor General said. *CBC News.* <http://www.cbc.ca/canada/story/2010/03/03/f-throne-speech-2010-wordle.html>

Condon, A., Frost, D., Guzdial, M., Sutner, K. & Williams, L. 2006. Foreword to the ACM model curriculum. In *A Model Curriculum for K-12 Computer Science: Final Report of the ACM K-12 Task Force Curriculum Committee,* Computer Science Teachers Association (ed.), I–VII. New York NY: CSTA. <http://www.csta.acm.org/Curriculum/sub/CurrFiles/K-12ModelCurr2ndEd.pdf>

Fligelstone, S. 1993. Some reflections on the question of teaching, from a Corpus Linguistics perspective. *ICAME Journal* 17: 97–109.

Freire, P. 1996 [1970]. *Pedagogy of the Oppressed.* (M. B. Ramos, Trans.). London: Penguin.

Goldschmidt, N. & Szmrecsanyi, B. 2007. What do economists talk about? A linguistic analysis of published writing in economic journals. *American Journal of Economics and Sociology* 66(2): 335–378.

Granger, S. (ed.). 1998. *Learner English on Computer.* London: Longman.

Granger, S., Hung, J. & Petch-Tyson, S. (eds). 2002. *Computer Learner Corpora, Second Language Acquisition and Foreign Language Teaching* [Language Learning & Language Teaching 6]. Amsterdam: John Benjamins.

Hockey, S. 2000. *Electronic Texts in the Humanities.* Oxford: OUP.

Johns, T. 1991. Should you be persuaded – Two examples of data-driven learning materials. *English Language Research Journal* 4: 1–16.

Kennedy, G. 1998. *An Introduction to Corpus Linguistics.* London: Longman.

Kirk, J. M. 1994. Teaching and language corpora: The Queen's approach. In *Corpora in Language Education and Research: A Selection of Papers from*

TALC 94, A. Wilson & T. McEnery (eds), 29–51. Lancaster: Unit for Computer Research on the English Language (UCREL).

Kirk, J. M. 2002. Teaching critical skills in Corpus Linguistics using the BNC. In *Teaching and Learning by Doing Corpus Analysis*, B. Kettemann & G. Marko (eds), 155–164. Amsterdam: Rodopi.

Lindquist, H. 2009. *Corpus Linguistics and the Description of English*. Edinburgh: EUP.

Louwerse, M., Benesh, N. & Zhang, B. 2008. Computationally discriminating literary from non-literary texts. In *Directions in Empirical Literary Studies: In Honour of Willie van Peer*, S. Zyngier, M. Bortolussi, A. Chesnokova & J. Auracher (eds), 175–191. Amsterdam: John Benjamins.

McCarthy, M., McCarten, J. & Sandiford, H. 2005. *Touchstone: Student's Book* 1. Cambridge: CUP.

McEnery, T. & Wilson, A. 1996. *Corpus Linguistics*. Edinburgh: EUP.

McEnery, T., Xiao, R. & Tono, Y. 2006. *Corpus-Based Language Studies: An Advanced Resource Book*. London: Routledge.

Meyer, C. 2002. *English Corpus Linguistics*. Cambridge: CUP.

Mukherjee, J. 2004. Bridging the gap between applied Corpus Linguistics and the reality of English language teaching in Germany. In *Applied Corpus Linguistics: A Multi-Dimensional Perspective*, U. Connor & T. Upton (eds), 239–250. Amsterdam: Rodopi.

Nesselhauf, N. 2005. *Collocations in a Learner Corpus* [Studies in Corpus Linguistics 14]. Amsterdam: John Benjamins.

O'Keeffe, A., McCarthy, M. & Carter, R. 2007. *From Corpus to Classroom: Language Use and Language Teaching*. Cambridge: CUP.

Opas-Hänninen, L. L. 2010. Multivariate analysis of stance in fiction: A case study. In *Literary Education and Digital Learning: Methods and Technologies for Humanities Studies*, W. van Peer, S. Zyngier & V. Viana (eds), 22–52. Hershey NJ: Information Science Reference.

Renouf, A. 1997. Teaching Corpus Linguistics to teachers of English. In *Teaching and Language Corpora*, A. Wichmann, S. Fligelstone, T. McEnery & G. Knowles (eds), 255–266. London: Longman.

Reppen, R. 2010. *Using Corpora in the Language Classroom*. Cambridge: CUP.

Semino, E. & Short, M. 2004. *Corpus Stylistics: Speech, Writing, and Thought Presentation in a Corpus of English Writing*. London: Routledge.

Simpson, J. & Weiner, E. (eds). 1989. *The Oxford English Dictionary,* 2nd edn. Oxford: Clarendon Press. <http://dictionary.oed.com/entrance.dtl>

Simpson, P. 1996. *Language Through Literature: An Introduction*. London: Routledge.

Sinclair, J. M. (ed.). 2004. *How to Use Corpora in Language Teaching* [Studies in

Corpus Linguistics 12]. Amsterdam: John Benjamins.

Stoddard, K. 2010, January 28. Obama's state of the union speech: How did the words he used compare to other presidents? As wordless. *Guardian.* <http://www.guardian.co.uk/news/datablog/2010/jan/27/obama-state-of-the-union-addresses-wordle-presidents>

Svartvik, J. 1992. Corpus Linguistics comes of age. In *Directions in Corpus Linguistics: Proceedings of Nobel Symposium 82,* J. Svartvik (ed.), 105–122. Berlin: Mouton de Gruyter.

Teubert, W. 2005. My version of Corpus Linguistics. *International Journal of Corpus Linguistics* 10(1): 1–13.

Teubert, W. 2007. Language and Corpus Linguistics. In *Corpus Linguistics: A Short Introduction,* W. Teubert & A. Cermáková(eds), 1–58. London: Continuum.

Thomas, J. & Short, M. 1996. Preface. In *Using Corpora for Language Research*, J. Thomas & M. Short (eds), ix. London: Longman.

Tognini-Bonelli, E. 2001. *Corpus Linguistics at Work* [Studies in Corpus Linguistics 6]. Amsterdam: John Benjamins.

Toolan, M. 2009. *Narrative Progression in the Short Story: A Corpus Stylistic Approach* [Linguistic Approaches to Literature 6]. Amsterdam: John Benjamins.

Tribble, C. & Jones, G. 1990. *Concordances in the Classroom: A Resource Book for Teachers.* London: Longman.

Viana, V. 2010. Authentic English through the computer: Corpora in the ESOL writing classroom. In *Effective Second Language Writing,* S. Kasten (ed.), 163–168. Alexandria VA: TESOL.

Viana, V., Giordani, N. & Zyngier, S. 2008. Empirical evaluation: Towards an automated index of lexical variety. In *Directions in Empirical Literary Studies: In Honour of Willie van Peer* [Linguistic Approaches to Literature 5], S. Zyngier, M. Bortolussi, A. Chesnokova & J. Auracher (eds), 271–282. Amsterdam: John Benjamins.

Viana, V. & Zyngier, S. 2008. EFL through the digital glass of Corpus Linguistics. In *Handbook of Research on E-Learning Methodologies for Language Acquisition,* R. de C. V. Marriott & P. L. Torres (eds), 219–236. Hershey NJ: Information Science Reference.

About the contributors

Guy Aston (guy@sslmit.unibo.it) is Professor of English Language and Translation at the University of Bologna's Advanced School of Modern Languages for Interpreters and Translators in Forlì, Italy. He did his doctorate in London under Henry Widdowson's supervision on the teaching of conversation, started using corpora as a language teaching tool in 1991, and co-authored the *BNC Handbook* (Edinburgh University Press 1998). He has been closely involved in the Teaching and Language Corpora (TALC) conferences. He edited the volume *Learning with Corpora* (Athelstan 2001), and has published various other papers in this area. He is currently working on the construction and use of speech corpora in language teaching and learning.

Paul Baker (p.baker@lancaster.ac.uk) is a Reader at the Department of Linguistics and English Language, Lancaster University. He has published ten books including *Using Corpora in Discourse Analysis* (Continuum 2006), *Sociolinguistics and Corpus Linguistics* (Edinburgh University Press 2010) and the edited collection *Contemporary Corpus Linguistics* (Continuum 2009). He is the commissioning editor of the journal *Corpora*. He is particularly interested in using corpus techniques to explore questions of discourse and ideology, and has carried out corpus studies on the representation of refugees, gay men and Muslims.

Geoff Barnbrook (g.barnbrook@bham.ac.uk) is a Senior Lecturer in English language at the University of Birmingham and has been involved in a number of EC-funded research projects, including PAROLE, SIMPLE and TELRI. He has worked at the University of Birmingham since 1989 and received his PhD from there in 1995 for work on the grammar of definition sentences and their automatic analysis, under the supervision of Professor John Sinclair. His main research interests are in contemporary and historical applications of Corpus Linguistics and Lexicography, and his publications include *Language and Computers: A Practical Introduction to the Computer Analysis of Language*

(Edinburgh University Press 1996) and *Defining Language: A Local Grammar of Definition Sentences* (John Benjamins 2002).

Tony Berber Sardinha (tony@pucsp.br) is Associate Professor of Applied Linguistics with the Linguistics Department and the Applied Linguistics Graduate Programme, São Paulo Catholic University (PUCSP), Brazil. He sits on the Executive Committee of RaAM (Researching and Applying Metaphor) and of ALSFAL (the Latin American Systemic Functional Linguistics Association). He runs a number of websites including the CEPRIL portal for online corpus analysis tools that hosts applications for automatic analysis of a range of linguistic features. He heads several projects, among which are the Brazilian Corpus, a 1-billion-word online resource, and Br-ICLE, the Brazilian subcorpus of the International Corpus of Learner English.

Ronald Carter (ronald.carter@nottingham.ac.uk) is Professor of Modern English Language at the University of Nottingham. He has written and edited more than 50 books and has published over 100 academic papers in the fields of literary studies, literary-linguistics, language and education, applied linguistics and the teaching of English. He has taught, lectured and given consultancies to government agencies and ministries in the field of language and literature education, mainly in conjunction with the British Council, in over thirty countries worldwide. In the UK he has worked as advisor in applied linguistics to successive ministries of Education on English in the National Curriculum and the Adult ESOL Core Curriculum. Recent books include: *Language and Creativity: The Art of Common Talk* (Routledge 2004), *From Corpus to Classroom* (CUP 2007) and *Cambridge Grammar of English: A Comprehensive Guide to Spoken and Written English Grammar and Usage* (with Michael McCarthy) (CUP 2006) which won the 2007 British Council International English Language Innovation Award. Professor Carter is a fellow of the Royal Society of Arts, a fellow of the British Academy for Social Sciences and was chair of the British Association for Applied Linguistics (2003–2006). He was awarded an MBE for services to higher education in the 2009 New Year's Honours List.

Susan Conrad (conrads@pdx.edu) is Professor of Applied Linguistics at Portland State University. She has been working in Corpus Linguistics for almost twenty years. She is co-author of several books that share Corpus Linguistics with different audiences, including *Corpus Linguistics:*

Investigating Language Structure and Use (for advanced undergraduate and graduate-level students – CUP 1998); *The Longman Grammar of Spoken and Written English* (a reference grammar for teachers and other professionals – Longman 1999); *The Longman Student Grammar of Spoken and Written English* (for teachers-in-training – Longman 2002), and *Real Grammar: A Corpus-Based Approach to English* (for ESL students – Longman 2009). Her other books and articles also apply Corpus Linguistics to the teaching of English grammar and writing.

Mark Davies (mark_davies@byu.edu) is Professor of (Corpus) Linguistics at Brigham Young University in Provo, Utah, USA. He is the creator of several large corpora that are used by nearly 100,000 users each month: the Corpus of Contemporary American English [COCA] (425 million words, 1990–current); the Corpus of Historical American English [COHA] (400 million words, 1810–2009), the TIME Corpus (100 million words, 1920s–2000s), BYU-BNC (100 million words), the *Corpus del Español* (100 million words, 1200s–1900s) and the *Corpus do Português* (45 million words, 1300s–1900s). All of these corpora are freely available at http://corpus.byu.edu, and additional information regarding word frequency data from these corpora can be found at http://www.wordfrequency.info. Dr. Davies is the recipient of several large grants (NEH and NSF) related to corpus creation and use, and is the author of more than fifty publications (including four books) dealing with corpus creation and use, word frequency, historical linguistics, and genre-based approaches to variation.

Stefan Th. Gries (stgries@linguistics.ucsb.edu) is Professor of Linguistics at the University of California, Santa Barbara (UCSB). He earned his MA and PhD degrees at the University of Hamburg, Germany in 1998 and 2000. He was at the Department of Business Communication and Information Science of the University of Southern Denmark at Sønderborg (1998–2005), first as a lecturer, then as Assistant Professor and tenured Associate Professor. In 2005, he spent 10 months as a visiting scholar in the Psychology Department of the Max Planck Institute for Evolutionary Anthropology in Leipzig, Germany, before he accepted a position at UCSB, starting November 1, 2005. From 1998 until 2005, he also taught at the University of Hamburg, and he was a Visiting Professor at the 2007 and the 2011 LSA Linguistic Institutes at Stanford University and the University of Colorado at Boulder.

Ken Hyland (khyland@hku.hk) is Professor of Applied Linguistics and Director of the Centre for Applied English Studies at the University of Hong

Kong. He was previously professor of Applied Linguistics at the Institute of Education, University of London and has taught Applied Linguistics and EAP for over 30 years in Asia, Australasia and the UK. He has published over 150 articles and 14 books on language education and academic writing. Most recent publications are *Academic Discourse* (Continuum 2009), a second edition of *Teaching and Researching Writing* (Longman 2010), *English for Academic Purposes: An Advanced Resource Book* (Routledge 2006), and *Academic Evaluation: Review Genres in University Settings* (edited with Giuliana Diani, Palgrave 2009). He was founding co-editor of the *Journal of English for Academic Purposes* and is now co-editor of *Applied Linguistics* and editor of the *Continuum Discourse Series*.

Stig Johansson (in memoriam) earned his PhD in Linguistics from Indiana University in 1968. He worked at a couple of renowned universities across Europe, including Lund University, the University of Lancaster, the University of Birmingham and the University of Oslo. In the latter, he was Professor of Modern English Language until 2008 when he was awarded the title of Professor Emeritus. He was among the founding fathers of the International Computer Archive of Modern and Medieval English (ICAME), and was involved in the compilation of some major corpora (the English-Norwegian Parallel Corpus, the Lancaster-Oslo/Bergen Corpus, the Oslo Multilingual Corpus, and the Norwegian component of the International Corpus of Learner English). In addition, he was a member of the editorial board of several journal and book series, and published widely in his life time.

Sara Laviosa (s.laviosa@lingue.uniba.it) holds a PhD in Translation Studies from the University of Manchester, UK. She is Lecturer in English and Translation Studies in the Faculty of Foreign Languages and Literatures, University of Bari 'Aldo Moro', Italy. She is also Visiting Lecturer in the Faculty of Humanities, University of Rome 'Tor Vergata', Italy as well as Tutor and Examiner for the MA Open Distance Learning Programme run by the Centre for English Language Studies, University of Birmingham, UK. From 1999 to 2002 she was Head of the Italian Section at the School of Languages, University of Salford, Greater Manchester, UK, where she taught Italian and Translation Studies. Her research interests lie in corpus-based translation studies and translation pedagogy. She has published numerous articles in scholarly journals and edited *L'Approche Basée sur le Corpus/The Corpus-based Approach* (Special Issue of *Meta*, 1998). She is also author of *Corpus-Based Translation Studies: Theory, Findings, Applications* (Rodopi 2002).

Geoffrey Leech (g.leech@lancaster.ac.uk) is Professor Emeritus of English Linguistics at Lancaster University (in England), where he has been for over 40 years. He has published many books and articles in the fields of English grammar, Stylistics, Pragmatics, Semantics and Corpus Linguistics. In the 1970s, he was a pioneer in the development of computer corpora, creating with Stig Johansson and others the first available corpus of British English, the Lancaster-Oslo/Bergen (LOB) Corpus. In the 1980s, with Lancaster colleagues, he pioneered corpus annotation by probabilistic automatic tagging and computer-aided tree banking. Later he led the Lancaster team as part of the BNC consortium that created the British National Corpus (1991–1995). His recent work has involved tracking recent change in English grammar using comparable corpora such as LOB (1961) and FLOB (1991). This research is reported in his latest book (with Marianne Hundt, Christian Mair and Nicholas Smith) *Change in Contemporary English: A Grammatical Study* (Cambridge University Press 2009).

Bill Louw (louwbill@gmail.com) is Chair of the English Department at the University of Zimbabwe. His interests have moved gradually from Stylistics to the provision of theory for Corpus Linguistics. He effectively started Corpus Stylistics as a discipline by publishing the first article in this area after presenting his first paper on the subject at St. Hilda's College, Oxford in 1987. His work with John Sinclair in the area of semantic prosody led to his interest in the interface between collocation, truth and the philosophy of language. His current research involves the use of corpora to determine subtext, based upon Wittgenstein's belief in natural language philosophy and the search for quasi-propositional variables. His findings bear out the application in Corpus Linguistics of Bertrand Russell's logical atomism and Rudolph Carnap's theory of the logical construction of the world. He believes that a Popperian approach to Quine's Third Dogma of Empiricism will falsify the cognitive and consolidate the role of collocation as instrumentation for language. Fifty years after Firth's death this would be gratifying.

Geoffrey Sampson (sampson@cantab.net) was born in 1944. He read Oriental Studies at Cambridge University, followed by graduate studies in Linguistics and Computer Science at Yale and a research fellowship at Queen's College, Oxford University. Sampson taught Linguistics at Lancaster and Leeds Universities and Informatics at Sussex University (Emeritus 2010–); he is now a research fellow at the University of South Africa. Sampson's career has also included periods as visiting researcher at British Telecom Research Labs, the Royal Signals and Radar Establishment, and the universities of Geneva and Cape Town. Sampson is best known for (i) his arguments against Steven Pinker's and Noam Chomsky's idea of a 'language instinct' (see particularly Sampson's book *The 'Language Instinct' Debate*, Continuum 2005) and (ii) his work on developing a 'Linnaean taxonomy' of grammatical structures in real-life written and spoken English (*English for the Computer*, Clarendon Press 1995). See his website www.grsampson.net for more detailed information.

Mike Scott (mike@lexically.net) is the author of WordSmith Tools (1st edition 1996 and subsequent ones ever since) and before that co-wrote MicroConcord with Tim Johns. Aside from his major activity as a software designer and programmer focusing on lexis, he was originally trained as an ELT teacher, and for many years worked in EFL and ESP, living in Brazil and Mexico. Since 1990 he has lived in the UK, initially working at the University of Liverpool. He now works at Aston University in Birmingham.

John M. Swales (jmswales@umich.edu) is Professor Emeritus of Linguistics at the University of Michigan, where he was also Director of the English Language Institute from 1985 to 2001. Although officially retired, he continues to present at conferences and to publish. The year of 2011 saw *Navigating Academia: Writing Supporting Genres* and *Creating Contexts: Writing Introductions Across Genres*, both with Christine Feak and published by the University of Michigan Press.

Vander Viana (vander.viana@gmail.com) is currently doing his doctoral research at Queen's University Belfast in the United Kingdom, where he also works as a Teaching Assistant at the School of English. His main research areas are Corpus Linguistics, English Language, Applied Linguistics, and Teaching English as a Foreign Language. He has contributed to several books, and is on the Editorial Board of seven international journals. His most recent publications include the co-editing of *Acting and Connecting: Cultural Approaches to Language and Literature* (LIT 2007) and *Literary Education and Digital Learning: Methods and Technologies for Humanities Studies* (IGI 2010).

Sonia Zyngier (sonia.zyngier@gmail.com) holds a PhD in Applied Linguistics from the University of Birmingham (1994), where she developed the concept of Literary Awareness under John Sinclair's supervision. She co-founded the REDES Project in 2002 aimed at developing researchers in the area of the Empirical Science of Literature. She has published widely in the area of stylistics, among which an article on pedagogical stylistics for the *Elsevier Encyclopedia of Language and Linguistics* (2006). She co-edited *Literature and Stylistics for Language Learners: Theory and Practice* (Palgrave 2006), *Directions in Empirical Literary Studies* (John Benjamins 2008), and *Literary Education and Digital Learning: Methods and Technologies for Humanities Studies* (IGI 2010). She also co-authored *Muses and Measures: Empirical Research Methods for the Humanities* (Cambridge Scholars Publishing 2007). Currently she works as editor to the Linguistic Approaches to Literature Series (John Benjamins).

Index

Stubbs 26, 31, 51, 144–145, 147, 202
style xxix, 54, 56, 109, 154, 170, 183–184, 205, 232
stylistics 53, 129, 133, 155, 183, 188, 204, 209, 255
Svartvik 31, 128, 138, 171, 252
Swales xxviii–xxix, 52, 118–119, 202, 242, 248–249
syntax xxviii, 17, 71, 75–76, 82, 87, 147, 173, 185, 199–200, 211, 218–220, 228–231

T

tagger 37, 42, 85, 173, 185
tagging 32, 36, 81, 86, 91, 180, 184–185, 244, 246
technology xxvii, 31, 37, 52, 70, 80, 84–86, 110, 128, 146–148, 157, 161, 171, 219, 236
term extraction tools 32, 161
terminology 11, 155, 157–158
Teubert 97, 151–152, 252, 263
text type xxiv, 3, 5, 8–11, 14–15, 140–141, 149, 159, 175, 183
theory xxiii–xxiv, 3, 13, 20, 32, 35–36, 45, 52, 56, 70–72, 110–111, 113, 117, 129, 132–133, 136, 144–146, 152, 157, 174, 178–179, 189, 192–193, 197–198, 201–202, 209, 220, 237
Tognini-Bonelli xxv, 129, 144–145, 147, 152–154, 252
Tono 2, 32, 252–253
Toolan 212, 255
transcription xxiii, 10, 38, 110, 135, 170, 177, 180–181
translation xxiv, xxix–xxx, 2–3, 7–10,

17, 62, 116, 129, 139–141, 144, 154–164, 172, 212
universals 158–159, 162
treebank xxviii, 226–228, 232
Tribble 184, 259

U

utterance xxiv, 15, 47, 55, 63, 90, 94–95, 124, 145, 172, 175

V

Viana xxv, xxxi, 250, 255, 262

W

White 36, 122
Widdowson 148, 155–156, 243
Wilson 19, 31–32, 41, 70, 155, 170, 252–253
Wittgenstein 189–192, 194, 197, 199, 203, 208
Wmatrix 42, 183
WordSmith Tools 32, 101, 111, 137, 235, 243

X

Xiao 32, 38, 252–253

Z

Zanettin 159, 162–163
Zyngier xxxi, 250, 262